ANDEAN WORLDS

A series of course adoption books on Latin America:

Series advisory editor: Lyman L. Johnson, University of North Carolina at
Charlotte

ANDEAN WORLDS

INDIGENOUS HISTORY, CULTURE, AND CONSCIOUSNESS UNDER SPANISH RULE, 1532–1825

Kenneth J. Andrien

UNIVERSITY OF NEW MEXICO PRESS

ALBUQUERQUE

Library of Congress Cataloging-in-Publication Data

Andrien, Kenneth J., 1951–
Andean worlds : indigenous history, culture, and consciousness under Spanish
rule, 1532-1825 / Kenneth J. Andrien.— 1st ed.
    p. cm. — (Diálogos)
Includes bibliographical references and index.
ISBN 0-8263-2359-6 (cloth : alk. paper) — ISBN 0-8263-2358-8 (pbk. : alk. paper)
1. Incas—Government relations.
2. Incas—Politics and government.
3. Incas—Social conditions.
4. Indians of South America—Andes Region—History.
5. Indians of South America—Andes Region—Social conditions.
6. Indians, Treatment of—Andes Region—History.
7. Spain—Colonies—America—Administration.
8. Peru—History—Conquest, 1522–1548.
9. Peru—History—1548–1820.
I. Title. II. Diálogos (Albuquerque, N.M.)
F3429.3.G6 A67 2001
980′.00498323—dc21
                                    2001001170

TO
JOHN J. TePASKE
TEACHER, SCHOLAR, AND FRIEND

CONTENTS

MAPS

LIST OF FIGURES

PREFACE

The origins of this book came in 1976, when I took my first trip to Cusco, Peru. I had spent several months already in Lima doing research on my doctoral dissertation and traveled to the old Inca capital for some additional archival digging in the city's Archivo Departamental. Although much of the reading I had done on the impact of Spanish colonialism emphasized how it had severely disrupted or even destroyed Andean societies over three hundred years, I was struck by just how vibrant the indigenous culture of Cusco remained in those days. People spoke Quechua everywhere in the city, and some Andean inhabitants used Castilian haltingly or with discernible accents, particularly in the main indigenous marketplaces. Likewise, the indigenous peoples still dressed in various types of traditional garb and favored Andean music over the "rock" tunes that so often blared from Lima's bars and sidewalk cafes. Inca walls remained visible and in nearly every respect, signs of a dynamic Andean culture abounded. Although Lima had experienced a visible influx of highlanders, particularly in the downtown area and the outlying shantytowns, the city's indigenous residents always appeared to be uncomfortable outsiders in the cosmopolitan, coastal capital. This was clearly not the case in Cusco, demonstrating that Andeans had managed somehow to preserve much of their own cultural heritage in the heartland of the old Inca Empire.

When I returned to Lima and later the United States, however, my memories of Cusco's Andean culture faded, as the chores of finishing a dissertation, beginning a job at Ohio State University, and publishing the fruits of my original research consumed my intellectual energies. Nevertheless, the idea of telling the intriguing story of the Andean peoples reemerged when my friend and colleague, Lyman Johnson, came to Columbus over the July Fourth weekend to work on a book that we were editing. Lyman had just received approval from the University of New Mexico Press to launch the *Diálogos* series, books for both scholarly and pedagogical use. He unexpectedly asked me to write a volume on the Andean experience under Spanish colonialism that would bring together the fruits of the latest scholarship, making it accessible to a student audience. I immediately suggested that he contact other authors whose work dealt more directly with these issues; yet he persisted. After much gentle persuasion, I agreed to undertake the task, but only after finishing my more specialized study of the Kingdom of Quito in the 1690–1830 period (published in 1995). If I had known the magnitude of the task, I would probably have followed my earlier inclination to decline the offer. Instead, I forged ahead. Now that the book is finished, however, I am grateful for Lyman's confidence and happy to have had the opportunity to tell at least a portion of the story about the endurance of a people and their history, culture, and consciousness, despite nearly three hundred years of Spanish colonial rule.

The foundations of this study rest on my own years of archival research in Andean history, and also on the work of numerous colleagues from an array of different disciplines. In Andean studies, the challenges of studying the diverse indigenous experience are well beyond the scope of a single academic discipline. Historians, anthropologists, archaeologists, art historians, geographers, demographers, and specialists in literary and cultural studies, to name only the most obvious fields, have used their varied methods to understand the complex changes in the lives of the Andean peoples from 1532 to 1825. As a result, this book attempts an interdisciplinary approach, reflecting the scholarly development of Andean studies. It also reflects the uneven evolution of the field. Some topics remain untouched, because scholars have ignored or given these subjects only scant attention. Other issues probably get what appears to be disproportionate attention. Moreover, I have had to eschew a more traditional chronological presentation, in favor of a series of topical chapters. Each of these chapters has its own distinct chronology: cultural affairs or religious evangelization, for example, moved at a different pace than socioeconomic trends or the evolution of the colonial state. As a result, I use the conclusion to compare the chronology of each topic and make some general comparisons about the overall story of the indigenous peoples during the long colonial era. I only hope that my readers will attain a deeper understanding of the intriguing evolution of the Andean peoples over nearly three centuries. It is a tale well worth examining, and I make no claim to speaking the last word on the subject.

At this point, I would also like to explain some technical matters relating to terminology and the spelling of Quechua and Aymara terms (defined in the glossary). Throughout the study I have avoided the common usage of "Indian" and instead, opted for the words Andean or Amerindian in referring to the indigenous peoples. Indian or its Castilian equivalent (*indio*) were terms introduced by the European invaders and applied in an undifferentiated and homogenizing way to label the multiplicity of Andean ethnic groups from the sixteenth century onward. To avoid this problem, I utilize words that are standard conventions in Andean studies, where anthropologists such as John V. Murra and R. Tom Zuidema have long attempted to sensitize fellow scholars about the ills of labeling the indigenous peoples with terms applied by their European overlords. Moreover, since the Andean peoples did not use alphabetic writing before 1532, their languages were first put into standard Latin script by the Spanish colonizers, particularly the first clergymen. The difficulties of this task meant that no "standard" orthography for even Quechua or Aymara words evolved. Even today, scholars routinely use different

renderings of even the names of important historical figures, such as
Túpac Amaru, Tupac Amaru, or Thupa Amaru; Felipe Guaman Poma
de Ayala or Felipe Waman Puma de Ayala; and Atahualpa or
Atawalpa. Even the word Inca is sometimes spelled Inka, and the
knotted cords used to convey meaning among the Inca are often
written as *quipu, quipo, khipu,* or *k'ipu.* As a result, I have chosen the
most hispanicized spellings, in order to make it easier for nonspe-
cialist readers to pronounce the words. Finally, I have chosen to spell
the capital city of the Inca as "Cusco" instead of the more common
"Cuzco," because that is how the people of that city spell its name.
After all, who has a greater right to authority than the people who live
in that lovely city?

Many people have aided me in preparing this study, and I gratefully
acknowledge their generosity. The College of Humanities and the
Department of History at Ohio State University awarded me leave time
in 1996–97, and 1999–2000 to do the bulk of the research and writing,
and they also provided funds for graduate research assistants
(Sherwin K. Bryant, Ana María Presta, and Andrea Smidt) to help with
innumerable tasks. David V. Holtby, of the University of New Mexico
Press, has always proven a patient, supportive, and congenial editor.
Lyman L. Johnson, the editor of the University of New Mexico Press's
Diálogos series, not only provided me with the opportunity to write the
book, he also encouraged me at every stage of the process and wrote
careful, constructive comments on the manuscript. My colleagues
Rolena Adorno, Kenneth Mills, Thomas Klubock, and Peter Bakewell
also read all or part of the manuscript, making many useful sugges-
tions for improvement and saved me from all too many embarrassing
errors. Barbara Mundy freely shared information from her research on
the Andean *relaciones geográficas.* Ron McLean, a graphics designer at
Ohio State University, did his customary fine work on the maps and
reproducing the artwork. I would also be remiss for failing to thank
the directors of the Museo Pedro de Osma (Lima), the Textile Museum
(Washington, D.C.), the Museo Inca (Cusco), and Enrico Poli of Lima
for granting me permission to use materials from their collections.
Thanks also go to Rolena Adorno and Editorial Siglo Veintiuno for
permission to reproduce drawings from Felipe Guaman Poma de

Ayala's masterpiece, El *primer nueva corónica y buen gobierno*. Moreover, I extend my gratitude to the archivists in Spain and in several Andean countries who have helped me so generously over the last twenty-five years of research. I also acknowledge my debt to the innumerable scholars from the different disciplines working in Andean studies whose books and articles have helped to shape this study. Any errors of fact or interpretation that remain, however, are my own responsibility.

Apart from these professional acknowledgments, I want to thank (once again) my indulgent wife, Anne, and our sometimes patient but always loving children, Jonathan and Elizabeth. My family has endured yet another of my scholarly projects with love and forbearance. Finally, I would like to dedicate this book to my friend, colleague, and teacher, John J. TePaske. Ever since I began graduate work under his direction in 1973, John has attempted to instill in me (and in his other graduate students) his own love of research and publishing and his indefatigable enthusiasm for taking on life's many challenges. Throughout his extraordinary career, John J. TePaske has distinguished himself as a scholar of international stature, a popular undergraduate teacher, a much beloved graduate mentor at Ohio State and Duke Universities, and a paragon of responsible leadership in the profession. It seems only fitting that I should dedicate this book, designed for both specialists and students, to my own former teacher, who has done so much over the years to shape my scholarly life. Given his recent retirement after thirty-two years at Duke University, I only hope that this book can serve as a partial tribute to his long and distinguished career.

Kenneth J. Andrien
Columbus, Ohio
31 JULY 2000

1

INTERDISCIPLINARY PERSPECTIVES
ON THE ANDEAN PAST

ACCORDING TO MOST CHRONICLES OF THE EVENT, on 16 November 1532 the Sapa Inca (literally "unique" Inca, meaning supreme ruler) Atahualpa and his lightly armed retinue of nearly six thousand entered the main square of Cajamarca to meet a Spanish expeditionary force of 168 men under the command of Francisco Pizarro.[1] After a brief exchange with the Spanish Dominican friar, Vicente de Valverde, the Inca stood up in his splendid litter to address his followers. Pizarro then gave the signal for his subordinate, Pedro de Candía, to fire the army's cannon into the tightly packed Andean retainers. As the Spaniards sprang from their concealment in the buildings surrounding the square, they shouted their war cry, "Santiago," and attacked the Inca's followers, offering no quarter. According to one Spanish participant, "[S]ince the Indians were unarmed, they were routed without danger to any Christian."[2] Amidst a terrifying din of horse hooves, weapons fire, and the clanking of armor, the Andeans panicked, trampling each other to escape from their entrapment in the enclosed square. Those at the rear flung themselves against a fifteen-foot wall on one side of the plaza, which finally gave way, as the terrified retainers desperately tried to flee through the opening. During this slaughter and mayhem, Pizarro and a small party captured Atahualpa, while the remainder of his army used their horses, lances, swords, and firearms to kill hundreds more Andeans, pursuing those who had fled through the wall onto the surrounding plain. Two hours later at nightfall, several thousand of the Inca's followers lay dead, and the Spaniards held Atahualpa himself captive. Within one year this small force and its indigenous allies would enter the Inca capital of Cusco in triumph, signaling the effective destruction of America's most powerful indigenous state.

This first violent encounter between representatives of the European and Andean worlds would have monumental implications for the world at large. After the carnage at Cajamarca, more Spaniards arrived, and over the next three centuries, initiated changes that profoundly altered traditional Andean modes of production, technology, commerce, politics, social hierarchies, patterns of diet and disease, and religion. At the same time, the indigenous peoples managed to incorporate these changes into their own political, economic, social, and religious orders, producing a constantly evolving mixture that was neither completely European nor Andean. Nevertheless, the Spanish invasion would usher the rich and complex Andean societies into an emerging global economy—a process that continues to shape the lives of people living there even today. This book deals directly with these transformations of Andean societies following the events at Cajamarca, as they became swept into this global arena during Spanish colonial rule (1532–1825).

The Human and Geographic Background

The origins of the Andean civilization began nearly twelve thousand years earlier, as human beings either migrated from Asia to the Americas across a land bridge that later became submerged and known as the Bering Straits, or as some scholars now argue, crossed the Pacific Ocean in boats. These peoples gradually migrated to the Andean region, where they produced a remarkable series of cultures and civilizations over the millennia. In the region from Ecuador through Peru to Chile in the south and extending eastward to Bolivia, a series of advanced civilizations evolved over time—the Chavín, Moche, Nazca, Tiahuanaco, Huari, Huanca, Chincha, and Chimú. The largest of these great imperial states was the Inca Empire or Tawantinsuyu—the empire of the four parts—which extended from its capital in Cusco to include this entire Andean region of 984,000 square kilometers. The extensive Inca domain encountered by the Spanish on that chilly November afternoon in 1532 represented a kaleidoscope of ethnic groups, languages, and cultures, which had boasted stunning achievements in art, technology, social organization, and state building.

The accomplishments of the Inca and those civilizations preceding them are all the more remarkable because of the daunting geographical obstacles posed by the fragmented Andean landscape. Parts of the northwestern coast of South America are lush and tropical, but further south, from northern Peru to Chile, cold ocean currents keep moisture from falling on the land, making it dry and desert-like. Over time, the indigenous peoples could only cultivate their crops—corn, beans, squash, and cotton—by employing extensive irrigation systems. In the Andean cordillera, the fertile valleys supplied corn, potatoes, tubers, and a wide variety of animals. The largest grazing areas, however, lay still higher in *puna or páramo* grasslands where huge herds of llama, alpaca, vicuña, and guanacos roamed. The eastern rain forest regions generally formed the periphery of the Andean world.

These ruggedly beautiful landscapes often remained divided from each other by geographical and climatic barriers that created a patchwork of different cultural groups, languages, and polities. Civilizations tended to emerge either along the coast or in the isolated, fertile Andean valleys. The spectacular achievement of the Inca was to build on the advances of their predecessors and to bring these varied civilizations and landscapes together under the sway of a single state. Although other important polities also developed in South America, this study will focus primarily on this expansive region included within the domain of Tawantinsuyu, which later served as the heartland of Spain's empire in South America.

Historical Sources on the Andean Peoples, 1532–1825

Scholars have been forced to utilize some very fragmentary and difficult sources in order to understand the complex history of Andean societies and the changes brought about by their incorporation into a larger Spanish imperial framework. One major difficulty has been the lack of a written alphabetic language before 1532. Instead, the Inca relied on the arrangements of knotted strings, called quipu, which the Andeans used to record their censuses, contents of state warehouses, and numbers of taxpayers. Some scholars have postulated that quipu may also have provided narrative accounts, perhaps even recording basic information about battles, dynastic successions, or other discrete historical episodes, but research in this area is still inconclusive. Art historians and anthropologists have also begun to extract meaning from the abstract, geometric designs on Inca textiles, ceramics, jewelry, and carvings. Other indigenous sources in the Andes come from the rich archaeological remains drawn from thousands of sites of pre-Columbian and later colonial occupation. These objects, buildings, and tombs, in conjunction with data from bones, plant remains, and waste materials have yielded rich information about indigenous cultural, artistic, and technological achievements. Finally, information comes from present-day descendants of the pre-Columbian Andean peoples, who can often explain to anthropologists many of the customs and traditions handed down through the generations, even from years long before 1532.[3]

Another important, but difficult to interpret, set of sources about the Andean past are the chronicles of European and indigenous writers, written after the Spanish invasion. The most abundant are accounts by Spanish settlers, priests, and bureaucrats (such as Pedro Pizarro, Francisco de Xerez, Pedro de Cieza de León, Juan de Betanzos, Agustín de Zárate, Bernabé Cobo, Juan Polo de Ondegardo, and Pedro Sarmiento de Gamboa) who sought to understand, govern, and even to justify their rule over the Andean peoples.[4] The few works produced by native Andean authors did not appear until the early seventeenth century.[5] The most famous, Felipe Guaman Poma de Ayala's El *primer nueva corónica y buen gobierno* was written to protest Spanish injustices, but it also provides much information on the culture, politics, socioreligious values, and economic practices of the Andeans before and after the Spanish invasion.[6] The work of Juan de Santa Cruz Pachacuti Yamqui and El Inca Garcilaso de la Vega (who lived most of his life in Spain) also supply some Andean perspectives on the past. The Huarochirí Manuscript, written in the official language of the Inca, Quechua, also tells about Andean provincial religious myths, rituals, and culture.[7] Regardless of their obvious value, however, each of these chronicles must be seen through a "double filter" that recognizes the limited understanding, biases, and miscomprehensions of both the Spanish observers and later Andean authors.

Another major source of information is the immense array of records generated by the Spanish civil and religious authorities after 1532. Most of these documents—such as treasury accounts, government and church correspondence, workbooks, trade records, policy proposals, judicial documents, censuses, reports from royal inspection tours, notary records, and the testimonies of clerical and public officials—are scattered in archival repositories in Spain and throughout the Andean region. In addition to these archival documents, scholars can glean much useful material from published laws, legal commentaries, diaries, genealogical studies, and historical dictionaries of Andean languages found in various research libraries. Nevertheless, each of these sources has its own limitations, reflecting the biases, misperceptions, and changing religious and administrative priorities of metropolitan, colonial, and local officials over time.

Modern Scholarship on the Andes

Much productive research utilizing these various source materials has been done by anthropologists and ethnohistorians, reconstructing patterns of culture and society in the Andes. Ethnohistorians have blended the methods of anthropology and history, often employing a mixture of techniques from both disciplines. In addition to relying on data from anthropological fieldwork and archaeological digs, many of these studies use a wide variety of materials, such as data from Spanish chronicles, accounts of Indian and mestizo (mixed European and Amerindian ancestry) writers, dictionaries of indigenous languages, analyses of religious traditions, and a wide variety of archival sources. These sources have provided a wealth of information on patterns of wealth and social stratification, methods of taxation, trade mechanisms, political practices, language and culture, religion, and family life in the Andes before and after the Spanish invasion.

The largest corpus of work on the Andean peoples between 1532 and 1825 has come from historians, drawing largely on written documents uncovered in the Spanish imperial archives and in the many national, regional, and local archives in the Andes. These historical works cover a wide range of topics, such as religious, demographic, and philosophical changes following the encounter in 1532; patterns of land tenure and labor practices; the emergence of a market economy and social classes; politics and colonial state formation; and forms of popular resistance to authority, such as crime, riots, or rebellions. Such studies deal most often with the points of interaction between Spaniards and various highland and coastal Amerindian groups between 1532 and 1825.

In recent years the scholarly fields experiencing the greatest growth in Andean studies have been in cultural/literary studies and art history. Some of these scholars have examined religious or messianic movements among the indigenous peoples, while others have studied how religious doctrine and popular religion provide insights into how Europeans, *castas* (people of any mixed racial ancestry), and Amerindians interpreted their own historical experiences. Most of these studies also have relied fundamentally on the relatively small number of canonical texts written by Europeans, mestizos, or indigenous authors. Moreover, a new generation of art historians is reinterpreting the paintings, frescos, and drawings from the colonial periods in the Andes. Many of the newest works in these fields, however, have begun to merge the information provided in literary or artistic texts with archival materials to produce a richer and more nuanced scholarship about Andean culture.

Methods and Organizational Framework of the Book

This impressive output of scholarly publications has come from a diverse mixture of disciplines (such as history, political economy, anthropology, literary studies, and art history). Each of these scholarly disciplines, however, has utilized its own approaches and methodologies to examine the diverse body of sources about the Andean past. This book, however, promises a multidisciplinary synthesis of this scholarship, focusing primarily on the contributions of the Andean peoples themselves to the formation of colonial society. Such an approach will examine the complex Andean indigenous societies and their evolution under Spanish colonial rule. It will also provide an understanding of the historical and cultural processes leading to the marginalization of the indigenous peoples, which today constitutes a salient problem facing the modern Andean nations. Finally, it will attempt to explain how persistent indigenous values mixed with European and African beliefs have endured to the present day.

To achieve such a synthesis, this book presents a methodological framework capable of integrating monographic Andeanist scholarship into a multidisciplinary perspective, merging the rich cultural world of the Andean peoples with large impersonal socioeconomic systems.[8] According to anthropologist George Marcus, for example, such an approach can create the "crucible for integrating the micro and the macro, combining accounts of impersonal systems into representations of local life as cultural forms both autonomous and constituted by the larger order."[9] As a result, this book will attempt to recreate the lives of real people in their broad historical context, but without reducing the human experience to a mere reflection of deep, long-term historical forces. In short, it will merge the detail and insights drawn from literary and artistic exegesis, ethnographic detail, and historical narrative to create a more interdisciplinary perspective for examining the Andean past.

Relying mostly on the work of anthropologists, archaeologists, and ethnohistorians, chapter 2 provides the social, economic, and political background of the diverse Andean societies that Tawantinsuyu comprised on the eve of the Spanish invasion. The subsequent two chapters rely almost exclusively on the work of anthropologists, ethnohistorians, and historians who have examined the published chronicles, archaeological data, ethnographies, and the rich archival documents generated by Spanish political authorities. Chapter 3 explores the changing methods of state control imposed by the Spanish colonizers on the Andean peoples from 1532 to 1825. Chapter 4 examines the transformation of regional economies of the varied Andean worlds upon their incorporation into the European global system of mercantile production.

The next two chapters address how Andeans interpreted and changed their cultural and religious traditions under Spanish colonial rule. The method of analysis shifts to consider document and artifact as "texts," drawing on work in history, art history, literary studies, and ethnohistory. Chapter 5 shows how these various forms of texts—chronicles, archival records, textiles, ceramics, ritual objects, and paintings—are seen as cultural productions, providing insights into the construction of colonial cultural identities over time. Chapter 6 evaluates attempts to impose Roman Catholicism in the Andes, focusing on how European and indigenous cultures came to coexist in a constantly evolving religious mixture. The foundations of this chapter rest on a variety of source materials—chronicles, religious myths, theological texts, paintings, and archival evidence (particularly trial records of Andeans prosecuted for lapsing into pre-Christian religious beliefs and rituals).

Chapter 7 uses some of these textual sources but depends more heavily on archive-based studies to examine the changing forms of Andean resistance, rebellion, and consciousness during the colonial period. Finally, the conclusion will compare and analyze the chronologies of each topic to examine the impact of the colonial experience on the history of the Andean population over time.

As this book attempts to demonstrate, the incorporation of the Andean region into the expanding economic and social system emanating from Europe produced profound historical and cultural changes influencing the lives of people in the region. The vast majority of these diverse ethnic groups gradually became an exploited peasantry, increasingly marginal to the social, economic, and political life of the newly independent nations of Peru, Bolivia, and Ecuador by 1825. This tragic side of the colonial heritage still haunts the Andean world today.

2
TAWANTINSUYU IN 1532

When [the leading citizens of Cusco] learned how near the enemy was, they made great sacrifices according to their custom, and decided to beg Pachacuti . . . to take charge of the war, looking to the safety of all. And one of the elders, speaking in the name of all, spoke with him, and he answered . . . that he had never aspired to assume the crown by tyranny or against the will of the people. Now that they had seen the Inca Urco was not fitted to be Inca, let them do what was their duty for the public good. . . . [After Cusco had been saved,] by unanimous consent of the people it was decided that Inca Urco should nevermore enter Cusco and that he be deprived of the fringe or crown, which should be given to Inca Pachacuti.

Pedro de Cieza de León, *The Chronicle of Peru*[1]

Made arrogant by his victory [over the Chanca], the disobedient youth [Pachacuti] Yngayupanqui resolved upon a deed so vile that its like was never seen or heard of by the people of that generation, either before or afterwards. Losing respect for his aged father and thinking nothing of

> his brothers, he snatched the royal fringe from Viracocha
> Ynga's head and put it on himself.
>> Miguel Cabello de Balboa, *Miscelánea Antártica:*
>> *Una historia del Perú Antiguo*[2]

AS HE ENTERED THE TOWN SQUARE OF CAJAMARCA on 16 November 1532 Atahualpa commanded the most sophisticated and successful state organization in the Americas, yet much of Tawantinsuyu's origins and early history remain only dimly understood. The quotations (cited above) from two Spanish chroniclers, Pedro de Cieza de León and Miguel Cabello de Balboa, for example, produce markedly different views about the rise to power of the empire's great military leader and reformer, Pachacuti Inca Yupanqui. In the first quotation, Pachacuti appears to be a noble citizen, who accepted power at the behest of his beleaguered people during a perilous period when the Inca's powerful enemies, the Chanca, had invaded the Cusco region in 1438. In the second he is depicted as an "arrogant" usurper, who used his victory over these enemies to wrest power from his own father and brother. Such contradictory assessments reflect the difficulties of attempting to reconstruct the empire's history from biased accounts written by Europeans long afterward.

Since Andeans had no formal system of alphabetic writing, the European chroniclers tried to assemble their histories from various informants, most often Andean keepers of dynastic oral traditions (*quipucamayocs*). These oral traditions differed greatly from European conceptions of historical change. Whereas Spanish chroniclers viewed the past as a linear progression— events unfolded over time, produced by historical processes that had preceded them—Andean peoples saw history as a cyclical process, moving from the creation of a civilization to its destruction. To the Inca, their rise to hegemony represented the fifth such cycle in Andean history. Moreover, they understood historical change as resulting from the intervention of both divine and human forces—religious beliefs and historical events were inextricably intertwined. Within this framework, the Inca saw their history as a heroic rise to domination. Other Andean peoples undoubtedly viewed it much less favorably, as the end of their own civilization's cycle of hegemony. As a result, contradictions and many differing viewpoints—liberally mixed with the intervention of divine personages—make any literal interpretation of Andean oral traditions and the chronicles based on them a very risky venture.

Even if the Spanish chroniclers could have uncovered an uncontested, unambiguous view of the Andean past, they invariably would have introduced their own biases and misrepresentations. Although these writers ostensibly subscribed to a European Renaissance view of history as "the unadorned reporting of the past, free of distortions or omissions," they never attained this ideal.[3] Embedded in their histories were ideological stands that sought both to justify the European invasion and to defend the pragmatic efforts of clergy, bureaucrats, or the conquistadors at controlling the indigenous populations. Even Andean writers, such as Guaman Poma or Santacruz Pachacuti Yamqui, presented self-interested accounts of the past, reflecting numerous personal, ideological, and intellectual biases that obviously colored their histories. Finally, many later Spanish and indigenous chronicles (particularly in the seventeenth century) were mere reworkings or even plagiarisms of previous accounts.

Although modern scholars have developed increasingly sophisticated techniques for filtering out some biases and distortions in the chronicles, they have also relied on other sources about the history of Tawantinsuyu. One important set of records is the early administrative, clerical, and legal documents of Spanish authorities that provide some remarkable information about the diverse Andean worlds before 1532.[4] These documents also reflect numerous administrative or religious biases, however, and because of the years of disorder following Cajamarca, few have survived. Another source of information comes from ethnographic studies of modern-day descendants of pre-Columbian peoples still living in the Andes. These people can explain many principles and customs of their ancestors, but this information too is replete with distortions and misunderstandings. After all, Andean societies have changed significantly over the ensuing five hundred years. Finally, the many archaeological digs in the Andean region have added an important dimension to an understanding of the cultural and material past of the indigenous peoples. Despite these problems in compiling and interpreting the evidence, modern scholars have begun constructing a basic outline of the political, social, and economic foundations of Tawantinsuyu from its period of expansion, beginning with the rise of Pachacuti in 1438, and ending with the violent encounter at Cajamarca in 1532.

The Expansion of Tawantinsuyu

The available sources indicate that Tawantinsuyu emerged from an era of endemic political disorder and conflict in the central Andes following the downfall of the powerful Huari and Tiahuanaco states from 800 to 1100 A.D. According to Inca dynastic oral traditions, their dynasty began with the legendary demigod, Manco Capac, who allegedly regenerated humankind and moved his people to the Urubamba Valley in the Cusco region. Soon the Inca began struggling with other ethnic groups for control of the area. Their first rulers were probably little more than war leaders, called *sinchis*, who led the Inca on raids to secure plunder, land, and water rights. The Inca did not begin permanent conquests in the Urubamba Valley until the reign of their eighth ruler, Viracocha Inca, who began solidifying state power through a regularized system of tribute and corvée labor exacted from the subject peoples. The military and diplomatic maneuverings of Viracocha eventually triggered an invasion in 1438 by the Inca's powerful rivals, the Chanca. The aging Viracocha and his chosen successor, Inca Urcon, retreated to their fortress at Calca in the hills beyond Cusco, leaving the defense of the capital itself to an ambitious young prince, Cusi Yupanqui, and two able generals, Apu Mayta and Wika Kiraw.

The Chanca invasion apparently came amidst heightened political infighting in Cusco, with various factions of nobles and commoners allied against Viracocha, Inca Urcon, and their policies of political and religious consolidation.[5] When Cusi Yupanqui and his generals decisively defeated the Chanca, they used their immense prestige and popularity to win over or eliminate this factional opposition in Cusco and to depose both Viracocha and his designated heir. Cusi Yupanqui then killed Inca Urcon, exiled (or killed) the former Sapa Inca, Viracocha, and proclaimed himself ruler. He next took the dynastic name, Pachacuti—meaning the earthquake or cataclysm, or he who turns the world upside down. Depending on which oral tradition later Spanish chroniclers utilized (supporting the faction of Pachacuti or his rival family members), Pachacuti Inca Yupanqui was portrayed either as the savior of his people from the Chanca menace or as the arrogant usurper of his father's kingdom.[6]

Although the chronicles differ about the exact details and chronology, it seems clear that once Pachacuti had consolidated control, he dramatically extended Viracocha's program of military expansion and state building in Tawantinsuyu. Beginning with the highland region surrounding Cusco, the armies of Pachacuti and his generals defeated their many foes and absorbed these local kingdoms into Tawantinsuyu. After securing the central Andes, Pachacuti next subdued the Chancas and began conquering the Aymara kingdoms around Lake Titicaca, eventually annexing lands extending even to the south coast. The Sapa Inca then dispatched his son and designated heir, Tupa Inca Yupanqui (also called Topa Inca), to Ecuador where he conquered new lands as far north as Quito. On the return homeward, Tupa Inca Yupanqui attacked and subdued the great coastal Kingdom of Chimor, which put up a stiff but futile resistance (see map 1).

After Pachacuti's death in 1471, Tupa Inca Yupanqui ascended the throne and continued to extend the borders of Tawantinsuyu to the north and south until his death in 1493. Imperial expansion continued, principally in the north, but on a reduced scale under Tupa Inca Yupanqui's successor, Huayna Capac. Indeed, this last

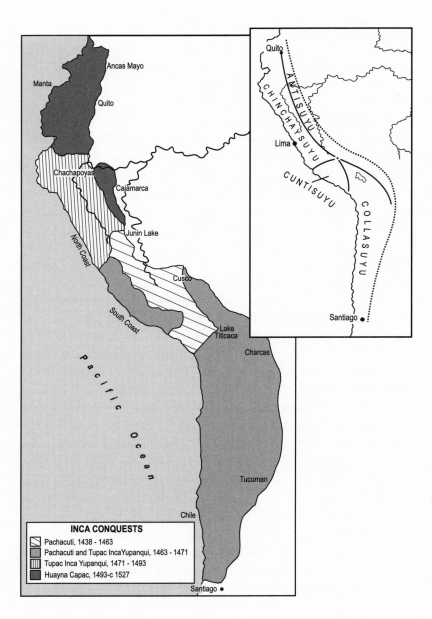

Map 1. The Expansion of Tawantinsuyu, 1438–1532;
the Four Divisions (suyu) of the Empire (insert)

ruler was on a military campaign in northern Ecuador when his army became infected with a terrible epidemic in 1527, probably smallpox or measles that had spread from the new Spanish settlements to the north. The mysterious disease devastated the Inca force, leaving Huayna Capac and his designated heir among the dead. His untimely death prompted a bloody civil war over the succession between the Sapa Inca's two most powerful sons, Atahualpa and Huascar, which produced a five-year bloodletting that greatly weakened Tawantinsuyu. Atahualpa eventually emerged victorious, only to fall into the trap set at Cajamarca by the small Spanish force under the command of Francisco Pizarro in November 1532.[7]

The Political Organization of Tawantinsuyu

The amazingly rapid expansion of Inca power, which allowed Tawantinsuyu to dominate most of the Andean cordillera and the coast in a mere three generations (1438–1532), was no historical accident. Exerting effective political control over this immense empire, with its diverse ethnic and cultural traditions, was an awesome task. Pachacuti and his successors undertook this challenge with a mixture of political ingenuity and ruthlessness. The Inca borrowed heavily from preexisting Andean political traditions, incorporating them into a centralized bureaucratic organization emanating from Cusco. The aim was to coordinate and control local political institutions, while minimizing the possibility of any armed challenges to Inca authority.

At the apex of the imperial state was the Sapa Inca himself, the supreme ruler over Tawantinsuyu, empowered to wear the royal fringed tassel or *mascapaycha*. The emperor, who traced his ancestry to the Sun god, Inti, ruled over an empire divided into four parts, or *suyu* (Chinchaysuyu, Antisuyu, Collasuyu, and Cuntisuyu). As map 1 indicates, these parts became unequal in size as the military expansion of the empire proceeded disproportionately to incorporate vast tracks of land to the north and south. Each was

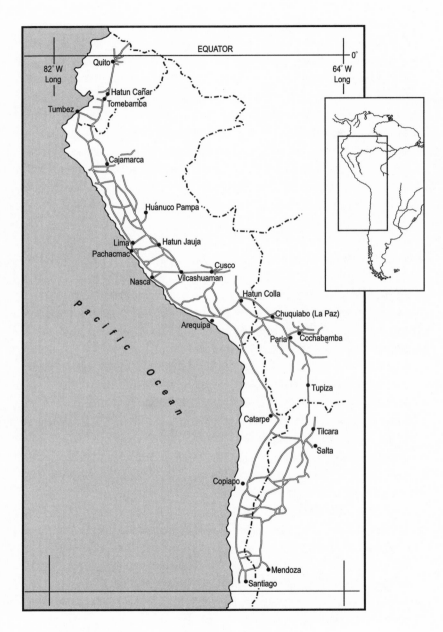

Map 2. The Inca Road System and the Major Settlements

governed by a member of the royal family, called a *capac apu*. These suyu were then subdivided into provinces (of varying sizes) under the control of a trusted kinsman of the Sapa Inca, who served as the governor (*torikoq*). The Inca, in turn, divided the provinces into two or three districts, called *saya*, which they usually placed under the command of Inca lords or trusted leaders from other ethnic groups. Finally, each of these saya was subdivided into *ayllu*— extended groupings of households linked by ties of kinship that formed the bedrock of Andean society from northern Peru to Chile and Bolivia.[8] Every ayllu or portion of these kin groupings was headed by an ethnic leader (*kuraka*), who formed the vital link in this bureaucratic chain extending from Andean kinsmen to the Sapa Inca in Cusco. Since ayllu varied in size and wealth, so too did the status of their kurakas within the imperial structure. Nevertheless, each of these ethnic leaders mediated between the demands of the state and the needs of their communities.

To facilitate administering their massive empire, the Inca arranged the various regions of the empire into hierarchically ordered decimal groupings of 10,000 households (called *hunu*), 5,000 (*piscahuaranca*), 1,000 (*huaranca*), 500 (*piscapachaca*), 100 (*pachaca*), 50 (*piscachuncha*), and 10 (*chuncha*). There is some evidence that each ayllu, depending on its size, roughly corresponded to one of these decimal units. Among the Lupaka (in Chucuito, near Lake Titicaca), for example, the ayllus approximately corresponded to pachaca units of 100 households. Nevertheless, each grouping of households, whatever its size, was partitioned into quarters (like the empire as a whole), and each quarter was subdivided into an upper half or moiety (called *hanan*) and a lower moiety (*hurin*). These moieties represented kin and religious divisions that had long predated the Inca in Andean societies, and traditionally the hanan moiety was the more important of the two. Each moiety had its own ruler and a subordinate, establishing a cooperative system of dual rulership within each unit of households. Government officials took periodic censuses of these household groupings and recorded their findings on knotted cords, called quipu, which served as the basis for collecting taxes and making state corvée labor assignments.[9]

Despite their best efforts, the Inca could never apply this decimal system uniformly throughout the extensive domain of Tawantinsuyu. Ethnic and cultural boundaries did not always conform to this convenient decimal organization, and Inca political control was often too recent and tenuous to organize or resettle people in conformance with administrative priorities. It seems clear from the archaeological evidence that the decimal system was applied most effectively in the central regions of the empire, while traditional forms of Andean administration prevailed in many outlying zones. In the region occupied by the former coastal Kingdom of Chimor (on the north coast of Peru), for example, political power remained dispersed among local lords loyal to the Inca, and the state made little attempt to regroup people into decimal units. In all regions of Tawantinsuyu, however, the decimal administrative hierarchy intersected with more traditional, localized forms of Andean political authority.

The rapid growth of Tawantinsuyu led to a proliferation of bureaucratic jobs, perhaps as many as three hundred thousand by the reign of Huayna Capac. Pachacuti organized the Inca nobility into eleven noble kinship lineages or royal ayllu, whose members staffed the most important bureaucratic positions. These nobles enjoyed many special privileges, and distinguished themselves by wearing the finest clothing and by using large, ornate earplugs. In fact, the Spaniards later referred to them as *orejones* or big ears, because their earplugs stretched the ear lobe in a very distinctive manner. The rapid growth of the empire, however, forced the Inca to grant the most loyal subject peoples (particularly near the Inca heartland in the Urubamba River Valley) the status of "Incas-by-privilege," and authorities in Cusco entrusted them with important but lesser bureaucratic posts. In this way, the Inca could recognize the abilities of important local citizens, providing an element of social mobility within the imperial state structure. The expanding number of administrative jobs finally even exceeded the numbers of the Incas-by-privilege. In the Mantaro Valley, for example, authorities relied on loyal Jauja and Huanca ethnic leaders to staff all positions from the district or saya level downward.

Apart from this extensive bureaucracy, the Inca established an elaborate system of roads to administer and defend their far-flung empire. Some of these roadways predated Tawantinsuyu, while most others were apparently constructed by the Inca. The main thoroughfare in this complex stretched from Quito southward through Cusco and terminated in northern Chile, a distance of nearly 5,800 kilometers (see map 2), while a secondary east-west highway connected the highlands with the coastal valleys. Including the various connecting roads, the entire highway system may have reached 30,000 thousand kilometers. Environmental constraints in the rugged Andean landscape were balanced against the state's need for a relatively straight, reliable route to facilitate communication and the transport of people and goods.[10] The roads varied from wide stone-paved surfaces to barely recognizable earthen footpaths. Moreover, the roads were primarily used for foot travel by animal and human caravans, since the Andeans did not use wheeled transport.[11] As a result, steps and rope or stone bridges formed part of the roadways. This massive complex of roads facilitated transportation, communication, and defense in the rugged Andean terrain.

The Inca state also maintained a far-reaching network of roadside inns, storage facilities, and strategic outposts along the road system. Small inns, called *tampus* (or *tambos*), were positioned approximately every twenty kilometers, the equivalent of one day's walk for an experienced messenger. In particularly rugged terrain, inns would be spaced more closely together. Estimates about the number of these inns vary, but in all likelihood at least two thousand such tampus provided food and shelter for travelers along the roadways. The tampus generally provided lodgings, food, firewood, and other necessities for travelers, or messengers (*chaski*), who constituted the Inca mail or courier system. State officials also kept numerous storehouses stocked with foodstuffs and arms, largely to supply Inca armies operating in various regions of Tawantinsuyu. Government storehouses may also have served to feed the local populace in times of famine or disease. Finally, the Inca erected large strategic outposts in places such as Quito, Cañete, and Huánuco Pampa, to serve as administrative and military centers (see map 2). These outposts also functioned as the focal point for important religious ceremonies, where state officials treated the local populace to ritual hospitality. This entire system of roads, roadside inns, and strategic outposts served as a major unifying force in the extensive domains of Tawantinsuyu.[12]

The Inca Economic Order

The expansion of the Inca state also created the need for an organized economic support system capable of draining productive resources from the Andean economies. The imperial state first achieved this goal by collecting taxes and corvée labor from indigenous ayllu. Later the Inca expanded their economic reach by dispatching colonists to various regions of the empire to engage in specialized economic production for the state. In effect, the political economy of Tawantinsuyu allowed imperial officials to intensify and redirect peasant production and to redistribute these goods and services for the benefit of the state.

While coastal civilizations used widespread irrigation to cultivate their lands, the rugged geography of the Andean cordillera posed daunting challenges to highland agrarian societies. Before the Inca conquests, Andean communities had developed a complex network of trade and production spanning multiple ecological zones up and down the mountainsides. Given the topographical and climatic constraints to commerce and cultivation in the Andes, ethnic communities often dispatched colonists called *mitmaq* (the plural is *mitmaqkuna* or *mitimaes*) to settle, grow crops, and supply goods to their ayllu of origin. As a result, the Andes became a vertical landscape, with neighboring groups at higher and lower elevations exchanging goods to expand their access to commodities not available in their own native climatic zones. These vertical "archipelagos" often extended for hundreds of kilometers from high altitude grasslands to jungle lowlands, but the entire system was very fragile and easily disrupted during times of prolonged ethnic conflict.

Within individual Andean communities, the ayllu was the basic unit controlling the distribution of peasant resources. Land was farmed communally, with kurakas determining each household's access to pastures, farmlands, and water rights. The kuraka in each community also controlled the amounts of tax and labor assessed to each household within the ayllu. Local kurakas divided these rights according to the needs of the ayllu—even the dispatching of mitimaes fell under their domain. In return, these ethnic leaders adjudicated local disputes, provided military and religious leadership, and tried to maintain amicable ties between their mitimaes and host communities at different elevations. Ethnic leaders also enjoyed the rights to lands and herds within the jurisdiction of their ayllu, assessed according to their rank and power. In short, the foundation of the Andean peasant economy rested on a series of reciprocal rights and obligations, largely controlled by kurakas on behalf of the ayllu.

In the North Andean and coastal regions, some specialized traders (*mindalaes*) supplemented these exchanges, most often by trading in luxury and some subsistence goods. These traders were usually dispatched by local ethnic leaders, and they exchanged goods with different ethnic groups along the coast. Farther south some coastal lords of Chincha sent large numbers of rafts up and down the coast, trading copper (from the highlands) for beads and spondylus shells (*mullu*), which were highly valued for their red color and frequently served as offerings to deities. The purpose of these exchanges was apparently not profit, but to gain inaccessible but highly valued goods. To date, there is no evidence of an independent merchant class, markets, or commerce for the accumulation of profits. Apparently, coastal commerce merely supplemented the system of reciprocity and redistribution traditionally carried out in Andean communities.[13]

These kin-based ethnic groups, with their networks of mitimaes spanning multiple ecological zones also provided an intricate web of interlocking economic relationships, which ironically facilitated later Inca conquests. Once a region fell under Inca control, the imperial state legally appropriated the rights to all the resources of its various ayllu and their mitimaes. This meant that Tawantinsuyu could even command the loyalty and resources of mitimaes not resident within its territorial limits. These connections gave the Inca economic, cultural, and religious power, which they could later use to extend their political control in regions where large numbers of loyal ethnic colonists resided. Such groups of mitimaes (loyal to the Inca) even could have served as a potential fifth column, undermining local authorities as Tawantinsuyu prepared to annex a given region.

In newly conquered regions, the Inca retained trustworthy local kurakas in power and replaced recalcitrant leaders with more pliable candidates. These ethnic leaders then worked with their imperial overlords to divide communal resources into three parts, determined by the state's dictates. As Spanish Jesuit chronicler, Bernabé Cobo, observed:

> When the Inca settled a town or reduced one to obedience, he . . . divided the fields and arable land within its territory into three parts. . . . [O]ne part he assigned to religion and the cult of his gods, another he took for himself, and a third he left for the common use of the people. . . . [I]t is known that in many places the division was not equal, but depended on the availability of land and the density of population.[14]

The people then worked all of these lands, tended herds, or harvested the produce of their efforts. In effect the ayllu provided labor and the wealth that it produced to the state and the Inca religious cults. Strictly speaking, however, the subject peoples owed only their labor and no material possessions to the Inca.

In addition to such agropastoral service, the state also required that each ayllu contribute periodic corvée labor, called the *mit'a* (or *mita*). Local kurakas usually attended state-sponsored ceremonial feasts and returned to their communities with gifts and assigned tasks to perform. This could involve having ayllu members weave cloth from wool or cotton provided by state storehouses, serve in the army or at a tampu, work in local mines, and construct or maintain public roads or storehouses. The most successful kurakas ensured the completion of these tasks without endangering necessary communal agrarian activities. The burdens of this mit'a labor were supposedly rotated equitably within the ayllu so that each household did its share and no more. In addition, local government officials traditionally provided all corvée laborers (the plural is *mit'ayuq*, *mitayus*, *or mitayos*) with hospitality—usually ample supplies of maize beer (*chicha*), food, and lodgings during their labor service to the state.

The Inca also expanded and transformed the traditional system of mitimaes. Whereas the kuraka had traditionally dispatched groups of colonists to expand ayllu access to economic resources, the Inca began resettling kin groups, sometimes forcibly, for the state's own political and economic purposes. Any rebellious or recalcitrant ethnic groups could be dispersed as mitimaes to new locations throughout the empire and their lands resettled with loyal groups. This happened to the Cañari peoples of southern Ecuador, for example, after their unsuccessful resistance against Tawantinsuyu. These resettled communities retained their distinctive ethnic identity and customs, but they were subject to authorities in their new locale. In some cases, the Inca removed especially skilled craftsmen, such as the famous Chimú artisans, simply to gain their services in Cusco. They also dispatched people with special artisan or agricultural skills to regions needing their services, called *camayoc*. In Pilileo, in the North Andes, the Inca sent camayoc from a variety of regions to tend local fields of coca.[15] In each case, the Inca manipulated traditional Andean methods of gaining access to additional resources for the benefit of Tawantinsuyu.

In other situations, the Inca settled large numbers of mitimaes in specified locations to produce commodities for the state. Huayna Capac, for example, resettled the Cochabamba Valley in

Bolivia with over fourteen thousand mitimaes who worked on state-owned farms producing corn for Inca storehouses serving the armies of Tawantinsuyu. State farms run by mitimaes in lowland areas also produced luxury crops, particularly coca. These changes dramatically expanded the power of the Inca state, which moved from redistributing ayllu agropastoral surpluses to establishing specialized labor systems that transformed the political economy of these Andean regions.

State Religious and Cultural Practices

Important religious and cultural practices in Tawantinsuyu served as an elaborate ideology of empire, which was critical in the consolidation and justification of Inca power. Many of these religious customs took form during the reign of Pachacuti, but they evolved over time as the empire grew. Religious authorities formulated a complete pantheon of gods and goddesses that they imposed on conquered peoples. This forced all ethnic groups in the empire to recognize the superiority of the Inca deities over their own religious traditions. For their part, the Inca also appropriated some of the gods and religious customs of other Andean peoples, tying them to their own state religion. As the Jesuit, Bernabé Cobo, observed:

> [T]he Incas were not always steadfast in their religion, nor did they . . . worship the same gods. At various times they took on many new rites and ceremonies. . . . They were prompted to make such changes because they realized that in this way they improved their control over the kingdom and kept it more subservient.[16]

The state also codified these practices by fashioning an elaborate religious calendar that prescribed the various rituals, pageants, and ceremonies each year. In this way, the Inca created a common set of religious rituals that provided greater unity within Tawantinsuyu.

The state religion defined a hierarchy of multifaceted gods whose powers and character often overlapped with each other.[17] At the pinnacle of this hierarchy was the androgynous creator god, Viracocha, whose divine personage represented all opposing forces of nature—sun and moon, male and female, day and night, and so on. Of these natural forces, the Inca singled out the male Sun god (Inti) as Viracocha's first descendant and the celestial power presiding over Tawantinsuyu. Inti was also the keeper of all masculine virtues, such as war or hunting. Since the Sapa Inca claimed direct descent from Inti, any popular veneration of the Sun also meant worshipping the head of state. Likewise, the Moon was the principal female deity, whose human manifestation was the Sapa Inca's principal wife, the *coya* (usually his sister). Such divine favor bestowed on their male and female leaders (as direct descendants of the Sun and Moon) helped to give the Inca a unique identity and provided them with a sense of having a "holy mission" to rule over other Andean ethnic groups.

According to Inca religious leaders, the center of their celestial universe was the Temple of the Sun (Coricancha) in Cusco. From this spot a series of forty-one sight lines, called *ceques*, extended outward to the far reaches of the empire. Between 328 and 400 of the most important Andean holy places (*huacas*)—which were most often features of the natural landscape, such as springs, boulders, hillsides, or mountains—were symbolically arrayed along these ceques, giving each one its own place in the Inca religious hierarchy.[18] Some of these holy sites, such as the shrine at Pachacamac, assumed great ritual importance and boasted a large priesthood, while others remained less significant, except to the local populace. Moreover, all of the ceques (except the first) were connected to groups of 1,000 households and pointed in the direction where each of them resided. These decimal groupings of households along the ceques, however, signaled the residence only of the Inca or Inca-by-privilege. The ceques, huacas, and the decimal groupings of households located along them were also tied to ritual celebrations designated each year by the Inca religious calendar.

The Sapa Inca participated in the most important and

elaborate ritual celebrations throughout the empire, establishing his religious primacy as the descendant of the Sun. On each occasion, the design of the Sapa Inca's tunics (*uncus*) worn on all holy occasions also was prescribed by religious tradition. The tunics were usually decorated with different repetitive designs, usually square, abstract patterns called *tucapu*. Textiles, particularly those worn by the Sapa Inca, constituted an important Andean art form, and their design identified both the ethnicity of the different indigenous groups and also the particular religious holiday. As a result, when the Inca traveled to different provinces performing religious rituals, he would wear a version of the local dress that associated him with these subject peoples and their cultural traditions (see figure 1). On the holy celebrations of the December solstice in Cusco (*Capac raymi*), the Inca apparently wore a special tunic that identified him with the shrines of the hanan and hurin moieties of the capital city.[19]

The Andean peoples had long venerated their ancestors and mummified the remains of their most important relatives (called *mallquis*), but the Inca institutionalized this process of ancestor worship by creating a system of religious corporations (*panacas*) to honor deceased rulers. The upper and lower moieties in Cusco were each subdivided into five panacas, administered by noble families and dedicated to venerating honored relatives. In time, these corporations came to be associated with a past Inca ruler. Each deceased Sapa Inca had a panaca, consisting of his most important male descendants, except the son who had succeeded him as ruler. Every new Sapa Inca had to form his own panaca. At the center of the religious celebrations for each panaca were the mummified remains of the dead Sapa Inca, which supposedly retained his spiritual presence. Lands and tributes also were reserved to support these panacas, and in time the corporations became quite wealthy, providing material support for celebrations to honor the dead ruler and also funds for his living relatives. In death, the Sapa Inca symbolically ruled over his panaca as he had ruled over all of Tawantinsuyu in life. To the Inca, this practice apparently affirmed both the immortality of

Fig. 1. *Royal tunic (uncu) of Tupac Inca Yupanqui.*
(*Guaman Poma, Nueva corónica*, 110, 110).

Author's note: Guaman Poma assigned page numbers to his original manuscript, but he made occasional errors, repeating a numerical sequence or failing to introduce some page numbers. As a result, in the images from his manuscript, I cite first the page number assigned to the drawings by Guaman Poma and then the corrected, consecutive page numbers used in modern editions of the manuscript.

their ruler and the cyclical nature of time, tying reverence for the dead with material goods produced by the living.

Inca religion also enacted subtle changes in the Andean hierarchy of gender relationships. Before the expansion of Tawantinsuyu, many indigenous religious traditions established parallel lines of descent for men and women, with males descending from a panoply of male-oriented gods and females from roughly an equivalent number of female-oriented gods. Even the contributions of men and women to economic production were divided symbolically along gender lines. Men, for example, traditionally hunted, cared for flocks, or waged war, while women took care of most agricultural duties, reared children, and wove cloth (which held important ritual and cultural significance). Each of these communal activities supported the Andean household structure in important and complementary ways. Under the state religion of Tawantinsuyu, however, the Sun god (Inti) and his descendant the Sapa Inca were clearly superior to their female counterparts. Likewise, men's work seems to have become more highly valued. Both of these subtle religious and cultural changes disrupted the apparently more equitable gender relationships that had prevailed among many Andean ethnic groups before the advent of Tawantinsuyu.[20]

The state religion also began controlling gender relationships more directly by demanding that Andean communities supply a quota of young women, called *aclla*, to serve the Sapa Inca and the religious community. As Guaman Poma described the practice:

> During the time of the Incas certain women, who were called acllas or "the chosen," were destined for lifelong virginity. . . . The so-called "virgins with red cheeks" entered upon their duties at the age of twenty and were dedicated to the service of the Sun, the Moon, and the Day-State. In their life they were never allowed to speak to a man. . . . There was also another class of acllas, only some of them kept their virginity and others not. These were the Inca's beautiful attendants and concubines, who were drawn from noble families and lived in his palaces.[21]

These "chosen women" engaged in different forms of state service, such as spinning and weaving, serving in local temples, and preparing food and maize beer for festivals. In essence, the labor, sexual behavior, and reproductive functions of the acllas were removed from the control of their ayllu and families, making these women emblems of the state's power over the daily lives of its subject peoples.

In essence, the state religion of the Inca provided an important unity throughout Tawantinsuyu. By imposing this hierarchy of gods and goddesses on subject peoples, the Inca asserted their religious and ideological authority over the diverse Andean landscape. Moreover, it gave the Inca a sense of divine election, which both justified their rule and gave them a sense of fulfilling a historic mission in conquering and ruling the Andes. Their intricate ritual calendar, with its elaborate ceremonies and rigidly prescribed forms of dress, also made Inca religion accessible to the populace under their control. Finally, the state religion of Tawantinsuyu introduced important social changes, particularly in gender relationships, which altered life in subtle but fundamental ways during their domination of the Andes.

Military Policies and Social Unrest in Tawantinsuyu

Despite the importance of the state bureaucracy and religion, the success of Tawantinsuyu also depended on a sound, well-developed set of military policies. The expansion of the Inca demanded an efficient military, and periodic frontier border wars and rebellions of discontented subject peoples only heightened the need for a strong, mobile army capable of moving quickly to quell revolts. Domestic strife, particularly over succession to the throne, often provided the pretext for such revolts, which sometimes exploded into full-scale civil wars. These various upheavals meant that the Inca state was involved in virtually continuous armed struggles from its inception in 1438 to its demise in 1532. As a result, military organization was an essential component of Tawantinsuyu's success.

Apart from several long-term border conflicts, one periodic hotbed of revolt was the Lake Titicaca Basin. The largest and bloodiest conflicts in this region occurred in the 1480s during the reign of Tupa Inca Yupanqui (1471–93). The Colla, an Aymara-speaking people living north of the lake, remained restive and troublesome under Inca rule, and they finally launched a full-scale rebellion when rumors spread of Tupa Inca Yupanqui's death. They killed all state officials in the region, raised a large army, and established a network of strategic fortifications. The rebellion involved many battles and protracted sieges, some lasting over three years. At one point, a desperate Tupa Inca Yupanqui was reduced to soliciting the assistance of other subjugated ethnic groups within the empire, and when several of these subject peoples refused, he threatened to burn their huacas and lay waste to their fields and herds. Finally, after twelve long years of struggle, the Inca prevailed. They took terrible vengeance on the Colla, humiliating and later flaying their leaders in Cusco, destroying their huacas, and expropriating much of their lands, which were given to loyal mitimaes who resettled the region. The Inca also stationed a permanent garrison in the region to prevent any further outbreaks of violence.

Another area where the Inca found it difficult to establish hegemony was along the northern frontier (modern Ecuador). Despite several military expeditions to the coastal regions and much slaughter, the armies of Tawantinsuyu never could completely conquer local indigenous groups. Huayna Capac, for example, apparently slew thousands on the island of Puná at the mouth of the Guayas River after they had assassinated several Inca ambassadors. Despite this brutality, he could never consolidate control over the surrounding coastal provinces on the mainland. Instead, the Inca settled for dispatching trading expeditions to acquire local exotic products, such as medicinal plants, feathers, wood, and spondylus shells. The Inca experienced similar frustrations trying to conquer the lowland jungle regions to the east of the North Andean cordillera. Even in the north sierra, many relatively small chiefdoms waged a bitter resistance to Inca expansionism. Tupa Inca Yupanqui apparently fielded several armies that together may have totaled two hundred thousand men in the North Andes, and both sides suffered heavy casualties. Later, the troops of his successor, Huayna Capac, for example, took several years to vanquish the Cañari peoples in southern Ecuador, devastating their homeland and killing much of the population. The remaining Cañari were then transferred to Cusco as mitimaes. Huayna Capac was so impressed by the heroic resistance of his enemies, however, that he used them as personal bodyguards and relied on Cañari troops as the mainstay of his army in the central highlands. Nonetheless, Inca excursions farther north continued slowly, and the region north of Quito remained an unsettled frontier zone even when the Spaniards arrived in 1532.[22]

The needs of an expanding power and the omnipresent threat of rebellion forced the Inca to develop a coherent military strategy for Tawantinsuyu, which apparently evolved from the reign of Pachacuti. The Inca armies had no tactical or technological edge over their enemies. Instead, much like their opponents, the armies of Tawantinsuyu relied on stone or bronze-tipped spears and projectiles, utilizing attacks with large numbers of soldiers. Slingers and archers usually began the combat providing concentrated volleys rather than attempting extremely accurate individual shots. These were often followed by an assault of massed formations of infantry, involving hand-to-hand combat with their enemies either in open terrain or in frontal assaults on hilltop fortresses (see figure 2). Nevertheless, the Inca could also display considerable tactical ingenuity in battle, feigning withdrawals followed by quick counterattacks, and ambushes in narrow mountain passes where they could roll boulders on their hapless adversaries. In most cases, however, the Inca relied on amassing superior numbers of troops to prevail over their foes.[23]

By the reign of Huayna Capac, Inca generals such as Chalcuchima and Rumiñahui allegedly commanded forces

Fig. 2. General Challcochima and his troops in battle.
(Guaman Poma, Nueva corónica, 161, 163)

ranging between twenty thousand and eighty thousand troops. The difficulties of the Inca in subduing the relatively divided North Andean chiefdoms indicate the problems involved in dealing with strategic and logistical difficulties in provinces far removed from Cusco. To raise, supply, and move such a host across the rugged and often barren Andean cordillera and coastal desert posed daunting difficulties. Nevertheless, the success of Tawantinsuyu depended on finding viable solutions to this logistical nightmare.

The Inca ultimately devised a military strategy of building self-contained fortresses and of employing mobile ground forces to move between them or defend them. In some cases, the Inca built these fortresses in sparsely settled regions, such as at Huánuco Pampa, while in embattled frontier zones they frequently established a cordon of well-provisioned forts among dense populations.[24] This last strategy was employed, for example, in the Quito region and in what is now eastern Bolivia. Other times the Inca simply kept permanent garrisons in existing fortresses, particularly in recently conquered territories where rebellion remained a threat.

Employing a network of forts proved so necessary because of the limited mobility of Inca armies in the Andes. Given the rugged mountainous and desert terrain, the lack of wheeled carts, and the relatively light load that llamas and human porters could carry, moving an army of 20,000 or more required a massive effort. Chalcuchima's army of 35,000 men stationed at Hatun Jauja in 1532, for example, would have required an equal number of human carriers, animals, and camp followers. The entire horde of 70,000 and their pack animals might have stretched over one hundred kilometers along the local roadway and taken many hours to cross a bridge or traverse narrow mountain passes. To avoid such problems, the Inca typically deployed large forces in sections, rather than single bodies of troops. Nevertheless, provisioning such a group was virtually impossible, and attempting to live off the land would have left devastation in the army's wake. The Inca resolved such logistical dilemmas with their system of roads, tampus, and storehouses. Moving from one network of storehouses to another along the extensive road network gave the Inca armies surprising mobility, allowing them to deal with most internal revolts and external threats. Moreover, since their enemies lacked these advantages, most could not penetrate the Inca defenses to the imperial heartland in Cusco, without receiving supplies from disgruntled subject peoples. Ironically, the greatest military threat to the Inca defense system would have been a small technologically superior enemy, who had even greater mobility and could resist the superior numbers that the Inca could muster against them. With the help of rebellious Andean ethnic groups, just such a small Spanish army managed to topple the Inca regime in a few short years.[25]

While the Inca maintained their control over Tawantinsuyu for many years (despite the periodic rebellions of subjugated ethnic groups), a major problem involved the dangerous conflicts emerging from cleavages within the Inca ruling classes, usually over succession to the imperial throne (*tiana*). The Inca had no clear-cut succession policy, and tradition demanded that only the most able of the ruler's sons should inherit the throne. Since the Sapa Inca usually had numerous wives and concubines, the number of possible claimants—all related to the most powerful of noble and royal ayllus in Cusco—could lead to constant intrigues among the various political factions. To succeed, any claimant had to consolidate his position among these important ayllu and panacas, and also establish alliances with important provincial ruling elites. In the relatively short lifetime of Tawantinsuyu, at least two major succession disputes arose. The first led to the accession of Pachacuti in 1438, who had unseated his own father to wear the mascapaycha of the Sapa Inca. The second succession crisis occurred in 1527 with the unexpected death of Huayna Capac and his designated heir, leading to the bloody conflict between his two sons, Huascar and Atahualpa.

Civil War and the Downfall of Tawantinsuyu

With the premature death of Huayna Capac, one of the Sapa Inca's powerful sons, Huascar, moved to consolidate his position among the influential political elites in Cusco, and initially he appeared the likely successor to the throne. The bulk of the empire's battle-hardened troops, however, remained in the north under the control of Atahualpa, another claimant. Atahualpa bolstered his power by gaining the support of the empire's three most distinguished generals—Chalcuchima, Rumiñahui, and Quisquis, who were all operating in the northern frontier region at the time. The chronicles give conflicting testimonies about which son had a more legitimate claim to the throne, but the Inca had no fixed system of succession, so "legitimacy" in this context was less important than raw political power.[26] A stalemate soon developed, with Atahualpa and his generals ruling in the north, and Huascar and his allies in Cusco controlling the imperial state apparatus and the remainder of the empire.

Relations between the two brothers deteriorated into an open civil war within a year. Huascar first attempted to invade his brother's northern strongholds in alliance with the disgruntled Cañari peoples. This combined army even captured Atahualpa and held him captive in Tumibampa (southern Ecuador) for a short time, until he escaped and rejoined his loyal troops billeted near Quito. Amidst this political disorder, rebellions also broke out in central Peru (among the Huancavelicas) and in northern Peru (among the Pacamoros). Nevertheless, the empire's best generals and troops, who had fought for over a decade with Huayna Capac in the north, united in support of Atahualpa and eventually drove Huascar and his Cañari allies relentlessly southward. In their drive toward Cusco, these northern troops also crushed the rebellions of the Huancavelicas and the Pacamoros.

In the end, Atahualpa and his generals prevailed. Rumiñahui stayed in command of the northern provinces, while Chalcuchima's troops pacified the central Andes. The remainder of the army under Quisquis inflicted the final defeat on Huascar's loyal supporters and captured Cusco. Quisquis and his soldiers then hunted down and executed Huascar's wives, children, kinsmen, noble supporters, and servants. The former Inca remained a captive, suffering various humiliations at the hands of his captors. As Guaman Poma relates: "Once he (Huascar) was in their power, they made cruel sport with him. They gave him human and dog's excrement to eat and urine to drink. They also concocted a mixture of human filth with medicinal herbs and made him chew it instead of coca leaves."[27] Huascar's humiliation indicated both the totality of his defeat and the bitterness of the conflict.

On his triumphant march south to Cusco at the conclusion of this bloody civil war in 1532, Atahualpa received notice that a small band of pale-skinned strangers had arrived in nearby Cajamarca. Flushed with his victories, Atahualpa apparently felt only curiosity about these intruders, and he marched boldly into that town's main square, expecting to receive signs of their fealty and promises of tribute. Pizarro and his men had recognized already the obvious signs of conflict in the devastation and slaughter left in the wake of Atahualpa's triumphant southward march. As a result, the Spanish leaders resolutely determined to use this opportunity to capture the Sapa Inca at the first opportunity and exploit the divisions within the empire, much as Fernando Cortés had done thirteen years earlier in Mexico. Their gamble paid off handsomely that November afternoon in Cajamarca when they captured the Sapa Inca and slaughtered many of his retainers. With Atahualpa a captive, the defeated allies of Huascar, particularly the Cañari, the Chachapoyas, and the Huancas proved only too willing to side with the Spaniards against their Inca overlords.

After demanding a ransom of gold and silver from the captive Atahualpa, the Spaniards ruthlessly executed the Sapa Inca and moved upland to Cusco. Before his death, however, Atahualpa had ordered the execution of Huascar to remove his brother as a possible threat. Even in captivity, Atahualpa apparently feared his brother more than the Spaniards. The death of Huascar also removed the last Inca leader capable of mustering an effective resistance to the invaders. After swelling their numbers with thousands of troops drawn from the allies of Huascar and other restive ethnic groups, the Spaniards finally entered Cusco in triumph on 15 November 1533, just one year after their bloody triumph at Cajamarca. The riches of Tawantinsuyu appeared within their grasp, a prize that promised to dwarf even the spoils of Cortés in Mexico.

3

The Colonial State

ON 6 MAY 1536 AN INDIGENOUS FORCE exceeding one hundred thousand men under the command of Manco Inca attacked the city of Cusco in an effort to drive the Spaniards from the Andean cordillera. Ironically, the Spanish invaders had handpicked Manco Inca to serve as the titular head of Tawantinsuyu only two and one-half years earlier, but eventually the proud Sapa Inca tired of enduring both personal indignities (including several beatings and Gonzalo Pizarro's seizure of his coya) and the oppression of his subjects at the hands of his erstwhile Spanish patrons. Finally, the exasperated Manco Inca fled Cusco by stealth and used his still considerable prestige and power to assemble this huge army and lay siege to the former Inca capital.

Only 190 Spaniards remained to defend Cusco, and they were completely surrounded when Manco Inca ordered his main attack. In their initial assault, Inca forces pushed the Spanish defenders from the fortress of Cora in the city's main square, and from that vantage point indigenous slingers shot red-hot stones, which set most of the thatched roofs in the city aflame. With the European invaders besieged in a few fortified buildings in the central district of Cusco, their chances of survival appeared bleak. Just a few months before, the conquistadors were masters of Tawantinsuyu; now they were in danger of losing their major Andean stronghold and their lives.

With a mixture of grit and determination, the desperate Spanish defenders survived numerous attacks, burning rooftops, and shortages of food and water to maintain their tenuous hold over the city. Nevertheless, the Sapa Inca's armies ambushed and annihilated four relief expeditions sent from Lima, trapping them in narrow Andean gorges where they hurled boulders on the Spanish horsemen and infantry. The Inca archers, slingers, and foot soldiers then finished off the survivors. Despite these many setbacks, at the end of May the Spaniards broke out from their encirclement in Cusco and retook the massive fortress of Sacsahuaman overlooking the city. Juan Pizarro, the twenty-five-year-old brother of Francisco, led the assault on Sacsahuaman and was killed by a stone missile to the head. Despite the capture of the fortress, his death was a great blow to the Spanish defenders of Cusco. Although the siege lasted an additional three months, the most immediate danger had passed.[1] The defeat of another Inca army besieging Lima in August 1536 further weakened Manco Inca's cause. Finally, in February 1539 the rebellion collapsed, forcing Manco Inca's retreat to his fortress in remote Vilcabamba. Just five years later the Sapa Inca fell victim to Spanish assassins; his dream of expelling the Spanish invaders and reestablishing Tawantinsuyu died with him.[2]

Accounts of these early turbulent years of Spanish power in the Andes, such as the great rebellion of Manco Inca, are largely found in the Spanish chronicles of the conquest era. Apart from these chronicles, however, a wide range of archival sources (located in Andean and Spanish repositories) contain detailed information on the remainder of the colonial period. As the Spanish invaders laid the groundwork for a more established state apparatus to rule over the Andes, the volume of these records—generated by the colonial bureaucracy—increased dramatically. Viceregal treasury accounts, government correspondence, workbooks, trade records, policy proposals, judicial documents, notary records, and reports from royal inspection tours all provide information on the evolution of the colonial state in the Andes. These documents are often dispersed, written in turgid prose, and present difficult paleographical problems (particularly the documentation for the sixteenth and seventeenth centuries), but they hold vast amounts of data on the relationship between the colonial state, the Spanish settlers, and the Andean peoples during the colonial period.

The Years of Turmoil and Crisis, 1533–69

Despite their suppression of Manco Inca's rebellion, the fractious Spanish invaders could not maintain order in the Andes. Trouble over the division of the spoils between Francisco Pizarro and his lieutenant, Diego de Almagro, began even before Manco Inca had retreated to Vilcabamba.[3] This friction soon erupted into open hostilities among the conquistadors. The Pizarro clan gained the early advantage, and on 26 April 1538 Hernando Pizarro's army decisively defeated and captured Diego de Almagro, executing him three months later. Almagro's son and followers continued the fight, however, and in 1541 they succeeded in assassinating Francisco Pizarro in Lima. Despite this setback, the Pizarro clan and their followers regained power a few months later. Nevertheless, disorder still prevailed in the Andes, threatening the entire Spanish colonial enterprise.

To avert losing its rich Andean holdings, the Spanish Crown dispatched the first viceroy of Peru, Blasco Núñez Vela, to dominate the unruly conquistadors and establish order. When Núñez Vela arrived in May 1544, he was determined to establish firm control over the willful Pizarro clan and the other conquistadors. Among his royal instructions were the infamous New Laws, which threatened to end the settlers' unregulated exploitation of the Andean population.[4] The most controversial provisions of the

New Laws of 1542 concerned the *encomienda* system, grants of indigenous towns to the first conquistadors, which allowed them to demand taxes and labor from their charges in return for military protection and religious instruction.[5] The New Laws, however, demanded: (1) an end to Amerindian slavery, (2) that no Amerindian be sent without cause to labor in the mines, (3) the establishment of a just and honest system of taxation for all Amerindians, (4) that all encomienda grants held by public officials and the clergy revert to the Crown, and most importantly, (5) that all encomienda grants pass to the Crown upon the death of the current holder. For their part, the independent-minded conquistadors had no intention of accepting such royal interference in the lands that they had won by force. Armed conflict between the Crown's officers and the conquistadors appeared inevitable.

Blasco Núñez Vela proved a vain, arrogant, and quarrelsome man who outraged many powerful Spanish families in Peru, particularly with his rigid stand about the immediate imposition of the New Laws. Núñez Vela's counterpart in Mexico, Antonio de Mendoza, proved more discreet; after realizing the disruptive potential of the New Laws, he delayed imposing them. As a result, he maintained the peace in Mexico until the Crown decided to modify the more controversial elements of the New Laws. But in Peru, the new viceroy's opponents grew in number, and they rallied around the charismatic Gonzalo Pizarro, who raised an army in Cusco to march on Lima in late 1544. Having alienated most of the political establishment in the capital city, the viceroy fled northward to the province of Quito, assembling his own army to oppose Pizarro.[6]

On 18 January 1546, Blasco Núñez Vela led his small ill-equipped force of less than four hundred to the plain of Añaquito, just north of Quito, to meet a battle-hardened army of seven hundred under the command of Gonzalo Pizarro. The struggle at Añaquito was not long in duration. The viceroy's hastily assembled troops were poorly trained, exhausted from their recent marches in the north, and badly outnumbered. Núñez Vela himself fought bravely, but late in the day he fell mortally wounded on the battlefield. As he lay dying, one of Pizarro's lieutenants found the ill-fated viceroy, ordered him decapitated, and had his head hoisted on a pike. When the victorious soldiers tired of this gruesome display, they put a string through the deceased official's lips and carried his severed head throughout the victorious army's march southward to Lima. Their trophy served as a reminder of the fall of royal fortunes in the Andes.[7]

Despite this apparently decisive victory at Añaquito, divisions quickly emerged once again among the conquistadors, who proved incapable of maintaining an orderly government in the former Inca empire. The Crown dispatched Governor Pedro de la Gasca, who quickly raised a new royalist army that defeated Gonzalo Pizarro at the battle of Jaquijahuana in 1548. La Gasca later ordered the rebel's execution. After another short-lived rebellion erupted in 1554, an uneasy peace prevailed as the royalist forces moved slowly to consolidate their hold over the Andes.

The slow rise of royal authority mirrored the gradual decline in the power of the conquistadors in the former Tawantinsuyu. The original invaders from Castile numbered under two hundred, and despite their courage and audacity, they only managed to overthrow the Inca by forging alliances with dissident Andean groups, such as the Huanca and Cañari peoples. The Europeans wisely used these alliances after the fall of Cusco in 1533 to consolidate their tenuous position in the Andes. Francisco Pizarro and his followers began this process by dividing the Andean villages loyal to the Inca into lucrative encomienda grants, giving them access to indigenous tax remittances and labor. The invaders relied on Andean kurakas to remit their communities' tax and labor quotas as they had done during the rule of the Inca. By 1542 these lucrative arrangements had netted the now 467 *encomenderos* in Peru the astounding sum of over 1.2 million pesos annually in rents and labor.[8]

The encomienda system of political and economic control in the Andes had begun to break down, however, even before the clash at Añaquito. The first encomenderos proved more adept at war than maintaining peace in the Andes. As the Amerindian population declined from the ravages of European epidemic diseases and the flow of Spanish immigrants increased, the balance of power shifted in favor of the Europeans. Many encomenderos used this leverage to seize the indigenous peoples' lands and to increase their demands for taxes and labor from communities now depleted by epidemics. Even their former Amerindian allies grew disillusioned with these greedy invaders, who seemed to bring only disease and devastation to the Andes. Within a generation, the productive capabilities of the Andean ethnic communities strained to support the escalating demands of their European overlords. Although many kurakas joined with the encomenderos in exploiting their ayllu, others resisted these heavy impositions. As the abuses of the encomenderos multiplied and the devastating diseases continued, however, many Andeans became more bitter and disillusioned.

In addition to the abuses of encomenderos, the European invasion brought a number of changes to the Andes that undermined the Amerindian communities and in turn weakened the encomienda. Before the arrival of Pizarro and his army, Andean communities had developed complex vertical exchanges using colonists to settle, grow crops, and return goods to their home ayllu. The fall of Tawantinsuyu, the demographic declines resulting from new diseases, and the depredations of the civil wars all disrupted these fragile vertical patterns of cultivation and trade, eroding the productive capacity of Andean communities. The encomienda system only worsened these difficulties; some grants even divided ayllu, which further eroded the vertical economies. Such problems intensified as the tax and labor burdens of the encomenderos came to weigh heavily on the diminished human and economic resources of indigenous communities. The response of some Andeans was resistance and rebellion, while many others simply fled to seek work on Spanish estates or at the region's proliferating silver-mining operations. Nevertheless, these wrenching changes weakened the very Andean communities that formed the basis for the political and economic power of the encomenderos.

Competition from other Spanish economic ventures also undercut the encomienda. Settlers who came from Europe after the 1530s usually found it impossible to secure a lucrative encomienda. Instead, they turned to other profit-making ventures in mining, agriculture, and trade. Moving to strategic cities such as Lima, Huamanga, and Potosí, these latecomers resented the encomenderos' control over the labor and surplus production of the Andean peoples. These rivalries only deepened as merchants or miners in important cities, such as the highland mining center of Potosí, found it difficult to attract mine workers and keep their urban marketplaces supplied with food at reasonable prices. These entrepreneurs blamed the encomenderos for blocking the open participation of their Andean charges in the emerging market economy, which inhibited economic development in the realm. Many encomenderos also engaged in these economic activities, but they enjoyed the competitive advantages of using cheap Andean labor and a steady flow of potential investment capital from their tribute collections. Needless to say, these benefits only heightened the friction between encomenderos and entrepreneurs who did not receive encomienda grants. In fact, this competition over Andean lands, material wealth, and labor helped to fuel the civil wars that plagued the first generation of Spanish rule.

Another vital factor in weakening the encomienda was the onset of European epidemic diseases. Waves of influenza, smallpox, measles, plague, and other forms of pestilence took a staggering toll throughout the Andes, where the indigenous people had no natural immunities. Disease spread rapidly among ethnic communities throughout the coastal and mountain regions, particularly as royal officials removed Amerindians from their dispersed traditional settlements and congregated them into larger settlements. In addition, as epidemics spread, the sick could not effectively cultivate their fields, creating food shortages that left the survivors in even more fragile health and lowered fertility rates. Mortality was particularly high among children, ensuring that the impact of the epidemics would extend to the next generation. These health problems only worsened with excessive labor and tax demands by Spanish authorities, which drained labor and resources from communities already suffering the impact of disease.

Despite the gradual weakening of the encomienda and the traditional Andean communities, the machinery of the colonial state grew slowly but steadily in the first generation after the European invasion in the former Inca heartland. Although the Crown gave broad powers to its viceroys, the fate of Blasco Núñez Vela demonstrated graphically the gap between the law and its observance. The Crown dispatched the first justices of the high court, or *audiencia*, in Lima with Núñez Vela in 1542 and granted them wide-ranging judicial and legislative powers under the viceroy's supervision. In time, the royal government established subordinate tribunals in Charcas in Upper Peru (Bolivia) by 1563 and Santiago in Chile by 1565. The Crown appointed only trained lawyers to staff these early tribunals, but each court had only four or five justices, whose control seldom reached beyond the larger cities. To curb the powers of the encomenderos in the countryside, by the 1560s Núñez Vela's successors began dispatching numerous royal treasury officials to collect royal duties and provincial magistrates (*corregidores de indios*) to control the Andean communities. Within a few years, however, the viceregal government had either yielded to pressure from the encomenderos to withdraw some of these corregidores or allowed conquistador families to gain control over these key positions. Nevertheless, the emerging colonial bureaucracy slowly began to fill the power vacuum left by the declining encomienda system.

By the 1560s the weakness of both the encomienda and the still embryonic colonial state contributed to a deepening political and economic crisis, which probably posed an even greater long-term threat to Spanish rule in the Andes than the rebellion of Manco Inca. The early colonial order, based on the extraction of surplus wealth and labor from the indigenous communities by the encomenderos, was in danger of collapsing. The disillusioned Andean communities faced a spiraling level of hardships, and while many turned to flight, others took up arms in open revolt. In the highland region of Huamanga (southeast of Lima), a millenarian religious revival called Taqui Onqoy demanded the rejection of European customs and a united effort to expel the Spaniards by 1564. The Huancas of Jauja, staunch former allies of the Pizarro expedition, even made their own metal pikes for a planned insurrection, but Spanish authorities uncovered the plot before violence erupted. And the Inca pretender, Titu Cusi, still raided Spanish settlements from his frontier stronghold at Vilcabamba.[9] Adding to these potential dangers, the silver-mining industry faced production declines, as labor shortages and the exhaustion of easily accessible higher-grade ores dramatically curtailed the profits of miners and merchants throughout the Andes. In short, the pillage/conquest economy established after 1532 had reached its limit, and only a drastic political and economic overhaul of the colonial system could revitalize Spanish rule in the Andes. Such a reform had begun slowly by Núñez Vela's successors and the growing viceregal bureaucracy, but the crisis of the 1560s demanded strong, more immediate action.

Francisco de Toledo and the Reform Period, 1569–81

The new viceroy dispatched by King Philip II in 1569 to deal with the emerging crisis in the Andes was Don Francisco de Toledo, the fifty-three-year-old younger brother of the powerful Conde de Oropesa, Fernando Álvarez de Toledo. Toledo was an experienced royal servant, but also a grim and unyielding autocrat, determined to suppress the fractious encomenderos and build a strong and effective colonial state on the foundations established by his predecessors. His twelve-year rule in the Andes marked a historical watershed, as this able official attempted to use a reinvigorated state apparatus to direct the socioeconomic development of the Viceroyalty of Peru. Although Toledo legislated on most aspects of Spanish-Andean relations, the primary focus of his reforms dealt with resolving three key problems: (1) congregating the indigenous peoples into large strategic towns, (2) imposing a regularized system of taxation, and (3) establishing a regimen of forced labor to support the silver mines of Peru and Upper Peru (modern Bolivia).[10]

After an extensive inspection tour (*visita general*) of the realm, Toledo put his administrative plans in motion by ordering all the Andean communities resettled into large Spanish-style towns, called *reducciones*.[11] The process of congregating the indigenous population, thinned by epidemic diseases, had already begun before Toledo's arrival, but he expanded the program dramatically. The viceroy also organized the reducciones into 614 administrative districts, or *repartimientos*, each headed by a kuraka and an appointed town council of Andean elders. These repartimientos were grouped into eighty larger provinces and placed under the control of a Spanish corregidor de indios. These magistrates controlled local justice, commercial relations between Spaniards and Andeans, and the collection of the head tax (tribute) levied against the Amerindians. In short, the corregidores served as local political and economic agents of the state who effectively took control of the countryside away from the more independent-minded encomenderos.

Toledo's forced resettlement plans were a massive undertaking, perhaps affecting over 1.5 million Andeans. Although historians have not examined the regional impact of the program in detail, for areas such as Yauyos, it involved congregating people from over two hundred separate villages into only thirty-nine new settlements.[12] The reducciones were patterned after Spanish towns, with a central plaza where key public buildings, including the church, and the houses of prominent citizens were located. Toledo also provided for the establishment of an indigenous city council and the normal array of other public offices found in Spanish urban centers. The congregation of dispersed groups into these new towns, however, also brought together different ayllus and even ethnic groups for the first time, and it further disrupted traditional Andean patterns of vertical exchanges. Nevertheless, with this forced relocation into the reducciones, Toledo could more easily impose effective labor, tax, and religious controls over the increasingly discontented Andean population.

Francisco de Toledo next focused on organizing the extraction of economic resources from the Andes and channeling them to the royal treasury. The first encomenderos had collected tribute from the outset of Spanish rule, and President Pedro de la Gasca[13] had set fixed tax assessments, but by 1569 these badly needed updating to account for migrations and population declines from disease. Toledo took a census of the Andean population and then established consistent, fixed tax rates (*tasas*) based on the material wealth of each region and its population. All adult males between the ages of eighteen and fifty paid this tribute, but the individual contributions varied according to the social status of the taxpayer. Kurakas were exempt, but members of the community clan structure (*tributarios*) paid the largest sums. Those outside the ayllu or kin structure (*yanaconas* or *yanakuna*) and recent migrants (*forasteros*) paid lesser amounts.[14] Taken as an average, each Andean tributary contributed between five and six pesos each year, which was considerably higher than the amounts collected in Mexico.

Toledo also established clear procedures for the collection and disbursement of tribute revenues. His legislation provided that the corregidor announce the tax assessments one month before collection on St. John's Day in June and Christmas. The magistrate determined the amounts from official tax lists and census data compiled from the local parish registers. If any population changes had occurred since the last collection, the kuraka could demand a new census and tax assessment (*retasa*). To simplify the collection procedures, Toledo also ordered that all tribute be collected in specie. When this was impossible, the viceroy entrusted the corregidor with setting the value of any taxes collected in kind according to the current market prices. Local kurakas actually collected the assessments and sent the proceeds to the chief town in the repartimiento, where the corregidor and his lieutenants registered the amounts. The corregidor then used the funds to pay his own salary, the parish priests, and any other administrative expenses. He sent the remainder to the local treasury office and the encomendero. To guarantee honesty, the Crown had the parish priest supervise the process. Moreover, the corregidor had to post a bond (*fianza*) as security against tribute debts and to undergo a judicial review (*residencia*) upon leaving office.

Another pressing problem facing Toledo involved fostering higher production at the silver mines, particularly the rich mining complex at Potosí. When the viceroy entered Potosí in December 1572, the formerly exuberant boomtown had fallen on hard times. The richest and most accessible deposits were becoming exhausted, and periodic labor shortages further inhibited production. The new amalgamation process, which used mercury to separate the ore from the rock, promised to rejuvenate mining operations in the town, but employing it involved large investments by the miners to build refining mills. Where mines flooded, owners also had to dig expensive drainage shafts, called adits, into the mountainsides to make their operations productive. Unless the viceroy could ensure adequate supplies of mercury and cheap labor, the miners refused to risk such large capital outlays.

Despite various misgivings, Francisco de Toledo dealt with the labor problem at Potosí by organizing a massive system of forced labor, which he called the mita, after the Inca system of state service. Once again, Toledo's predecessors had organized the first forced labor drafts for the silver mines, but the viceroy expanded and reorganized the system. He designated sixteen highland provinces, stretching some six hundred miles from Cusco through much of southern Peru and Upper Peru, to provide laborers for Potosí. One-seventh of the tributary population of these provinces served at the mine heads once every seven years—some 13,500 men annually. Toledo even specified the wages, working hours, and jobs of the corvée labor force (mitayos or mitayus). The corregidores and the local kurakas had to ensure that the Andean communities met these specified quotas. Along with the voluntary wage laborers (*mingas*) who migrated to Potosí, this infamous draft supplied the workers to run the mines and keep silver flowing to fill the royal coffers of Spain.

Toledo kept supplies of mercury available by subsidizing production at the quicksilver mines in Huancavelica, near Huamanga in Peru. The Crown declared all subsoil deposits of mercury a royal monopoly in 1582, and only leased the right to extract the mineral to the local mining guild. In return, the state would fix the price of mercury, pay a yearly subsidy to the guild, and provide an adequate supply of cheap mita labor from the region between Huamanga and Jauja. The viceroy also entrusted the corregidores and the local kurakas with providing the necessary mitayos. Despite periodic adjustments, this system furnished a steady supply of mercury to the silver mines until late in the seventeenth century.

The last remaining task for Toledo was to secure the capitulation of the Inca regime in exile at Vilcabamba. The viceroy continued the efforts of his predecessors to negotiate with the Inca, Titu Cusi, about leaving the fortress and accepting a Crown pension. These talks reached a peak in 1568, when Titu Cusi accepted baptism into the Catholic Church. All negotiations ceased abruptly in 1571, however, when the Sapa Inca died unexpectedly and was succeeded by his militantly anti-Christian brother, Tupac Amaru. Within a year Toledo had abandoned plans for a peaceful settlement and resolved to reduce Vilcabamba by force of arms. His army engaged in bitter fighting outside the Inca fortress, but on 24 June 1572 the Spaniards took the city, captured Tupac Amaru, and returned him to Cusco. Following a hurried trial, the young Inca was sentenced to death, and beheaded in the central square of Cusco on 24 September 1572. The last hope for an independent Tawantinsuyu perished with him (see figure 3).[15]

During his viceregency, Don Francisco de Toledo attempted to do more than wrest control of the Andes from the encomenderos, quell Inca resistance, and end the socioeconomic crisis of the 1560s. Moreover, by his departure, a strong bureaucratic state was in place, composed of a network of audiencias and numerous provincial officials, which would remain the bedrock of Spanish power in the Andes until its reform in the eighteenth century (see map 3).

Fig. 3. The execution of Tupac Amaru I.
(Guaman Poma, Nueva corónica, 451, 453)

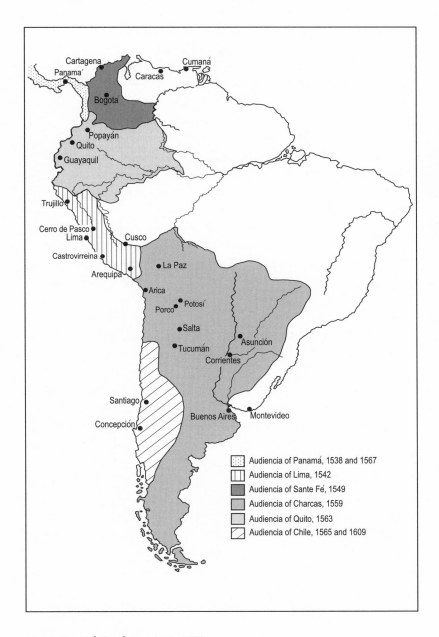

Map 3. Spanish South America in 1650

The viceroy also wished to use the state to plan and manage the emerging colonial Andean society and economy. This ambitious design involved more than merely governing. Through his labor and tax policies, Toledo hoped to redirect the flow of labor and goods from the Andean communities to Europe. Moreover, the viceroy's reforms deprived the Andean ethnic communities of access to political power and their traditional settlements and huacas. The Toledan laws also failed to recognize Andean ethnic divisions, treating the indigenous peoples as a common mass of undifferentiated "Indians," with the responsibility for providing tribute and labor to the colonial regime. In short, Francisco de Toledo attempted to use this new institutional framework of the colonial state to siphon the wealth of the Andes to meet the economic needs of Spain and to create a new colonial society, supported by the labor and taxes of a rural Andean peasantry.

Corruption and the Decline of Royal Authority, 1581–1765

Viceroy Francisco de Toledo's ambitious attempt to create a strong unified state, capable of directing the socioeconomic development of the Andes, was probably doomed from the outset. His entire program revolved around retaining the already wavering Andean system of production and controlling its surplus labor and wealth. To achieve this end, the state had to operate at an unprecedented level of honesty and efficiency. Within a few years after their implementation, however, the Toledan reforms began to fail, and by the early seventeenth century dishonesty and bad government had undermined the smooth operation of government. Regional creole elites abetted this process by forging economic and social ties with dishonest officials to block or alter objectionable Crown policies.[16] In addition, the declining Andean population and their resistance to Crown policies further subverted the Toledan system. Taken together, these factors promoted a host of socioeconomic changes unforeseen by the viceroy and his advisors.

The first of Toledo's programs to falter was the system of reducciones. The Andean peoples bitterly resented leaving ancestral homes, with their ties to traditional holy places (huacas) so important to indigenous religions. The resettlement program also wreaked havoc with traditional Andean vertical systems of landholding and settlement, and further disrupted established patterns of social interaction, production, and exchange. Pulling different communities into larger towns in some cases separated ethnic confederations or even split ayllu. This in turn weakened the reciprocal ties of allegiance between kurakas and their people. In addition, concentrating Andeans in the reducciones often proved utterly impractical, since villagers had to walk long distances to reach their fields or pasture lands. Moreover, villages opposed having Spanish corregidores dictate landholding patterns, tax and labor burdens, and governmental relations inside the reducciones. Gathering the Andeans into larger communities even promoted the spread of European epidemic diseases that killed thousands and further undermined the social fabric. Finally, many Amerindians opposed Spanish efforts to manipulate the law and acquire the best lands for their ranches and farms. In short, the whole pattern of resettlement restricted traditional forms of Andean liberty and led to greater potential for exploitation. Recognizing these problems, native Andean lords even offered to pay the Crown eight hundred thousand pesos for abandoning the reducciones, but Toledo refused.[17] According to the cynical viceroy the Andeans only wished to remain near their "pagan" religious shrines and depraved ways, cohabiting "with sisters and even daughters."[18]

A key factor behind the deteriorating quality of life on the reducciones and the decline of Toledo's reform program was the wanton corruption of some corregidores. Too often these Crown officials falsified their census and tax rolls to undercount the number of tributaries in the towns in order to embezzle money taken from those not legally listed on the tax ledgers. Another related ploy involved forcing the Andeans to pay taxes for those who had died or left the reducciones, as well as the aged and others legally exempt from taxes. In these cases the tax rates applied to each repartimiento apparently reflected the illicit whims of the corregidores, rather than any legal rates set by Toledo. Some contemporaries even asserted that unscrupulous magistrates assessed abnormally low values to tribute collected in kind, which cheated both the taxpayers and the Crown, but allowed the corregidor to make a tidy profit when he sold these goods at the real market price. The corregidores also withheld tribute monies belonging to the Crown in order to finance their own local business ventures. Moreover, some magistrates allegedly used unpaid Andean laborers to advance their personal enterprises. In 1580, for example, a Crown inspection of the corregimiento of Cañete south of Lima revealed that the corregidor used unpaid Amerindian laborers from the town of Carabayllo to plant and harvest his wheat fields in the province. This last abuse of the law occurred under the very eyes of government authorities in Lima during the final years of Francisco de Toledo's viceregency.

Over time, such abuses became increasingly common, particularly by the early seventeenth century. Abundant evidence from royal inspections, for example, indicates that the corruption of the corregidores and the loss of tax revenues were even more widespread in the interior provinces. According to members of the viceregal audit tribunal (*tribunal de cuentas*), by 1630 several generations of corregidores had failed to remit over 1,654,057 pesos in tribute to the Crown. These debts undoubtedly resulted from governmental inefficiency and outright corruption by colonial officials. The rich highland provinces of La Paz (180,786 pesos), Cusco (399,588 pesos), and Potosí (1,005,282 pesos) recorded the largest debts. These problems only worsened with time. An inspection of the corregimientos conducted in 1663, for example, found shocking evidence that 2,449,286 pesos in debts had accumulated since 1600.[19] This process of institutional decline took place gradually, but by the mid-seventeenth century the administrative procedures and tax rates imposed by Francisco de Toledo were clearly in shambles.

The ties forged between partisan Spanish and creole groups with local corregidores de indios played a key role in undermining the Toledan state. From the outset, local interests gained leverage over important government posts. In Cañete, for example, the powerful encomendero, Nicolás de Rivera, had his eldest son named the first corregidor of the district, and his family managed to control the office and other neighboring corregimientos for several generations. Some viceroys even contributed to these abuses by selling the positions clandestinely, which gave wealthy local elites a perfect opportunity to control the assignment of mita laborers or tax collections throughout the rural zones. These problems only worsened by the 1630s when the financially strapped Crown began selling high-ranking appointments to colonial treasuries. By the 1680s the Madrid government openly sold corregimientos and audiencia judgeships; even the viceregal throne went to the highest bidder by 1700.[20] With appointments to such important offices sold outright, creole elites bought these positions and used them for their own benefit, regardless of the dictates of authorities in Lima or Madrid.

Even efforts to tighten administrative controls over government officials, such as the security bond or fianza, merely reinforced these alliances between bureaucrats and regional magnates. The purpose of the bond was to discourage tribute debts, but since few magistrates could meet the obligation with their own savings, most found prominent local citizens to post the bond. After all, the powers of the corregidor over local commerce, labor, and taxes made him an important ally for Spanish merchants, landowners, or miners. Even the judicial review (residencia) that took place when the corregidores left office seldom altered their ties to local elites. Partisan prejudices, unreliable witnesses, and uncooperative local officials all hindered the judicial process, but the most glaring weakness involved the Crown's insistence on having the successor of the corregidor conduct the inquiry. Most often the corregidor-designate had a stake in covering up illicit business practices, graft, or abuses, which he himself hoped to continue after taking office. As a result, local needs too often overwhelmed state institutional controls.

By the early eighteenth century, the most grievous governmental abuses centered around the *repartimiento de comercio*—the forced distribution of merchandise by local corregidores to the Andean communities. The repartimiento de comercio probably began informally in the early eighteenth century, but the Crown legalized the process in 1751. As two young Spanish officials, Jorge Juan and Antonio de Ulloa, described the practice in Peru and Upper Peru (Bolivia) by the 1740s, even before receiving royal sanction,

> Repartimientos consist of mules, merchandise from Europe and the Indies, and food. . . . Since Lima is the principal market for merchandise in Peru, corregidores obtain their stock here. They get the needed goods from the warehouse of some merchant on credit and at a very high rate of interest. . . . At the same time, he must borrow the money from the merchant to buy the consignment of mules needed for the trade in his district.[21]

In essence, the repartimiento represented an alliance between creole merchants and local corregidores to force Andean communities to purchase and consume items, whether needed or not. These contracts, however, reaped great profits for the merchants and the official, since only the corregidor could compel local ayllus to purchase and consume merchandise. In fact, by the eighteenth century the price each corregidor paid for his appointment in Peru was largely determined by the profitability of the local repartimiento. Needless to say, the Andean communities were the great losers—they were forced to buy goods at inflated prices by the very officials ostensibly placed there by the Crown to protect them from such economic exploitation.

Problems with the mita system and the need for deeper, costlier mining operations also led to terrible abuses and further undermined Crown efforts to rejuvenate the mining economy. Although the mita initially contributed to a mining renaissance in Potosí and Huancavelica, by the 1620s production declines became a pressing concern at both sites. At Potosí, the infusion of mita laborers and the use of amalgamation in the 1570s allowed miners to draw ore from the slag heaps left by nearly thirty years of mining. These tailings were easy to collect and using mercury allowed the miners (called *azogueros* because they used mercury, or *azogue* in Spanish, to refine silver) to extract any silver left from less efficient refining methods used earlier. As the slag piles diminished and the miners had to return to digging deeper subterranean shafts, production costs rose and yields diminished. The gradual decline of the Andean population in the highlands also curtailed the number of cheap mita laborers available for the mines, exacerbating these technical problems. In addition, flooding in the mine shafts and gradual declines in ore quality further contributed to rising costs and falling profits. Similar conditions obtained at the mercury mines of Huancavelica, which also experienced a sharp downfall in productivity.

Working conditions at the mines deteriorated rapidly for mita laborers as the financial woes of the miners increased. Mining foremen assigned mitayos to the most dangerous and taxing jobs. More highly skilled, lucrative jobs went to Amerindian or mestizo (mixed Spanish and Andean ancestry) wage laborers, called mingas. Most mita workers served as ore diggers, who often worked, ate, and slept in the mine shafts for six consecutive days. Other mitayos had to haul heavy loads of ore up long rope ladders in tunnels lit only by the candles they carried. Mita laborers were also beaten, whipped, and forced to work long hours to meet the illegal quotas set by miners. Conditions at Huancavelica were complicated further by the presence of toxic mercury dust. Sickness and death were omnipresent, and the corrupt corregidores installed by Toledo to prevent abuses proved useless at enforcing the law. By the end of the sixteenth century, the mistreatment of the mitayos and the devastating effects of epidemic diseases made the mita quotas from the reducciones hard to fill. The mita, in its original form, simply ceased to exist; in its place was an abusive and corrupt system that weighed heavily on the Andean communities.

Andean resistance to the mita of Potosí and Huancavelica also undermined the labor system put in place by Francisco de Toledo. Some Amerindians fled their villages to avoid the draft, while others petitioned the courts to eliminate abuses or escape service altogether.[22] Others even utilized a legal loophole that allowed any Andean to buy his way out of the mita by paying the wage of one minga laborer. By 1606 the head of the Audiencia of Charcas, Maldonado de Torres, noted that the miners customarily received 20 percent of their mita service from such *indios de faltriquera* (literally pocket or purse Indians) who paid cash to avoid serving. Only thirty years later entire communities escaped the mines in this way, and as much as half of the mita labor was met by such cash payments. By this period, it was clear to all concerned that the mita was little more than a heavy tax burden, whether paid in labor service or in purchasing an exemption, on the already exploited Andean communities.

The miners also encouraged this deception, which provided them with needed cash at a time when the silver lodes began to decline. The law required the miners to use these deliveries in silver for hiring substitute workers, but by the mid-seventeenth century they seldom did so. Instead, cash subsidies contributed to further production declines, as the azogueros left their less productive mines unworked and lived off the cash payments provided by the indios de faltriquera. These abuses required the collusion of the local corregidores, who most often proved willing accomplices in deception. Viceroy Toledo would have raged at such a flagrant distortion of his carefully planned system of labor subsidies to the all-important silver mines.[23]

Successive viceroys during the seventeenth century tried unsuccessfully to reform the mita to restore the flow of indigenous laborers to Potosí. In 1633, for example, the Conde de Chinchón (viceroy, 1629–38) dispatched a special inspector, Juan de Carvajal y Sande to Potosí, to assign a new labor draft, excluding any miners from receiving mitayos if they had abused the cash payments from indios de faltriquera. Carvajal y Sande's actions provoked widespread unrest among the miners and local officials, who lobbied the Council of the Indies to suspend the reform effort. In 1659 the viceroy, the Conde de Alba de Liste (1656–61) attempted new reforms. He sent Francisco de la Cruz (bishop-elect of Santa Marta, in New Granada) to Potosí, with instructions from Spain to eliminate abuses of the mita and to assign a new labor draft that incorporated more provinces in Upper Peru. Once in Potosí, Francisco de la Cruz vigorously implemented his reform program, gaining an important ally in the president of the Audiencia of Charcas, Francisco Nestares Marín. Both men quickly ran afoul of local miners and Crown officials, however, and in 1660 they were found poisoned, undoubtedly murdered by powerful enemies. Finally, authorities in Lima became so frustrated with past failures at reform that on 4 July 1670, the viceroy, the Conde de Lemos (1667–72) recommended abolishing the mita altogether. Local miners countered by threatening to suspend their operations in Potosí, and the Council of the Indies refused to implement the measure. In the end, the abuses continued and silver production at Potosí continued its decline.[24]

Apart from abuses of the mita, another factor undermining Spanish administrative control was the tendency of Andeans to resist the abuses of the corregidores and the mita by fleeing their reducciones. Once away, the former tributaries could claim forastero status, which gave them a lower tax rate and exemption from the feared mita. Others simply sought protection from local miners or estate owners by working as wage laborers (often called *gañanes, conciertos,* or yanaconas). As Viceroy Luis de Velasco wrote in 1604: "[I]n order to escape from the work and vexations they suffer in the reducciones, they leave and flee and hide on haciendas, in mountainous or brush areas, and ravines, which has resulted in the desolation of the reducciones."[25] This decline of the reducciones caused much alarm in Lima, as the increasing numbers of forasteros made it impossible to monitor and control the mita and tribute systems. In 1616 and 1628 the Crown even tried to round up the forasteros and send them home, but to no avail. The problem was particularly severe in the provinces subject to the Potosí mita, where royal inspectors estimated that disease and flight accounted for the loss of over 3,100 tributaries by 1633. As a result, flight from the reducciones continued apace.

By the late seventeenth century the rising number of forasteros had so seriously undermined the inflow of tribute monies and the supply of mitayos to Potosí that the Madrid government demanded immediate and drastic action. In 1682 the viceroy of Peru, the Duque de la Palata, began this reform process by conducting a census of the thirty corregimientos of Upper Peru. The results were shocking; the Toledan systems was in shambles. In the sixteen provinces subject to the mita, the number of registered tributaries had declined by 50 percent. In the remaining corregimientos over 75 percent of the inhabitants claimed forastero status, with its lower tribute rates and exemptions from forced labor. To renovate the system, the Duque de la Palata proposed an end to legal distinctions between forasteros, yanaconas, and tributaries, making every Andean responsible for paying tribute in his place of residence, instead of in the town of his birth. In addition, the viceroy made several additional provinces responsible for supplying forced laborers to the mines. All of these changes, however, depended on active support from the kurakas and compliance from the Andean population; both failed to materialize. Instead, a groundswell of protests arose from the Andean communities, echoed by the azogueros, who also deemed the viceroy's reforms both impractical and threatening to their practice of receiving cash subsidies from the indios de faltriquera. Amidst these protests, the Crown abandoned the whole idea. As a result, the migration of Andeans, the decline of tribute receipts, and the breakdown of the mita continued apace.[26]

The Crown did not address the problem again until 1720, in the wake of a major epidemic that swept through the Andes killing at least three hundred thousand people. The epidemic forced local officials to take a new census of the Andean population, and in the process of assessing new tax rates, viceregal authorities decided to force all forasteros with access to land to pay the full tribute rate, wherever they resided. Transients without lands paid a lower rate. It was the first successful effort to revise the tribute system since Toledo.[27]

Local Spanish and Andean groups played a major role in undermining the system established by Francisco de Toledo and later attempts to reform it. While Toledo wanted the state to direct the economy through his tax, labor, and settlement programs, regional Spanish and Amerindian groups often conspired to control local economic surpluses, instead of dutifully directing them to the colonial treasuries in Lima and Madrid. Spanish estate owners, for example, profited as Andeans left the reducciones to work on their farms, while kurakas gained as their kinsmen avoided the mita and tended community flocks, worked their lands, and produced commodities for local needs. Ambitious European elites also benefited from forging alliances with dishonest local officials or even Andean groups to modify or block any objectionable royal policies. This process began even before Toledo left Peru, but it gained momentum over time. The exact configuration of such local factional groups constantly shifted, depending on the resources at stake, but by the late seventeenth century this collusion had seriously undermined royal authority in the Andes.

As Francisco de Toledo's ambitious designs to create a state-controlled colonial economy in the Andes faltered, tax receipts fell dramatically in the 1660s. Apart from the decline of state tax, labor, and settlement policies, mineral wealth in the Andes proved a wasting asset. As the productivity of the silver lodes in Potosí and elsewhere declined, so too did mining taxes. Along with the recession in the transatlantic trade with Spain, these falling tax receipts threatened to undermine the fiscal strength of the colonial state. State revenues had dropped to barely 2 million pesos by the 1680s, the lowest levels since Francisco de Toledo left the Andes one hundred years earlier. These problems only worsened in the eighteenth century. Between 1700 and 1750 total state revenues fluctuated between 710,000 pesos (1711–15) and 1,650,000 pesos (1746–50).[28] Officials in Lima and Madrid tried to rejuvenate the colonial state and expand the tax base of the realm, but official corruption and the resistance of both creole and Amerindian groups stifled all of these later fiscal initiatives. By 1750 the colonial state had exhausted its options and faced bankruptcy. The monumental efforts of Francisco de Toledo and several generations of high-ranking Crown officials to create a unified, fiscally solvent, and efficient colonial state lay in near ruins by the eighteenth century.

The Bourbon Reforms and Attempts to Revitalize State Power, 1765–1825

While the colonial state in the Andes slowly lapsed into decadence, in Spain itself a period of reform had commenced with the rise to power of the new Bourbon dynasty by 1716. The reforms gained renewed momentum, with the fall of Havana, Cuba, to the English in 1762. The loss of this major Caribbean stronghold forced King Charles III and his advisors in Madrid to shore up the colonial defense system. The expenses incurred in supporting defense outlays also prompted the Crown to tighten administrative controls and raise taxes throughout the empire. This involved a major effort to rethink the colonial relationship, and initiate policies designed to enhance royal authority throughout the empire, including the Andean provinces.

Crown officials had already taken steps to eliminate the sale of high-ranking bureaucratic appointments by 1750, which curtailed creole access to the colonial bureaucracy. This was followed in 1776 by an ambitious fiscal, commercial, bureaucratic, and defense program aimed at further renovating royal authority in the colonies. To this end, the powerful minister of the Indies, José de Gálvez, dispatched a series of powerful special investigators first to conduct full-scale inspections (*visitas*) of each important region and then to impose needed administrative, commercial, and defense reforms. This task was even more important in the Andean region, where the Viceroyalty of Peru had already been diminished by the transfer of territories to two newly created viceroyalties in South America—New Granada in 1739 and the Río de la Plata in 1776 (see map 4). This separation of Upper Peru from the old viceroyalty was particularly devastating to the fiscal structure of the state, because it removed the wealthiest silver mines (particularly Potosí and Oruro) from Lima's control.

The special investigator for the Viceroyalty of Peru was Antonio de Areche, an experienced subordinate of Gálvez, who soon recognized the magnitude of the task before him. After beginning his visita in 1777, Areche despairingly wrote to a colleague in Mexico:

> Peru is being ruined by a lack of honest officials, forced Indian labor, and the forced trade (repartimiento de comercio) conducted by district judges. The corregidores are concerned solely with their own interests. . . . [H]ow close we are to losing everything here, unless these disgusting abuses are corrected. . . . Here everything is private interest, nothing public good.[29]

The need for such strong measures was made even more obvious by the outbreak of several Andean rebellions, led by Tomás Katari, Tupac Amaru II, and Tupac Katari between 1780 and 1783. Among the grievances most frequently cited by rebel leaders were the abuses perpetuated by the corregidores de indios, particularly concerning the repartimiento de comercio. As a result, Areche and his successor in 1781, Jorge Escobedo, initiated a number of strong measures to shore up the colonial state, raise needed revenues, and maintain order in the Andean provinces.

The most important reform affecting the Andean peoples was the establishment of the intendant system in Peru in 1784.[30] The Crown appointed seven intendants who represented a new layer of colonial officialdom, linking provincial magistrates with the audiencias of the major cities and even the viceroy. Intendants were responsible for the administration of public policy, royal finances,

Map 4. *Spanish South America in 1785*

justice, and military affairs. The intendants even controlled patronage to some key ecclesiastical institutions. These powerful officials also supervised the activities of fifty-eight subdelegates, who would replace the corrupt corregidores. Concurrent with imposing the new system, the Crown also outlawed the hated repartimiento de comercio. Although tribute rates remained stable or increased only slightly during this period, the government hoped the new administrative system would collect this tax (and others) more effectively. The intendancy reforms had proven effective in raising revenues in Upper Peru after its imposition in 1776, and officials in Peru expected similarly positive results. By appointing these powerful, well-paid intendants and abolishing the old system of corregidores, the Crown hoped to eliminate bureaucratic abuses and to raise significant new amounts of tax revenue from the Andean population, and extend royal power in both the cities and the countryside.

The fiscal impact of the intendancy system justified the high expectations of Escobedo and the Madrid government. In the years immediately following the system's introduction, treasury income rose to nearly 6 million pesos, despite the loss of the rich provinces in Upper Peru. In most of the viceroyalty, tribute, mining levies, and commercial taxes contributed to this increase. They remained at this high level until the disruptions of the wars of independence in the nineteenth century. Tribute returns, for example, rose steadily from over 752,000 pesos in 1785 to over 1.3 million pesos by 1811—the gradual demographic recovery of the Andean population and more stringent efforts to collect tribute assessments largely accounted for this upsurge in tax revenues.[31]

Despite the increase in tribute receipts, the intendancy system was less effective at eliminating corruption at the local level. Subdelegates often continued many illicit practices of the corregidores. These subdelegates received no annual salary, only 3 percent of their tribute receipts. As a consequence, they began extorting tribute from their Andean charges above the legally established rates, and many even carried on the odious repartimientos to supplement their incomes. In consequence, bad government, corruption, and inefficiency continued unabated in much of the Andean countryside. Only the escalating tax load distinguished the new "reformed" regime from the system established by Toledo over two hundred years earlier.

Conclusions

The resurgence of central authority under Viceroy Francisco de Toledo proved a passing phenomenon in the Andes. When Toledo came to Peru in 1569, King Philip II entrusted him with ruling a kingdom torn by civil war and mired in a deepening economic crisis. Given the threat of a renewed outburst of civil strife and the danger of an Amerindian uprising, led by either the Inca Tupac Amaru in Vilcabamba or a number of other dissident Andean chieftains, the colonial bureaucracy and the Spanish colonists were temporarily receptive to the reformer's schemes to unify the kingdom under a strong central government. In 1569 a powerful state apparatus seemed the only way to avoid economic chaos and political tumult. Like a true representative of the Crown, Francisco de Toledo took advantage of his temporary political leverage to build on the efforts of his predecessors to solidify state power, to control the socioeconomic relations between Spaniards and Andeans, and to channel the flow of economic wealth to Spain.

Toledo's attempts to plan and direct the dynamism of the emerging colonial economy to meet the Spanish and international demands for silver, however, proved overly ambitious. As a result, the corregidores de indios (and later the subdelegates) continued abusing their powers in alliance with an ever changing series of local, regional, and supraregional networks of Spanish and Andean groups to undermine objectionable royal policies. In addition, as the exploitation of the corregidores and their allies worsened, many Andeans fled the alien world of the reducciones to seek work in Spanish towns, mines, and estates. The numbers making this transition began as a trickle, but swelled steadily during the seventeenth century, further complicating the task of colonial authorities in Lima and Madrid seeking to monitor and control the Andeans. In fact, by 1660 these factors contributed to the decline in tax revenues flowing into the viceregal coffers, which continued until the Bourbon Reform period in the 1760s.

Rampant corruption, indigenous resistance, and the decline in royal revenues finally prompted a new effort to revive royal authority in the Andes during the eighteenth century. This process of rejuvenating the colonial state and making it more responsive to the Crown culminated in the intendancy reforms of the 1780s. In the end, even these innovations failed to ensure Crown control, and by the early nineteenth century royal authority had declined once again. All that remained of the reformers' program was high tribute levies. The emerging market economy did provide opportunities to acquire wealth for some, and noxious institutions such as the dreaded mita were undermined. But, so were the minimal paternalistic state controls established by Francisco de Toledo (and later the Bourbon reformers), which helped marginally to protect the Andeans from the unfettered exploitation of the creole and peninsular elites.

Spanish colonial policies treated all the diverse indigenous groups as "Indians," which tended to blur ethnic and cultural divisions in Andean societies over time. Pushing ethnic communities into larger settlements or reducciones, for example, often redefined preexisting ethnic boundaries. Attempts to extirpate local Andean religions and promote Roman Catholicism in these new settlements also advanced this process of cultural amalgamation. So too did the viceroys' demands for labor and tribute in specie, which too often ignored the traditional ways that service to the community or state had taken place before 1532. In this way, the Spanish state curtailed the power of old indigenous ethnic elites over time, which diminished the importance of traditional ethnic distinctions between groups such as the Huanca, Colla, or Lupaka. Only the ayllu remained as an important administrative boundary. In the end, ethnicity remained a potent force in the Andes, but Spanish colonial policy still recognized only the homogeneous category of "Indian."

4

THE COLONIAL SOCIOECONOMIC ORDER

The very celebrated, always illustrious, August,
magnanimous, noble and rich town of Potosí; a world in
miniature; honor and glory of America; center of Peru;
empress of cities and towns of this new world; queen of her
opulent province; princess of native places; mistress of
treasures and fortunes . . .

> Bartolomé de Arzáns de Orsúa y Vela, 1705–36[1]

Some [Andeans] absent themselves from their communities
to avoid going to the mines where they would suffer agony
and martyrdom, and in order to avoid experiencing such
hell, hardship, and torment of the devils, others flee the
mines, and still others take to the roads to avoid the mines
and would rather chance dying suddenly rather than to suffer
a slow death . . .

> Felipe Guaman Poma de Ayala, 1615[2]

THE SPANISH INVASION OF THE ANDES began the gradual process of integrating the indigenous peoples into an expanding nexus of regional markets, which were connected to an emerging global economic arena. The introduction of European-style market exchanges began slowly at first, as the conquistadors divided most indigenous communities into encomiendas, which simply drained surplus production from the existing Andean economic system. The discovery of vast reserves of gold and silver, however, led to an accelerated expansion and integration of regional market economies. Historian James Lockhart has used the railroad metaphor of "trunk lines" and "feeder lines" to describe this expanding network of markets in the Andes. The principal avenue for market exchanges, or trunk line, extended from the viceregal capital of Lima, first by sea to the port of Arica (today in northern Chile) and then inland through the rugged Andean cordillera to Arequipa and from there through the populous indigenous zones of Upper Peru to its terminus at Potosí, the "mistress of treasures and fortunes" (as Bartolomé de Arzáns so effusively described it in the quotation above).[3] Any Spanish or Andean communities located along the trunk line complex became progressively drawn into market exchanges, while those on the subsidiary feeder lines took longer to feel the influence of the new economic order (see map 5). From its inception, however, the colonial market system could only grow and prosper with the active participation of indigenous peoples who served as workers, consumers, and producers of needed goods and services. Indeed, many of the reforms initiated by Viceroy Francisco de Toledo in the 1570s—the tribute system, corvée labor, and the reducciones—were designed to expropriate indigenous resources and to compel the participation of reluctant Andean communities in the emerging market economy.

As larger numbers of Spaniards and Andeans took part in market exchanges, an evermore prosperous and complex nexus of trunk and feeder lines evolved throughout the Viceroyalty of Peru during the seventeenth century. At first, much of the impetus behind the development of this integrated web of market economies was silver mining, but as the boom years for this industry slowly passed,

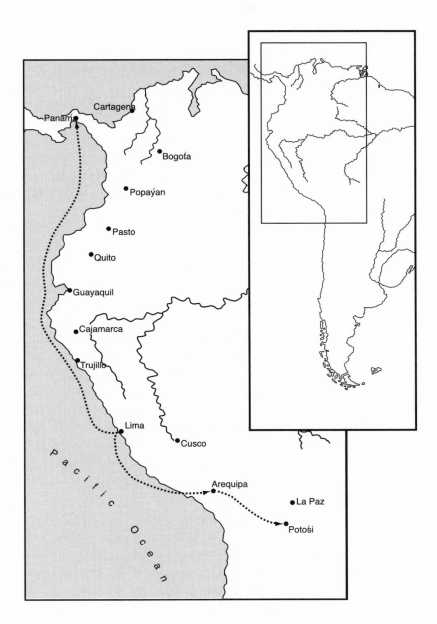

Map 5. The Trunk Line and the Principal Economic Centers
in the Viceroyalty of Peru

regional economies—based on agriculture, artisan crafts, manufacturing, and intercolonial trade—began to develop more independently of the trunk line running from Lima to Potosí. This more diverse complex of regional markets certainly had its cycles of prosperity and recession. Between 1687 and 1730, for example, a series of earthquakes and epidemics struck different regions of the Andes causing economic repercussions felt throughout the trunk and feeder line system. Nevertheless, by the 1760s a recovery in silver mining and the transatlantic trade produced new levels of prosperity. Indeed, this economic upswing encouraged the Bourbon monarchy in Spain to initiate a second major reform era to tax and control those economic sectors that had developed since the Toledan Reforms.

Over time, the expansion of the market economy provided daunting challenges but also new opportunities for Andean peoples. Market pressures, epidemic diseases, and excessive tribute and mita quotas took a heavy toll on indigenous communities, prompting the lament (in the second quotation above) from Felipe Guaman Poma de Ayala about "the torment of devils," and a "slow death" in the mines. Despite the diseases and economic exploitation that accompanied colonial rule, some Andean ethnic groups resisted, survived, and prospered. Indigenous communities participated in market exchanges to endure the challenges of Spanish rule, and some kurakas even made vast personal fortunes. The majority were less fortunate, however, prompting wholesale migrations from traditional communities to flee excessive tribute and mita obligations or to take advantage of economic opportunities elsewhere.

Because of the state's important role in the evolution of colonial markets, government organizations provide a wealth of data on the material life of Amerindian communities in the Spanish Andes. The colonial state, for example, generated many different types of data on demographic trends, such as lists of taxpaying Andean tributaries and by the eighteenth century, more detailed censuses (*padrones*). In addition, official economic data found in fiscal accounts (*cuentas*) from the local treasury offices (*cajas reales*); administrative reports; the records of Spanish estate owners, merchants, and miners; court proceedings; and notary materials (dealing with contracts, wills, and a variety of other mundane matters) provide a cornucopia of information about the socioeconomic evolution of the Andean provinces. Much of this archival data can be supplemented by archaeological materials and ethnographic information to provide clues about numerous additional matters, such as how indigenous economic attitudes and beliefs shifted over time.

The Initial Phase: Conquest and Settlement, 1532–69

The first Spanish invaders of the Andes came with self-serving, but realistic, entrepreneurial goals—plunder and profit. After the overthrow of Tawantinsuyu, the conquistadors quickly attempted to promote a vigorous market economy. The first institution established to govern the Andes, the encomienda, merged this European mercantile mode of production with the preexisting Andean notions of kin-based reciprocity and redistribution. The early encomenderos used profits from controlling Andean tribute and labor to engage in a diverse assortment of supplementary economic activities—acquiring lands to raise stock and crops for local markets, speculating in urban properties, founding mines and textile mills, and taking part in a wide range of commercial exchanges. Although some encomenderos accumulated great fortunes from such ventures, control over the labor, wealth, and productive capacity of their Andean charges formed the center-piece of their business enterprises. In short, the encomienda allowed the first generation of settlers to harness indigenous modes of production and to connect them to an expanding network of regional markets, linking the Andes to Europe and beyond.[4]

Despite its importance, the encomienda caused a series of problems within indigenous communities that undermined its long-term effectiveness for exploiting Andean resources. The Andean societies were not organized for the production of goods and services demanded by a rapidly increasing European population. The fall of Tawantinsuyu, the persistence of Inca resistance, and the depredations of the civil wars also disrupted fragile vertical patterns of trade and production in the Andes. Moreover, encomiendas sometimes divided Andean confederations or separated individual communities from their ethnic colonists (mitimaes) living at different ecological levels. By the 1550s and 1560s, for example, encomienda grants had so disturbed traditional lines of ethnic authority in Cochabamba that highland and valley kurakas squabbled incessantly in colonial courts for control over the lands and production of different groups of mitimaes.[5]

Social tensions in the Andes only worsened as excessive tax and labor demands of some encomenderos posed heavy burdens on the diminished economic resources of indigenous communities. Such abuses often led to conflicts between encomenderos and local kurakas. From the earliest years of the colony many powerful ethnic leaders had allied themselves with sympathetic Spanish clergymen, such as Fray Domingo de Santo Tomás, to oppose abusive encomenderos. A few strident Andean leaders even petitioned Spain, offering the Crown money to end the encomienda and to restore their own authority over indigenous communities. In 1582, ethnic lords in Charcas, for example, sent a petition to the King, listing their noble genealogy and asserting: "[W]e alone are the counts and marquises of this realm."[6] These indigenous leaders further demanded privileges at the Potosí mines and knighthoods in the Royal Order of Santiago. Nevertheless, the Crown ignored the requests, implementing instead its own socioeconomic vision in the Andean provinces.

The onset of European epidemic diseases, however, provided another blow to the embattled encomienda system. According to historical demographers, waves of European diseases (influenza, smallpox, measles, plague, and other forms of pestilence) caused the pre-invasion population of what is now modern-day Peru to drop from approximately 9 million to just under 1 million by the arrival of Toledo in 1569. By 1630 diseases—compounded by famine, overwork, excessive taxes, and the loss of traditional lands—had reduced the population further to approximately 600,000.[7] Densely populated lowland regions suffered the greatest losses, while the Andean population in the more scattered mountain valleys generally experienced less severe mortality rates. Similar patterns obtained throughout the rest of the Andean cordillera and the coastal regions. In the Audiencia of Quito, for example, the indigenous population fell from approximately 1.5 million in 1520 to less than 250,000 by the end of the sixteenth century. Population losses were staggering everywhere in the north, but as in Peru they reached the highest levels in coastal regions, where over 95 percent of the population died. Although less is known about the impact of epidemics in Upper Peru, studies by historical demographers indicate that epidemics caused catastrophic losses throughout the region, where the Amerindian population in several important provinces fell by over 60 percent between 1561 and 1683, making the demographic catastrophe comparable to other regions of the Andes.[8] The indigenous population of the Andes did not stabilize and begin to recover from the onslaught of disease until the 1650s, only to suffer another major setback following later waves of severe epidemics that hit the North Andes (modern Ecuador) in the 1690s and in the central and southern Andes between 1719 and 1730.

The decline of the encomienda and traditional indigenous communities by the 1560s led to a deepening political and economic crisis, which posed a serious threat to Spanish rule in the Andes upon the arrival of Viceroy Francisco de Toledo in 1569. The energetic but ruthless viceroy responded to these daunting problems by reinvigorating the power of the colonial state. Through his labor (mita), resettlement, and tax policies, Toledo used this colonial state apparatus to force Andean participation in market-oriented production and exchange. In this way, he hoped to stabilize and control the economic development of the Andes and siphon off a considerable portion of its resources to metropolitan Spain.

The Silver Metropolis, 1569–1620

The Toledan reforms solidified Spanish control over the Andes and established the foundations for a network of regional markets, branching off from the trunk line running from Lima to Potosí. The economic core of this emerging market economy revolved around silver and gold mines in highland Peru and Upper Peru, and the transatlantic trade centered in the viceregal capital of Lima. Mines at Castrovirreyna, Cailloma, Pasco, San Antonio de Esquilache, Carangas, Laicocota, Oruro, and of course, the "empress of cities," Potosí, produced legendary amounts of silver for markets in Europe and even the Far East, yielding immense profits to Spanish colonists and to the Crown.

The origin of this emerging Peruvian trunk line was the viceregal capital of Lima, known officially as the "City of the Kings." Enterprising traders in the city facilitated the exchange of silver and other colonial goods for European products, tying the Andes to a wider global commercial arena. From 1566 the Crown established a regular system of convoys to protect the valuable commercial lanes to the New World and restricted direct participation in this trade to only a few cities in the Indies. Lima was the licensed port to serve the Andean region, and its merchant guild became a powerful link in the transatlantic commerce in silver and European goods. Peru became a silver metropolis in the minds of contemporaries, and tales of its legendary wealth circulated widely. According to one observer in 1595: "Many [Lima] merchants, having a treasure of three or four hundred bars and ingots of silver, each worth about five hundred *escudos*, pile them up and then spreading mattresses on them, use them as beds for sleeping."[9] These merchants also played a key role in supplying the city of Lima itself with needed foodstuffs to fuel its urban growth. By 1610 the viceregal capital had expanded to twenty-five thousand inhabitants, which annually consumed 240,000 *fanegas* (approximately 384,000 bushels) of wheat, 25,000 of corn, 3,500 head of cattle, 400 sheep, 7 tons of rice, and 200,000 bottles of wine. This produce came from markets scattered throughout the viceroyalty and even from faraway centers in Europe and later Asia (see map 5).

This meandering Peruvian trunk line ended at Potosí, whose legendary "red mountain" yielded dazzling amounts of silver. Whereas Lima served as the region's gateway to Europe and the global economy, mining centers such as Potosí became the growth poles for an integrated network of internal markets. Estimates of Potosí's population are notoriously imprecise, but from a ramshackle mining town of 14,000 persons shortly after its foundation in 1545, the city's inhabitants may have reached over 150,000 (largely from the influx of Andean corvée and wage laborers) in its heyday between 1600 and 1650. Potosí allowed producers and merchants to make fortunes supplying luxury goods, wine, brandy, and fish from coastal Peru, while sugar, preserves, fruit, wine, wheat, corn, meat, cotton, clothing, and coca came from inland centers such as Cusco, Chucuito, Tucumán, Paraguay, Santa Cruz, and Cochabamba (see map 5). According to contemporaries, the daily volume of trade in Potosí alone in 1549 (when the city was scarcely four years old) averaged sixty thousand silver pesos.

To supply the cities and mining zones a burgeoning rural economy emerged along the trunk line and the various feeder lines, which specialized in livestock, agriculture, and manufacturing enterprises. Spanish encomenderos and other settlers quickly began taking possession of vacant lands, forming the beginnings of commercial agriculture and livestock raising in the Andes. The size and type of estate depended on a range of variables—climate, the crops or livestock raised, the availability of investment capital or good land, and most importantly, the distance and strength of local markets. In addition, virtually all Spanish estates relied extensively on inexpensive Andean laborers.

Spanish landed estates most often emerged on lands left vacant by depopulation or in areas not intensively cultivated by the indigenous societies, such as regions near the more remote mines. Individual entrepreneurs usually gained access to this land through grants from Crown officials or by direct purchase from indigenous communities. In some regions local kurakas even sold ayllu land to enrich themselves, indicating that European notions of private property were beginning to overcome Andean traditions regarding communal property ownership and reciprocity. When offers of direct purchase were rebuffed, some unscrupulous Spaniards resorted to illegal seizures of indigenous property. By the late sixteenth century the chaotic process of granting land had produced so many conflicting claims to property that the Crown ordered an inspection of land titles in 1591 (*venta y composición de tierras*). Those without a legal title had to pay a tax to maintain their property. The process was repeated in 1631, but it too brought a host of protests from indigenous communities about the abuses of local Spanish landowners, land inspectors, and sometimes unscrupulous kurakas. Regardless of the widespread chorus of complaints surrounding the emergence of Spaniard estates, these landholdings formed a key link in the emerging market economy, supplying needed agropastoral products to growing urban centers and mining zones.

Despite the importance of regional markets, by 1600 indigenous communities remote from the complex of trunk and feeder lines still resisted European modes of production. On the north coast of Peru, for example, the Spanish invasion caused considerable unrest but little direct market participation by indigenous communities. After all, Andeans had traditionally gained access to goods outside of their own ecological zones through vertical exchanges, not by utilizing any widespread form of market transactions. In the cities and rural regions where the encomiendas predominated, the indigenous communities often proved unwilling to produce goods demanded by their Spanish overlords or to sell their labor services to outsiders. As a result, under extreme pressures from Spanish authorities native lords forcibly mobilized local labor for the task, leading ordinary Amerindians to resist by fleeing their communities for frontier zones. Sometimes these refugees were individual males, but more often entire families or kin groups fled the demands of the

Spaniards and those traditional ethnic leaders who served the Europeans' interests. This exodus became so serious that local kurakas held a meeting in 1558 to discuss how to force the return of escapees to their ayllus. Nevertheless, the problem endured for many years, and market exchanges expanded in northern Peru only gradually.[10]

Andeans in the provinces nearer the trunk and feeder lines responded far differently than those living in more remote settlements along the north coast of Peru. Local kurakas, for example, participated in colonial markets from the outset, and some ethnic lords even began to make vast fortunes. The fabulously wealthy and powerful Diego Caqui, kuraka of Tacna, provides only one particularly vivid example. Tacna was situated amidst a major southern grape-producing region, which exported considerable quantities of wine and brandy to mining centers in Upper Peru, particularly to Potosí. When Diego Caqui died in 1588, his will specified that the kuraka owned an estate worth 260,000 pesos, including a coastal vineyard with forty thousand plants and three ships engaged in coastal trading. Nevertheless, Diego Caqui used his wealth in the manner of a traditional Andean kuraka, employing the produce of these lands to meet tribute quotas, to support local festivals and ceremonies, and to provide gifts for his people. In short, some enterprising kurakas, such as Caqui, could participate in local markets to gain personal wealth, while still fulfilling their traditional economic functions of redistribution and reciprocity within their local communities.[11]

The emergence of a market economy in the Andes by the 1570s had produced profound socioeconomic changes, offering both pitfalls and opportunities for traditional indigenous communities and their ethnic leaders, the kurakas. In some cases, such as the north coast of Peru, local ethnic leaders simply accommodated themselves to the colonial regime by increasing the pressures on their communities to meet Spanish labor and tribute demands. In areas where the emerging market economy offered alternatives to such direct exploitation, ethnic lords such as Diego Caqui participated actively in local market exchanges, easing the burdens on their communities and at the same time amassing great personal fortunes. While the leaders Tawantinsuyu had built their empire on the foundations of the old Andean ethnic mosaic, the introduction of fundamentally new modes of European mercantile production brought much more far-reaching socioeconomic changes to the Andean world.

Regionalism and Economic Diversification, 1620–1730

During the seventeenth century growing economic diversification in the viceroyalty slowly prompted a series of realignments in the simple network of trunk and feeder lines that had emerged after the conquest. The decline of silver mining and the transatlantic trade provided a powerful stimulus for developing a wider array of regional and local economic sectors between approximately 1620 and 1687. The Viceroyalty of Peru was rich in natural resources, which eventually served as the foundation for an ever widening nucleus of regional market economies. Although mining declined, it never shrank to economic insignificance; even in the worst years of the period, Potosí produced large amounts of silver, and its output still compared favorably with the yields of Mexico's largest silver mines. Nevertheless, mining and transatlantic commerce no longer attracted so much of the available investment capital, which now flowed to more vibrant economic sectors, such as agriculture, manufacturing, and artisanal production. Although these regional economies experienced periodic cycles of expansion and contraction, the overall trend was toward greater self-sufficiency and diversification, at least until late in the seventeenth century.

These gradual socioeconomic changes also promoted wider participation by Andean communities in colonial markets. While not all indigenous communities became utterly dependent on them, commercial exchanges emerged as an important factor in the prosperity and the economic survival of indigenous communities. Sometimes the tribute and labor policies of the colonial state encouraged this market participation. In other cases, the Andeans responded creatively to the allure of economic gain. Regardless of the motivation, larger numbers of Andeans continued to participate in market exchanges and to work in the mines or on Spanish estates. As European modes of production expanded, the indigenous peoples adapted their kin-based norms and institutions to the rapidly changing economic landscape. Nevertheless, Andean peoples often did so without completely sacrificing their own cultural matrix, which still shaped so many of their market activities.

After the Toledan reforms, state demands for tribute in specie played a key role in encouraging Andean communities to take a more active role in local markets. As the Jesuit José de Acosta pointed out in his criticisms of Toledo's system of tribute collection in 1577: "[S]ince the Indians do not have silver in their lands, except only for those who have mines, they now have to earn money with hard labor and leave their homes in order to find waged employment."[12] Forcing Andeans to substitute money payments for tribute in kind, for example, encouraged them to sell their goods and labor to Europeans, in order to get the cash needed for their tax assessments. Moreover, the exorbitant rates assessed to some communities served as an added stimulus to market participation. Spanish authorities in the Audiencia of Quito, for example, assessed rates of four to nine pesos annually, which effectively forced Andeans to seek work at low wages (set by the Crown) in the region's textile mills (*obrajes*). Similar patterns obtained in Upper Peru, where high tribute rates forced indigenous groups in the region of Chaqui to enter the market economy by raising and selling barley, using their llamas for transporting goods, and working for wages in nearby Potosí.

Apart from tribute exactions, state-imposed mita obligations also forced reluctant Andean laborers to work for long periods in Spanish mining towns. The mita of Potosí, for example, established an annual quota of approximately 13,500 corvée laborers from sixteen highland provinces to the mining town. Many of these workers later stayed on to work as wage laborers (mingas) or independent ore cutters (*kajchas*), which contributed to the dizzying growth of that city's population to nearly 150,000 by the 1650s. In short, the mita helped to create an indigenous labor market where Andeans worked for wages instead of just performing tasks on community holdings.

Spanish rural estates also attracted indigenous workers seeking cash to meet tribute obligations, to escape mita service, or just to find more productive employment. Since most Spanish estate owners did not receive mita allocations, they used a variety of devices to lure Andean workers to their mills, farms, and ranches. Despite offering relatively low wages, estate owners often succeeded in enticing seasonal laborers (*jornaleros*), eager to earn cash to pay their tribute assessments. In the provinces of Huacho and Végueta near Lima, for example, by the 1620s Spanish landowners hired highlanders as seasonal labor on local wheat and grape estates. Spanish landowners also attracted Andean laborers to work as full-time wage laborers. Estate owners usually offered laborers a cash advance, a small plot of land to cultivate, and food or tools allowances. Spaniards also provided full-time wage laborers with protection from mita service and met each worker's tribute obligations. Since wages were low (and employers deducted all tribute payments from a worker's earnings), many workers fell into debt. Debtors were then legally bound to work for their employers until they paid off their financial obligations. This system of debt peonage effectively kept indigenous laborers in servitude. Many Andeans undoubtedly escaped debt peonage, but it remained one more way that the colonial market system altered traditional indigenous forms of production and labor.

By 1600 the explosive growth of remote mining towns, such as Potosí, led to massive imports of goods, many traversing the rugged Andean cordillera in indigenous caravans, called *trajines*. These trajines became a central link connecting the various segments of the Peruvian trunk line, crossing the densely populated indigenous lands between Arequipa and Potosí. Much of the responsibility and the burdens of these trajines fell on the

Aymara-speaking communities along the major routes, particularly the Lupaka and Pacajes living around Lake Titicaca. Such ethnic communities provided the pack animals (sometimes mules but more often llamas), the manpower, and whatever other resources were needed to maintain the trajines. The caravans shipped Arequipan wine and brandy over 150 leagues to Cusco, La Plata, and ultimately Potosí, the major marketplace. Likewise, large amounts of coca leaf (a popular stimulant chewed by Andean mine workers) moved along routes from estates in the lowland *yungas* around Cusco and La Paz to the mining towns, a distance of at least 160 leagues.

Merchants organized the caravans, but from the sixteenth century the Crown ordered local corregidores de indios to assist in mustering resources needed for the trajines. With the intervention of the corregidores, supporting the trajines became an onerous form of state service, much like the mita. Wages for Andean workers were low, barely covering the cost of food, drink, and coca, let alone providing adequate compensation for being away from typical agrarian tasks. Moreover, the merchants organizing the caravans only paid workers for the one-way trek to the various mining towns, not the return trip. As a result, the cost of furnishing llamas or mules for the round trip, and the various risks entailed in the hazardous two- or three-month journeys heightened the communal burdens of supporting the caravans.[13]

Despite the exploitative nature of the trajines, enterprising Aymara herding communities, such as the Lupaka, still managed to find ways to profit from them. The llama caravans allowed indigenous communities to carry and sell specialized trading articles, such as coca, salt, and livestock products, along crucial central and south Andean commercial routes. Supplementary profits from these transactions often counteracted the potential losses incurred in the caravans. Moreover, the importance of trajines and the large llama herds supporting them allowed Aymara groups to resist the incursions of Spanish landowners seeking to divest them of communal pasture lands. After all, most Spanish merchants and corregidores were loathe to have anyone expropriate the lands and other resources from communities maintaining the vital trajines supplying the urban markets of Upper Peru. Thus, participating in trajines throughout the central and south Andean trade routes allowed some communities to turn this exploitative system into a profitable activity that helped to maintain traditional ayllu.

Spanish cities and towns became another important theater for Andean participation in the market economy. In mining centers, such as Potosí and Oruro, most Andean residents undoubtedly worked in various tasks associated with the extraction of silver. Other cities with more diverse economies, however, offered a wider variety of employment options. In seventeenth-century Cusco, for example, nearly 50 percent of the labor contracts involved Andeans joining mule trains to the mining centers, followed in importance by service sector jobs (particularly as domestics and food sellers) at 30 percent, skilled artisan trades at 10 percent, and agricultural service with 10 percent.[14] The bulk of the indigenous population surrounding the north Andean provincial capital of Quito also cultivated communal lands or small freeholds supplying produce for the urban market. Moreover, Amerindians (mostly women) in Quito served as hucksters (*regatonas*) and peddlers (*gateras*) to distribute these goods in the city markets.

While some Andeans owned city property or small shops, most lived on the margins of urban society where they frequently suffered exploitation from their creole and mestizo employers. Domestic servants in La Paz, for example, were usually unattached women who eked out a meager living, seldom formed stable marriages, and often labored to raise several illegitimate offspring.[15] Andean hucksters and market women in cities like Quito also suffered exploitation and abuse by European merchants and store owners, who resented the competition from these Andean men and women working in the local marketplace. Likewise, in Potosí a large number of petty merchants imported vital supplies of coca, crude woolen and cotton cloth, and local produce into the city, but these motley, small-scale traders usually earned only a pittance.[16]

By the seventeenth century, Andean responses to the expanding network of trunk and feeder lines often involved some forced or voluntary migrations from the ayllu. Whether the indigenous peoples moved to fulfill their mita obligations, to resist colonial oppression, or to take advantage of new employment opportunities in regional market economies, migration became a commonplace adaptive strategy for indigenous groups from Quito to La Paz. Indeed, by the 1680s much of the Andes had become a virtual beehive of human activity, with individuals and families moving constantly.

The devastating losses from epidemic diseases, heavy tribute and mita obligations, Spanish usurpations of community lands, and even the lure of market participation led many Andeans to leave their ayllu permanently. Migrations had long been a part of Andean history, even before the expansion of Tawantinsuyu, as communities sent colonists to different ecological regions to gain access to needed economic resources. The Inca state allowed this practice to continue and also relocated some ethnic groups by force to satisfy its political and economic designs. The system of reducciones imposed by Francisco de Toledo, however, vastly increased the level of forced resettlement. As one Spanish observer, Melchor Suárez de Poago, indicated in 1634: "[T]he Indians, or almost all of them, leave their villages and flee to distant and remote parts ten, twenty, thirty, and fifty leagues away where neither the corregidores nor the caciques nor Indian governors nor the appointed tax collectors can collect tribute from them."[17] As the exploitation of the Andean peoples on these strategic hamlets continued apace, a steady swell of migrants left their ayllu, apparently severing ties with their kinsmen permanently.

Few areas in the Andes experienced more out-migration than did those provinces of Upper Peru subject to the Potosí mita. According to the law, only male tributaries between eighteen and fifty years of age residing in their natal communities (*originarios*) were subject to mita. As epidemics thinned the population in these regions, the burdens of corvée labor became more onerous in many ayllus, encouraging many community residents to migrate to other regions. Once ensconced in another community, the Andeans could become forasteros, who were outsiders with no rights to community lands. This legal status also allowed the forasteros to claim a lower tribute rate and an exemption from the mita. By 1646 over 36 percent of the population in these provinces were officially listed as forasteros; by the census of the Duque de la Palata in 1683 that number had risen to 54 percent. The provinces experiencing the greatest out-migration were those in the altiplano, which traditionally had supplied the greatest number of mitayos to Potosí. These migrants found refuge in urban areas and those rural zones not subject to the mita, such as the lowland yungas, where Spanish commercial estates provided employment opportunities for refugees.

Despite the pervasiveness of migration throughout the Andean cordillera, significant numbers of migrants continued to maintain links with their original ayllu for spiritual, social, and material support. Much of the migration in the Cusco region, for example, was relatively short-range, as Andeans sought jobs in the city or took over unoccupied agricultural lands. Nevertheless, these migrants often continued contributing tribute and labor services to their home communities. Similar patterns emerged by the seventeenth century in Upper Peru, where some highland kurakas even retained control over ayllu migrants who had left their communities to find work or farmland elsewhere. In 1702, for example, María Orcoma, a woman from the town of Jesús de Machaca died, leaving an estate that included rental property in Oruro. Her kuraka claimed this real estate for the community, maintaining that Orcoma had resided most of her life in the local ayllu one hundred miles from the mining city. In short, even when Andeans left their ayllu, participated in local markets, and accumulated wealth, they often retained traditional ties and obligations to their ancestral homes. The case of María Orcoma also indicates that some indigenous leaders still brought court cases to defend communal ownership rights over notions of individual private property as late as the early eighteenth century.

When migrants severed ties with their ayllu, a process called ethnogenesis often took place, leading to the reformulation of traditional lifestyles, social practices, and cultural identities in new communities. In rural zones many forasteros acquired land among other ethnic groups through sharecropping, rental, or outright purchase, sometimes being absorbed into the communities where they had come to reside. In other cases, groups of migrants constituted a separate ayllu of forasteros in rural areas, representing a mix of different ethnic groups. Over time, these forasteros intermarried, took on a blend of cultural values, and through this process of ethnogenesis, formed an entirely new community, with its own social, economic, and cultural patterns. On the North Andean estate of Guachalá (in Cayambe, Ecuador), for example, migrants from several different ethnic groups throughout the northern portions of the Audiencia of Quito came to seek work. Each group originally retained its characteristic ethnic surname after arriving on Guachalá, but by the late eighteenth century the number of such surnames on the estate diminished significantly. Apparently members of the ethnic groups had intermarried, abandoning their old surnames, and forging a new eclectic mix of ideas about community and ethnicity on the estate.[18] Regardless of where it took place, the process of ethnogenesis still produced communities that maintained primarily traditional Andean rather than Spanish customs.

State policies and the market economy also produced significant changes in the role of kurakas, as ethnic leaders adjusted to new socioeconomic circumstances. Sometimes these pressures caused them to lose status and power. Throughout the Andes, colonial officials frequently imprisoned or replaced kurakas who did not meet state tax or labor quotas in their communities. Other regional Andean leaders, however, used their pivotal position between the ayllu and Spanish society to attain wealth, power, and even a precarious status in both societies. The kuraka of Asillo (in Azángaro, Peru), Bartolomé Tupa Hallicalla, for example, used his position to amass a considerable personal fortune, through his activities as a merchant, miner, and landowner. He also managed to control a huge grazing estate with four thousand sheep and llamas for the community of Asillo, which he managed for his people. In this way, he fulfilled his responsibilities to secure the prosperity of his community as a kuraka, while still gaining a considerable personal fortune. Moreover, when armed clashes broke out in the frontier town of Laicacota between rival mining clans, this kuraka donated nine thousand pesos in cash, livestock, foodstuffs, wine, and grains to viceregal authorities trying to reestablish order. To reward him for this assistance, the viceroy of Peru, the Conde de Santisteban, named Tupa Hallicalla captain of the local indigenous infantry in 1661, an honor that allowed him to ride a horse, bear weapons, and enjoy military immunity from certain types of civil prosecution. As a Christian and a wealthy local entrepreneur, the kuraka also married a prominent creole woman, establishing important kinship ties to European society, which served him well for many years. When Bartolomé Tupa Hallicalla became implicated in an aborted indigenous rebellion in 1667, for example, his allies apparently helped him to emerge unscathed. It was not until Tupa Hallicalla ran afoul of the church over a series of disputes with local clergymen in the 1680s that he eventually suffered imprisonment and death.[19] While skillful kurakas, such as Bartolomé Tupa Hallicalla, might gain wealth and status, their social position always remained subordinate and often precarious.

By participating as consumers, laborers, and producers in Andean regional economies, the indigenous peoples played an integral role in the economic evolution of the colonial order from the 1620s to the 1680s. Where they survived, indigenous ayllu supplied agricultural, mining, and manufacturing laborers, and food for urban markets. Their migrations from decaying rural economies to areas of greater prosperity also allowed agriculture, business, and trade to flourish. Despite these considerable contributions to the economic development of the Andes, however, the indigenous peoples suffered heavy tribute and corvée labor obligations, which drained resources from their communities. This interweaving of Andean subsistence sectors with regional markets gave added flexibility, dynamism, and strength to the colonial economy, but the limited benefits Andeans derived from this colonial market economy never matched their contributions. While traditional forms of Andean economic exchange based on reciprocity and redistribution eroded, indigenous ethnic groups still tried to participate in colonial markets on their own terms. Despite the overtly exploitative nature of colonial tribute and mita levies, many Andeans migrated to work in the mines, on Spanish estates, or in urban centers as a survival strategy for reproducing traditional family and community life. Forasteros often remained in touch with their traditional communities, returning when mining jobs or seasonal labor on Spanish estates had ended. Even when migration did lead to a complete break with traditional ayllu, communities of forasteros created new lifeways on Spanish estates, on the rural holdings of different indigenous ethnic groups, or even in urban areas. The process of ethnogenesis created new communities, but the material and cultural matrix that governed them was much more Andean than European. Even along the trunk lines, the incursions of the colonial state and European modes of production altered but seldom destroyed Andean culture and society.

The more diversified colonial order that emerged during the seventeenth century suffered a series of reversals—earthquakes, epidemics, and the further decline of silver mining—which eroded the vibrancy of the economy in many regions. In 1687 the viceregal capital of Lima and the entire central coast of Peru suffered a series of devastating earthquakes. Within five years the capital city's population had fallen from nearly eighty thousand to under forty thousand inhabitants, and the irrigation systems that had sustained coastal agriculture were devastated, prompting a sustained agrarian crisis. These shocks were followed by a series of epidemics and earthquakes in the Audiencia of Quito beginning in the 1690s, which undermined the buoyant regional textile industry of the north-central highlands. Meanwhile, the mining industry also continued its decline, particularly at Potosí, where production fell from over 800,000 marks (a measure of weight equal to one-half pound) of silver in the 1590s to under 100,000 marks by the 1740s.[20] Amidst these difficulties another wave of epidemics—plague, influenza, and measles—ravaged Peru and Upper Peru between 1719 and 1720 and again in the 1730s. Not every region suffered the effects of this series of disasters equally, or even endured prolonged economic recessions, but collectively they produced a severe setback to the integrated network of colonial markets that had evolved since the 1620s.

By the early eighteenth century transatlantic commerce between the Viceroyalty of Peru and Spain had declined, further weakening the economic primacy of Lima and its merchant elite. The system of convoy fleets that had carried so much silver from the Andes to Seville had become moribund by this period. Transatlantic fleet sailings declined from twenty-nine in the period 1600–1650, to nineteen between 1650 and 1700; between 1700 and 1740 only seven convoys left Spain. French and British contraband traders plied the Pacific with near impunity during much of the 1700–1730 period, supplying many of the luxury goods previously imported from Spain. The Madrid government first dealt with the problem by attempting to revive the convoy system. When this proved futile, the Crown ended the system of licensed fleets dispatched from Spain in 1740, relying instead on periodic licensed-registry ships to carry goods to and from the Indies.[21]

Along with the eclipse of Potosí, these fundamental economic changes led to a dramatic realignment in the nexus of trunk and feeder lines that had emerged in the sixteenth century. Changes in market linkages had been underway since the seventeenth century, but the economic shocks of the 1687–1730 period accelerated the trend. Colonial textile manufacturers in the Audiencia of Quito, for example, began to sell more of their woolens to markets in New Granada rather than Lima. Likewise, the mining centers of Upper Peru began trading with Buenos Aires, instead of relying on the old trunk line running from Potosí to Lima. Even the indigenous trajines originating in the Lake Titicaca region began moving from the mines to northern Argentina, instead of just operating between southern Peru and the mines of Upper Peru.

Economic Revival and the Bourbon Reforms, 1730–1825

By the 1730s the discovery of new silver mines and the more efficient exploitation of older deposits led to an overall renaissance in mining and commerce in Peru. Internal commerce began to revive and the move to licensed registry ships by the 1740s prompted a revival of commerce with Europe. Nevertheless, the overall diversification of the colonial economy and the fundamental realignment of the colonial market system continued apace. Mining taxes collected in Peru rose from a mere 60,570 pesos (1700–1709) to nearly 870,000 pesos (1790–99). Mines in Upper Peru, including Potosí, saw less impressive gains, rising from a low of less than 350,000 pesos (1740–49) to a high of over 620,000 pesos during the 1780s.[22] This rising output from the silver mines also energized the transatlantic commerce through Lima, particularly after the introduction of imperial free trade between 1778 and 1789.

Despite this commercial revival, the monopoly of the Lima merchant class, already weakened by the decline of the fleet system, continued its slow decline during the century. At first guild members attempted to compensate by investing more heavily in intercolonial trade routes, but various natural disasters afflicting the capital city and much of the Andean region between 1687 and 1730 curtailed the profitability of such commercial outlets. The next blow to Limeño dominance came in 1776 when the great silver-mining provinces of Upper Peru became part of the newly created Viceroyalty of the Río de la Plata, with its capital in Buenos Aires. Finally, between 1776 and 1789 the Crown gradually allowed free trade within the empire, which further undermined the commercial domination of the viceregal capital.

The Lima merchants did benefit from the overall rise in commerce following imperial free trade, but their monopoly of South American commerce had ended.

The erosion of their commercial supremacy prompted many Lima merchants to seek investment opportunities in the Andean hinterland, particularly after the internal economy began to revive in the 1730s. This involved opening up the vast market potential of indigenous communities in the interior provinces. The repartimiento de comercio (the forced distribution of merchandise) was an important device for tapping the wealth of the interior provinces. Limeño merchants supplied local corregidores (who had a legal commercial monopoly in the indigenous communities) with a variety of goods from their storehouses, particularly mules, American and European cloth merchandise, and iron or steel products. The prices charged for this merchandise were highly inflated, which cheated the Andean peoples but reaped enormous profits for the merchants and the corregidores. By the 1730s, for example, repartimiento quotas in the province of Chilques y Masques allegedly amounted to 84,500 pesos annually, and contemporaries estimated that an "able" corregidor could net 50,000 pesos in profits during a five-year term. In short, Lima merchants used their economic power and political connections to force larger numbers of Andeans to participate in the market economy on terms that were increasingly unfavorable to the indigenous communities. The Crown did not end the practice until the wave of Andean rebellions erupted in the 1780s.

Apart from relying on the repartimiento de comercio, Spanish and creole merchants also began sending merchandise to interior markets utilizing a complex network of internal trade routes. The increase of the Andean population in Peru and Upper Peru undoubtedly encouraged these increasingly vigorous commercial exchanges in the internal economy. Although some merchants dispatched large caravans, such as the trajines moving between Arequipa, Cusco, and Potosí, most often small-scale traders plied these arduous overland routes carrying one or two mule-loads of American or European merchandise. Such commercial ties extended throughout the Andes, supplying the interior with a wider variety of merchandise. These trade routes tied the indigenous peoples, mestizos, and Spaniards in the hinterland to the large commercial houses in cities such as Lima and Buenos Aires.

By the 1760s metropolitan authorities recognized that much commerce in the interior escaped taxation, so the Crown began extending a network of customs offices (*aduanas*) to collect the sales tax (*alcabala*) on all market transactions. Although Andeans were not theoretically subject to paying sales taxes, customs agents often collected the levy anyway, which increased transaction costs and lowered profits. The Crown also began taxing the various goods being sold in urban centers, and much of this produce traditionally had been marketed by Andeans. Given the already high tribute assessments and repartimiento quotas weighing on Andean communities, these added fiscal exactions only heightened the economic burdens on the Andean ayllu, limiting the potential gain from market transactions.

Throughout the Andean region from the 1770s the Crown also implemented a series of administrative changes to collect tribute revenues and meet mita quotas more effectively. Whether imposing the intendancy system or special agencies to supervise the head tax, royal officials managed to clarify the tax status of the Andeans, adjust tribute rates, and enroll thousands of unregistered males between the ages of eighteen and fifty. The result was an unprecedented upsurge in the numbers of indigenous males subject to the mita and in the amounts of tribute flowing into Crown coffers by the 1780s. In the Viceroyalty of Peru, for example, tribute receipts rose from nearly 85,000 pesos (1690–99) to over 1 million pesos (1790–99); in Upper Peru tribute returns increased from 88,000 pesos (1720–29) to nearly 890,000 pesos (1800–1809). In both Peru and Upper Peru, Amerindian tribute actually became the largest single source of revenue for the colonial state, outstripping even levies on mining and commerce.[23] This growth in tribute revenues far exceeded population growth or any increases in regional economic activity;

it merely meant far heavier tax burdens on the beleaguered Andean population.

In the first half of the eighteenth century, complaints about the abuses of the colonial system escalated. A number of these early protesters were literate, hispanicized Andean kurakas, who complained in formal, written petitions to the Crown about the pernicious effects of the repartimiento de comercio and abuses of the tribute and mita systems. Many of these members of the Andean elite held the title of *procurador*—a legal representative residing in Spain entitled to act on behalf of local interest groups in the Indies. One of the most famous and influential of these memorials was written by Vicente Morachimo, a kuraka of Chimo y Chica near the city of Lambayeque in 1732. Morachimo's report provided a blunt, straightforward recitation of the economic costs of rampant corruption by local officials and parish clergy, citing the specific laws violated in each case. Indeed, the Council of the Indies thought so highly of the text that they eventually published and sent it to pertinent government officials in the Andes.

According to Morachimo, most malfeasance by Spanish magistrates revolved around tribute abuses, the repartimiento de comercio, and the mita. He argued that corregidores made a practice of collecting tribute from unwary Andean travelers, children, cripples, and many others exempted by law. Moreover, Morachimo argued that each magistrate distributed between 100,000 and 200,000 pesos in merchandise every two years, regardless of the wealth or poverty of his district. The corregidor of Collao (near Lake Titicaca), for example, even forced forty or fifty of his Andean charges to transport his flocks of cattle and sheep for distribution to local indigenous communities near Lima. This was a flagrant abuse of the system of trajines and of the laws governing the repartimiento. Spanish officials also required Andeans to serve as mitayos in textile mills, on coca farms, and on public works projects, despite specific imperial and local laws forbidding the practices. When kurakas attempted to protest or take the local magistrate to court, the corregidores and their allies among the parish priests usually conspired to intimidate, abuse, jail, or even replace the ethnic leader with a more pliable candidate.

Later protests by Andean leaders went even further than Morachimo, formulating specific reforms to alleviate colonial exploitation. One Andean member of the Franciscan order, Fray Calixto de San José Tupak Inka, wrote a special memorial to the King in 1749, proposing that Spain turn power in the indigenous regions of Peru over to local kurakas. As Fray Calixto admonished the King: "[O]pen your innocent eyes and you will see the whip and the club of the Spaniard, corregidor, judge, landowner, and priest, exploiting the Indian towns of all the Americas."[24] Apart from calling for an end to the mita and the repartimiento de comercio, Fray Calixto suggested that Andeans obtain appointments as corregidores and local parish priests, receive access to schooling, and serve in a new tribunal (composed of Spanish, mestizo, and Andean leaders that would be independent of the viceroy and local audiencias) to set policy for the viceroyalty. Although Fray Calixto never challenged the legality of Spanish rule, he did propose sweeping changes in the colonial system that would have allowed Andeans unprecedented access to self-rule and economic power.

These more orderly protests were not the only response by Andean groups to eighteenth-century changes within the empire, as violent rebellions disrupted the Andes from the 1740s to the independence era (1809–25). The Bourbon program of imperial reorganization led to a whole range of commercial, economic, and political innovations that disrupted life in numerous highland indigenous communities. From the rebellion of Juan Santos Atahualpa in Cerro de la Sal in 1742 to the great rebellions of the 1780s, increasing numbers of Andeans felt forced to gamble on violent upheavals to protest the injustices created by the reforms. In short, the political struggles touched off by the Bourbon Reforms set in motion a complex series of power struggles among metropolitan reformers, creoles, mestizos, and the indigenous communities, unleashing forces that would engulf the region in disorder and violence for generations to come.

Conclusions

The colonial market economy was imposed gradually in the variegated Andean landscape, which had previously utilized networks of vertical exchanges relying on kin- and state-controlled systems of reciprocity and redistribution to exchange goods and services. By the end of the sixteenth century, however, a market system based on a trunk line running from Lima to the mining metropolis of Potosí emerged, serviced by a growing number of secondary feeder lines. As more Spaniards and Andeans took part in these exchanges, the entire market system became more complex and less tied to the original trunk line with its dependence on silver mining and the transatlantic trade. A more diversified market system eventually began to produce multiple trunk and feeder line complexes, particularly after the period of crisis between 1687 and 1730. Indeed, the administrative changes of the Bourbon monarchy in Spain, including the establishment of new viceroyalties in New Granada (1739) and the Río de la Plata (1776), effectively took account of these preexisting socioeconomic realignments.

At times the Andean peoples resisted the incursions of the European market economy, but gradually they adapted their kin-based institutions and modes of behavior to the changing economic circumstances. While indigenous communities resisted excessive repartimiento, tribute, and labor burdens, they also began selling produce, contracting their labor for wages, and migrating to new locations. Although these strategies failed to reverse mercantile penetration, they often allowed Andeans to shape the nature of these exchanges and to maintain the integrity and prosperity of their traditional communities. By the late colonial period, these strategies became more difficult to employ, particularly in regions close to large markets. Many communities either disintegrated or became radically transformed through the process of ethnogenesis, where ethnic groups reformulated customs and their own sense of ethnicity. Nevertheless, indigenous groups usually maintained a cultural matrix that was more Andean than Spanish.

The socioeconomic changes occurring during the colonial era highlighted the two very different economic cultures of the European and Andean peoples. Ethnic groups in the Andes generally sought to attain community self-sufficiency to ensure the survival of the ayllu, along with its complex of cultural and religious values. Even the limited trade conducted by mindalaes in the North Andes and the dispatching of colonists (mitimaes) only allowed communities access to goods not available in the ecological niche inhabited by the ayllu. Relations with the Inca state were arranged by a kin-based system of reciprocity, wherein the rulers and the subject peoples exchanged obligations, goods, and services. The Europeans, however, defined resources according to different values. From the outset their society was oriented around a market-based system of exchange that tied the Andean peoples to forces of supply and demand in a European and even a global economic arena. Gold and then silver were the key resources, along with the foodstuffs and services needed to sustain them. Indigenous commodities, such as cochineal, cacao, tobacco, and indigo only had value because they could be sold in colonial, European, and global markets. Spaniards introduced familiar foods and products, including a wide array of European animals and crops—horses, pigs, cattle, sheep, wheat, barley, and grapes. When these two economic cultures conflicted, the more powerful Europeans usually managed to force changes in the subordinate Andean system. Nonetheless, the two systems merged and altered each other in large and small ways, changing the economic culture of both groups.

Despite their more subordinate socioeconomic position, recent ethnographic work by anthropologist Olivia Harris seems to confirm that some Andean ethnic groups maintain vestiges of traditional economic attitudes. An indigenous group near Potosí, the Laymi, have engaged in cash-based exchanges since colonial times, but these people ascribe values and meaning to money that reflect Andean, not market-oriented, cultural norms. The Laymi, for example, prefer to conduct barter negotiations in their own province, using cash primarily for long-distance payments, such as purchasing livestock or making tax or religious payments. Quite apart from their value as a means of exchange in a market economy, coins also have ritual meanings to the Laymi associated with the fertility of people, herds, or the local mines. Coins also have come to symbolize the pact between the Laymi and the Bolivian state, because cash payments have been required since the colonial period for taxes. In short, the Laymi accept the realities of the market economy, but traditional cultural attitudes about economic exchange linger. The socioeconomic changes imposed during the colonial era were certainly pervasive and real, but more traditional Andean cultural attitudes persist even to the present day.[25]

5

ANDEAN CULTURE AND SOCIETY
UNDER COLONIAL RULE

BY HIS OWN ACCOUNT, in the year 1615 an aged Andean named Felipe Guaman Poma de Ayala began a long overland trek from his native province of Lucanas in the central Andes to the Spanish viceregal capital of Lima, accompanied only by his young son, a horse, and two dogs (see figure 4). Despite his humble appearance, Guaman Poma represented an emerging class of bicultural Andeans, called *indios ladinos*, who knew both Castilian and their indigenous tongue, and he carried in his possession a massive manuscript (1,189 pages with 398 illustrations) that he had personally written over a period of thirty years, entitled *El primer nueva corónica y buen gobierno*. This impressive tome, written in a mixture of Castilian and his native Quechua, detailed life before and after the foundation of Tawantinsuyu, along with the abuses visited upon native Andeans by their Spanish overlords since 1532. The intended audience for the text was none other than King Philip III. Upon finishing his opus, Guaman Poma was nearly eighty, impoverished, and scorned by colonial authorities, yet he bolstered his right to speak for the Andean peoples by claiming the status of an indigenous prince, having descended on his father's side from the Yarovilca dynasty of Huánuco, which predated Tawantinsuyu, and on his mother's from the Inca royal family. Beset by robbers, vagabonds, low-born indigenous ne'er-do-wells, and a host of rapacious Spanish officials and priests on the road to Lima, Guaman Poma still managed to reach the capital and arrange for his precious manuscript to be sent to Madrid. Although it is unlikely that King Philip ever read El primer nueva corónica y buen gobierno, the work remains an outstanding artifact of the hybrid colonial culture that had emerged in the Andes by the early seventeenth century.

Guaman Poma's achievement in writing El primer nueva corónica y buen gobierno is all the more impressive because the Andean peoples had no alphabetic writing before the European invasion. As a result, Spanish friars entrusted with converting the Andeans to Catholicism had to learn the principal indigenous languages and translate them into European alphabetic script. The complexity of this task delayed until 1560 the appearance of the first Quechua-Castilian dictionary by Fray Domingo de Santo Tomás. More complete versions of Quechua and Aymara dictionaries and grammars came only in the early seventeenth century, roughly contemporaneous with the publication of Guaman Poma's work. At the same time, European missionaries opened schools to teach Andeans Castilian, the most common language in Spain. Both of these enterprises ultimately made possible the production of literary texts written in that language and in indigenous tongues, such as El primer nueva corónica y buen gobierno. About the time that Guaman Poma finished his opus, the Andean author Juan de Santa Cruz Pachacuti Yamqui Salcamayhua already had written his Relación de las antigüedades deste reyno del Pirú, and the mestizo author, El Inca Garcilaso de la Vega, also had produced the first segment of his famous history, Comentarios reales de los Inca y historia general del Perú. Meanwhile, the Spanish priest, Francisco de Avila, had compiled a series of religious traditions, written entirely in Quechua, known as Ritos y tradiciones de Huarochirí. By this time other indigenous forms of artistic representation (such as painting,

Fig. 4. The author, Felipe Guaman Poma de Ayala, on the
road to Lima. (Guaman Poma, Nueva corónica, 1095, 1105)

textiles, ceramics, and wood carving) merged with Spanish modes of expression, leading to a distinctive colonial culture that was neither entirely European nor Andean. By the seventeenth century European rule had not destroyed indigenous culture; instead the European and Andean cultures became "mutually entangled," producing a complex and constantly evolving mixture. European cultural forms may have dominated in most spheres, but as time progressed colonial artistic production represented an interweaving and integration of the Spanish and the Andean.[1]

Any effort to address how indigenous culture and society changed under colonial domination must rely on a wide array of sources, most quite different from those utilized in previous chapters. Here, the method of analysis shifts to consider written documents, paintings, and other artifacts as "texts." Analyzing these cultural productions—chronicles, archival records, textiles, ceramics, ritual objects, and paintings—can illuminate Andean efforts to understand and reinterpret their past, merging it with their views about the colonial society taking shape around them. These varied cultural representations reflected changing patterns of language and literacy, artistic production, history, law, and concepts of geographical space, which all provide valuable insights into the construction of indigenous identities in the Andes over time.

Literacy and Numeracy in the Andean World

The cultural ramifications of imposing both European-style alphabetic writing and the Castilian language have provoked considerable debate from the sixteenth century to the present. Some modern scholars have viewed the expansion of alphabetic literacy from Europe to parts of the world where it did not exist, such as the Andes, as a positive or even as a "civilizing" process. From this perspective literacy was a "tool" that allowed the Andean peoples to benefit from translating their own thoughts and words into signs or alphabetic symbols that could be read and understood by all. According to this viewpoint, alphabetic literacy was merely a useful "technology of the intellect."[2] The compilers of the Huarochirí manuscript presented literacy in this light, seeing writing as a new way to preserve the past. As it was expressed at the beginning of the manuscript: "If the ancestors of the people now called Indians had known writing in earlier times, then the lives they lived would not have faded from view, until now. As the mighty past of the Spanish Viracochas is visible until now, so too would theirs be."[3] Seen in this light, writing provided the power to transform thoughts and ideas into permanent, understandable symbols, capable of linking the past to the present.

Since the sixteenth century many other scholars have connected the introduction of alphabetic literacy with colonial domination and Andean cultural subservience. From this perspective, literacy and language depended on deeply embedded societal beliefs and institutions.[4] Teaching Andeans to spell was not merely transmitting a "technology of the intellect," but enforcing alien methods of belief, understanding, and learning that had little to do with indigenous cultural experiences. The early Spanish friars certainly viewed literacy in this way, as a vehicle for evangelization and spreading European culture. One modern scholar has even termed the expansion of alphabetic writing as the "darker side of the Renaissance," enforcing a "colonization of language, of memory, and of (geographical) space."[5]

Other specialists then and now have taken stands somewhere between these two positions. They tend to link the expansion of European languages, law, and religious beliefs more than alphabetic writing with the colonial subjugation of the Andean peoples.[6] Regardless of whether alphabetic literacy produced cultural subservience or represented a mere "technology of the intellect," it clearly formed part of a sequence of cultural changes that had a profound long-term impact on the Andean peoples between 1532 and 1825.

The sixteenth-century expansion of Spain into the Andes coincided with efforts in the late Middle Ages and early

Renaissance to codify Castilian grammar, vocabulary, and orthography, and to privilege the use of alphabetic writing over oral traditions. Just as Spain entered its period of global expansion in 1492, the humanist Elio Antonio de Nebrija published his grammar of Castilian, followed in 1517 by his orthography, which both linked the invention of the alphabet and language with the consolidation of a Christian empire ruling over less "civilized" peoples. The ideas of scholars such as Nebrija provided the rationale for teaching Castilian to the indigenous peoples, and they also laid the foundation for allowing the colonizers to use the Latin alphabet and Castilian grammar to transform Andean tongues into written languages.

Despite the ideas of Castilian humanists about the importance of language and writing as civilizing tools, the first Spanish invaders of the Andean world had no such grandiose ideas. Most were unlettered or only functionally literate men themselves, and their immediate goal involved simply communicating with Andean peoples. The most pragmatic solution was to rely on indigenous interpreters (called *lenguas*), who were fluent in both Castilian and Andean languages. The most famous of these early lenguas was Felipillo, apparently a coastal Amerindian (and thus not a native Quechua speaker) captured in an earlier Spanish invasion of South America, who accompanied the Pizarro expedition from Cajamarca to Cusco. Nevertheless, the limitations and potential dangers of using interpreters such as Felipillo, particularly for the friars intent on converting the Andeans, soon became obvious. As this letter from 1542 (only a decade after the initial Spanish invasion) warned:

> The interpreters in this land are native Indians who know something of the Castilian language. . . . It should be made known that in certain important situations when it is against the interests of the Spanish, and as these Indians are lacking in any moral conscience, they say what they please or what they have been told to say, and it may be in their own interest or because they have been frightened

> into doing so, and thus, in matters of importance, the
> truth will not be known as it should be . . . [7]

By the early 1540s, the invaders understood that governing the Andes and the process of religious conversion required both the spread of Castilian among the indigenous peoples and that some priests and colonial officials learn indigenous tongues. Both tasks involved teaching alphabetic writing in Andean societies.

Indigenous civilizations in the Americas could communicate specific, concrete, and abstract ideas in a manner that resembled European writing systems, but they did so in very different ways. In Mesoamerica, the Nahuas and the Maya had developed advanced types of pictoral and even some forms of phonetic writing, so that transferring their languages into European script came relatively quickly and easily. Within the first generation, Amerindian scribes produced texts in their native tongues and in Castilian, a practice that continued throughout the colonial era. In the Andes the situation was much more complex, and European alphabetic symbols proved more alien and difficult to learn.

In Tawantinsuyu the only analog to European written symbols was the quipu, a system of knotted cords arranged to present ideas. Quipus communicated meaning through the color, texture, size, form, and arrangement of the knotted cords, but they were not an attempt to reproduce phonetic sounds as in European script. Instead, they imparted numerical information and some basic narrative ideas much as mathematical symbols or international road signs do (such as the common red, octagonal "stop" sign), without using any form of alphabetic symbols. Interpreters of the quipus, known as quipucamayocs, deciphered this information both by touching and looking at the knotted cords. They could communicate this information to interested parties, much as literate European scribes did (see figure 5). As José de Acosta—one of the most important early Jesuit scholars responsible for creating the first Quechua-Aymara-Castilian catechisms, sermons, and other doctrinal materials— commented:

> The Indians of Peru, before the Spaniards came, had no
> sort of writing, not letters nor characters nor ciphers nor
> figures, like those of China or Mexico; but in spite of this
> they conserved no less the memory of ancient lore, nor did
> they have any less account of all their affairs of peace, war
> and government.[8]

Like most Mesoamerican writing systems, quipus were not tied to a phonetic reproduction of sounds in any single language or dialect, which was particularly advantageous in regions with a multiplicity of different languages. Whereas a Frenchman could not necessarily understand a document written in English (if he was not conversant in the language), a Mexican pictogram or an Andean quipu could be understood by an indigenous "reader" of the text, independent of any system of phonetic signs associated with a specific language or dialect. Nevertheless, as a system of communication quipus differed in fundamental ways from European writing, and so the tradition of indigenous scribes using alphabetic script to write in Quechua, Aymara, Uru, or any of the plethora of Andean tongues never became common as in Mesoamerica.

According to Spanish chroniclers, quipus were used primarily as mnemonic devices to record and communicate numerical information. Quipucamayocs could use the knotted cords arranged on a quipu to add, subtract, multiply, and divide quantitative information. The tribute assessments of Tawantinsuyu, for example, were recorded on quipus. Since taxes were levied in labor, the numbers of workers assigned to perform state service could be registered on quipus in decimal units of 10, 20, 50, 100, and so on. These groupings and the tasks assigned were encoded in the arrangement, color, texture, and size of the knots for each kinship group and moiety. Such quipus were also used by Inca authorities to record the amounts of corn, potatoes, freeze-dried meat, and maize beer (chicha) kept in storehouses along the network of Inca roadways. Likewise, quipus recorded calendrical information, listing the number of days and months in their various lunar or

Fig. 5. A *quipucamayoc*. (*Guaman
Poma, Nueva corónica*, 360, 362)

solar cycles. The Inca used different calendars to organize time for religious rituals and public affairs, and each of them would have been recorded on quipus. Moreover, quipus were not merely "legible" or understandable to the original maker of the arranged cords, but to any local official trained in interpreting them.[9]

In early legal disputes over taxes and labor services, Spanish authorities often relied on quipus and the interpretations of quipucamayocs. Spanish officials understood that quipus recorded the past, law, ritual, business matters, and to a limited degree, written information in much the same way as alphabetic writing. As José de Acosta stated:

> And in every bundle of these, so many greater and lesser knots, and tied strings; some red, others green, others blue, others white, in short, as many differences as we have with our twenty-four letters, arranging them in different ways to draw forth an infinity of words: so did they with their knots and colors, draw forth innumerable meanings of things.[10]

In 1578, for example, in a court case in La Plata (present-day Sucre) in Upper Peru (Bolivia), a dispute over tribute assessments between a local encomendero and the Andean community of Sacaca led the judges to summon local quipucamayocs for testimony. By feeling the knotted cords and using some stones (apparently to determine exact quantities), the quipucamayocs verified the types of items required and the amount of laborers assigned to make them (see figure 5). In this way the quipu communicated both nouns (the items) and their quantities. Since the required tasks demanded different labor assignments, however, these quipus may even have encoded a number of different verbs, indicating the various types of labor service being performed (i.e., to make, to take, to guard, to plant, to carry, etc.).[11] While this does not necessarily make the quipu a formal system of writing, the knotted cords probably served some of the same purposes, even if they could not relate complex narratives or abstract thoughts about particular events and ideas.

Despite their importance early in the colonial period, Spanish authorities became suspicious and later hostile to evidence drawn from quipus. The information contained in quipus was only decipherable by an Andean quipucamayoc, and it could not be independently verified by European scribes. Clerical authorities also feared that the mysterious quipus represented a link with Andean religious beliefs and hence idolatry, particularly after the 1560s, when the millenarian Taqui Onqoy movement emerged in the central Andes.[12] After the Third Lima Church Council in 1582, colonial authorities began systematically destroying quipus and ignoring the evidence presented by quipucamayocs. These early concerns continued into the next century, prompting the famous seventeenth-century jurist, Juan de Solórzano y Pereyra, to complain:

> I would not venture to give any or such great faith and authority to the quipos [sic], because I have heard it said . . . that the manner of making and explaining them is very uncertain, deceitful and convoluted; and furthermore, I do not know how it can be affirmed that the quipo-keepers are selected with the authority of the general public for this post. . . . When all is said and done, they are Indians, whose faith vacillates, and thus also, they will equivocate in the explication they give of their quipos.[13]

In essence, the quipu represented a form of communication that was too exotic and unintelligible to Spanish settlers of the Andes, so these devices had to be discredited and later destroyed. Spaniards could not invest the power of record keeping solely to native leaders and quipucamayoc, and besides, they judged the knotted cords much inferior to European alphabetic writing. Although in Solórzano's lifetime Andeans still used some simple quipus, this important indigenous form of communication had largely given way to alphabetic writing in Castilian, and to a lesser extent, in the principal indigenous languages, Quechua and Aymara.

Language, Writing, and the New Colonial Order

After rejecting the use of quipu, Spanish authorities relied exclusively on alphabetic writing in establishing a stable colonial political and religious order. Roman Catholicism and Castilian law were the twin pillars of the colonial regime in the Andes and both depended fundamentally on alphabetic writing. Christianity was a religion based on a book, the Bible, and without the spread of literacy among the Andeans, even this canonical Christian text had little practical value in everyday religious rituals. Moreover, Castilian law was codified in written statues, which the Andeans had to learn and obey for the stability of the colonial regime. As a result, the Crown ordered that schools be established for Andeans so that they could learn "Christianity, decent morals, good government, and the Castilian language."[14]

Since the promulgation of the Laws of Burgos (1512–13), the Crown demanded that encomenderos teach their charges to read and write Castilian. This program was later amended by King Charles I in 1535, when he transferred this responsibility to the regular clergy. The "Statutes Concerning the New Discoveries and Settlements in 1563" well summarized the aims of this educational impulse:

> Teach them good manners; have them dress and wear shoes and let them have many other good things heretofore prohibited to them. Take away their burdens and servitude; give them the use of bread, wine, oil, and other foodstuffs, cloth, silk, linen, horses, cattle, tools, arms and all the rest that Spain has had; and teach them the arts and trades by which they may live honestly, and that all of these things may be enjoyed by those who come to the knowledge of our holy Catholic faith and to Our obedience.[15]

These sentiments were echoed in the royal instructions given to Viceroy Francisco de Toledo in 1569, who implemented this royal mandate by ordering the foundation of schools to instruct the indigenous peoples, beginning with their hereditary leaders, the kurakas. By 1594, the Crown and the clergy had even issued a set of formal instructions for teachers in indigenous schools, directing them to provide a broad religious, social, and academic program for their students. Decrees ordering the spread of primary schools throughout the Andes continued even into the late eighteenth century, indicating that the task of spreading literacy was far from complete in the late colonial period.[16] The principal dilemma, however, was how to provide effective instruction for Andeans, given the many indigenous languages spoken by different ethnic groups living in the former Tawantinsuyu.

From the early writings of Elio Antonio de Nebrija, many Spanish intellectuals and policymakers favored teaching Castilian as the standard language for the entire empire, arguing that language, religion, and civilization were deeply intertwined. Given the practical difficulties of converting people and conducting public business in a multiethnic empire with so many different Andean languages, successive monarchs encouraged school instruction in Castilian. In the indigenous Colegio de San Andrés in Quito, for example, teachers taught Andean students in Castilian for two reasons: first, because the indigenous peoples spoke some twenty different languages within forty leagues of the city, and second, to train a generation of indigenous interpreters who could then spread European religious and cultural principles. A royal edict in 1605 explained additional compelling reasons for using Castilian in indigenous schools:

> Because it has been stated that in the best and most perfect language of the Indians it is not possible to explain well or properly the mysteries of the Faith, but only with much difficulty and imperfection, and that even though chairs have been established where the priests who indoctrinate the Indians have been taught, this is not a sufficient remedy because of the great variety of tongues;

but since it would be more common and practical to introduce Castilian, I order you that you should, in the best way possible and with the least trouble to the Indians and without cost to them, provide teachers for those who voluntarily wish to learn the Castilian language . . . [17]

Some colonial authorities even felt that maintaining indigenous languages and cultural traditions would allow Andeans to hatch conspiracies against the Crown and even persist in the heretical religious beliefs.

To encourage the spread of Castilian and Roman Catholic doctrine, the Crown, clergy, and local colonial authorities focused their initial educational efforts on Andean leaders, the kurakas. At the request of the first bishop of Cusco, Fray Vicente de Valverde, colonial authorities founded a school to educate Andean lords and their male offspring in 1535. Only five years later, the Crown also enjoined local officials to found similar schools in every major town or village. King Philip II issued two additional edicts to implement this program: in 1576 he gave the task of instruction in the academies for kurakas to the Jesuits, and in 1578 he ordered that funds from vacant encomiendas be set aside to support the effort.[18] Two of the most famous and long-lasting of these schools for indigenous leaders were the Priest's Academy in the indigenous sector (*cercado*) of Lima founded in 1616, and the Academy of San Francisco de Borja, established in Cusco in 1621. The Jesuits operated both schools, and although some of the faculty were fluent in indigenous tongues, Castilian remained the primary language of instruction.

The religious orders and the secular clergy apparently served as the principal force behind founding schools for Andean kurakas and even for commoners throughout the Andes by the seventeenth century. The numbers of schools, the clientele admitted, and the quality of instruction undoubtedly varied. In the Audiencia of Quito, for example, the Mercedarians, Augustinians, and Jesuits operated schools scattered throughout the district, while local secular clergy supplemented these efforts by providing some rudimentary instruction in local parishes. Details about the quality and extent of such educational efforts remain sketchy, but by the early seventeenth century these schools apparently served as an important vehicle for spreading alphabetic literacy in Castilian among Andeans.

While the Crown vacillated about promoting indigenous literacy in Castilian, many regular clergy favored following the dictates of the Council of Trent (1545–63), which called for utilizing indigenous languages to spread the faith. The incredible linguistic diversity of the Andes, however, seriously complicated this task. According to José de Acosta, there were over seven hundred languages spoken in the former Inca domains, and some eyewitnesses argued that "every village and every valley has its own language."[19] The expansion of Tawantinsuyu did encourage Quechua as the principal administrative language in the empire, but there is no real evidence that it became widely spoken in everyday life before 1532. Faced with this plethora of tongues, members of the regular clergy decided to focus their energies on learning Quechua and Aymara, a major language of the highland peoples in Upper Peru, particularly around Lake Titicaca. To this end, the Dominican, Fray Domingo de Santo Tomás (a strong advocate of indigenous rights and a collaborator of the legendary Fray Bartolomé de Las Casas), compiled the first Quechua-Castilian dictionary in 1560. In addition, during the Third Provincial Council of Lima (1581–83) clerical authorities published the first standard catechisms, confessionals, and sermons in Quechua and Aymara.

Another problem in establishing Quechua and Aymara as standard languages in the Andes was the difficulty in converting them to the phonetic Latin alphabet. The Crown ordered the establishment of university professorships in the sixteenth century both to teach indigenous languages and to begin turning them into alphabetic languages. While the first dictionary of Domingo de Santo Tomás clearly advanced this process, it was not until 1607–8 that the Jesuit, Diego González Holguín, published his more complete, standard Quechua grammar and

Quechua-Castilian dictionary. This was followed in 1612 by a similar grammar and dictionary for Aymara by a fellow Jesuit, Ludovico Bertonio. Making these landmark works available to regular and secular clergy greatly facilitated instruction and proselytization in both languages. Indeed, the indigenous language sermons of preachers, such as Francisco de Avila and Fernando de Avendaño, became famous in the Andes as eloquent tools to advance the process of evangelization. Some modern linguists have even argued that the process of converting Quechua and Aymara into a more standardized phonetic alphabet and using them as languages of religious conversion may have been a principal force in making them so widely spoken in the Andean world by the end of the colonial era.[20]

Overall, the Crown and the church pursued two distinct language policies in the Andes simultaneously, a strategy that sometimes worked at cross-purposes. The Crown usually encouraged education in Castilian, but at various times it also supported efforts by clerics, particularly the Jesuits, to use Quechua and Aymara in evangelizing. Such activities facilitated the conversion of these languages into alphabetic script during the sixteenth century, a process that was completed by the publication of the grammars and vocabularies of González Holguín and Bertonio in the early seventeenth century. Utilizing Quechua and Aymara, however, also prompted considerable criticism. The Council of the Indies recommended that the Crown ban any official use of both languages in 1596, as it had outlawed Arabic in the Iberian peninsula a generation earlier. King Philip II refused to do so, but his successors grew increasingly skeptical about instruction in indigenous languages, giving an added impulse to teaching Andeans Castilian. These periodic shifts in language policy continued throughout the colonial period, as authorities periodically feared that preserving Andean languages ensured the continuation of native religious heresies and even fomented periodic rebellions. Nevertheless, it is important to point out that the use of Quechua and Aymara never led to the creation of any large-scale production of routine administrative documents by indigenous officials during the colonial period, as happened in New Spain. Instead, indigenous scribes in the Andes commonly wrote in Castilian.

An Andean Literary Awakening

By the early seventeenth century, the spread of alphabetic writing and Christianity in the Andes led to the production of three major literary-historical texts—one by the mestizo author El Inca Garcilaso de la Vega, and two by Andean writers, Juan de Santa Cruz Pachacuti Yamqui Salcamayhua and Felipe Guaman Poma de Ayala. Each in his own way sought to place the disruptions of the early colonial era within the context of the Andean past, in an effort to understand, explain, and better the plight of the subjugated indigenous peoples. El Inca Garcilaso de la Vega wrote in an elegant Castilian prose, which drew inspiration from Renaissance humanism current in Europe. For their part, Santa Cruz Pachacuti Yamqui and Guaman Poma employed a mixture of Castilian, Quechua, and pictorial representations to present their ideas. Each of the three authors entered actively into the ongoing intellectual and political debates about the formation of a new colonial order taking place around them. In their hands, writing became a political act.

In his two-part opus, *Comentarios reales* (1609) *y historia general del Perú* (1617), El Inca Garcilaso de la Vega attempted to write an account of the Inca past and the Spanish conquest, capable of empowering the indigenous peoples. His father had been a prominent Spanish conquistador and his mother an Inca princess, which gave Garcilaso an opportunity to learn stories about the Inca past and to experience the turbulent early conquest era. Some time after his father abandoned his indigenous partner in favor of a European bride, Garcilaso made his way to Spain in 1560, where he spent the remainder of his life and composed his literary works.

Whereas most European accounts of the conquest celebrated the triumphal victory of the Christian invaders over the "pagan"

Andeans, El Inca Garcilaso attempted to use his history to reconcile both worlds. Garcilaso argued that the Incas governed according to the dictates of natural law, venerating a single god and imposing justice and order in their empire. In his account of the conquest, the Inca voluntarily submitted to the Christians, rather than being conquered militarily. Garcilaso used this argument to undermine Spanish jurists who sought to justify European rule in the Andes by right of conquest. Moreover, his portrayal of the many misdeeds of the conquistadors and the first viceroys (particularly Francisco de Toledo) represented a thinly veiled criticism of Spanish colonialism. Using a variety of rhetorical strategies to convince his European reading audience, Garcilaso sought to demonstrate that a stable, colonial society could only emerge from a fusion of Andean and European cultures.[21]

While El Inca Garcilaso de la Vega drew on ideals of Renaissance humanism to write his history, the indigenous author Juan de Santa Cruz Pachacuti Yamqui Salcamayhua used a mixture of Castilian, Quechua, and pictorial images to reconcile his vision of Andean history with the conquest era. According to his autobiographical statement in the *Relación de antigüedades deste reyno del Pirú* (1613), Santa Cruz Pachacuti Yamqui was born in a region halfway between Cusco and Lake Titicaca into a prominent Andean family, which was among the first voluntary converts to Christianity. According to Santa Cruz Pachacuti Yamqui, the apostle St. Thomas had arrived in the Andes long before the Spaniards. Although Andean peoples rejected the apostle's preaching, his presence in the Andes had paved the way for the region's eventual evangelization after 1532. The principal aim of this relatively brief work, using both bilingual literary and visual codes, was to present "a history of the evangelical preparation of Peru" to receive Christianity.[22] While Juan de Santa Cruz Pachacuti Yamqui's literary work pales in comparison to the complex and elegant arguments of El Inca Garcilaso de la Vega, his *Relación de antigüedades* represents one Andean's attempt to use an alien medium, alphabetic writing, to rewrite the history of his people and to reconcile their traditions with those of the European conquerors. For Santa Cruz Pachacuti Yamqui, writing was a way to correct the misleading accounts of European chroniclers and to resist the subordination of his people by the colonial regime.

The use of writing to rework history and to oppose European domination emerged most eloquently in the richly complex study of Felipe Guaman Poma de Ayala, *El primer nueva corónica y buen gobierno* (1615).[23] Guaman Poma, a self-proclaimed Andean nobleman, apparently learned to write Castilian from his half-brother, a priest, and from his service as an interpreter in the campaigns of Cristóbal de Albornoz to root out the Taqui Onqoy movement. Although he declared his account an objective history of events from the creation to his own day, Guaman Poma actually wrote a polemical contribution to contemporary political debates. He condemned Spanish clerics and colonial officials alike, arguing that Andeans were the only "civilized" Christians in Peru. Coming from an Andean ethnic group conquered by the Inca, Guaman Poma also denounced Tawantinsuyu as an illegitimate pagan empire that had usurped power from the preexisting polities. Like Santa Cruz Pachacuti Yamqui and El Inca Garcilaso, Guaman Poma also argued that a Christian prophet, in this case St. Bartholomew, came to the Andes and taught the indigenous peoples (who were "white" descendants of Adam) how to live according to Christian precepts. This moral order was later extinguished by the Inca usurpers, who brought pagan beliefs and idolatry to the Andes. Furthermore, Guaman Poma drew on arguments advanced by two prominent Dominicans, Fray Bartolomé de Las Casas and Fray Domingo de Santo Tomás, to propose that the Crown give political power to the indigenous peoples themselves. Specifically, he urged the King to establish a sovereign Andean empire, with Guaman Poma's own son as ruler, but still loyal to King Philip III, the intended reader of the manuscript. Guaman Poma used Castilian, Quechua, and a host of pictorial images to fashion his complex but cohesive argument—repudiating the Inca past, scornful of clerics and colonialism, but pro-Andean and orthodox in his Christianity.[24]

Despite claiming that the first portion of his manuscript, *El primer nueva corónica*, represented an accurate, objective history of the Andes, Guaman Poma used a number of discursive strategies to advance his own "moral vision" of the past. He used Andean oral traditions and earlier European chronicles to construct a history of the indigenous peoples from the creation of humankind to the first troubled decades after the Spanish invasion. Guaman Poma's argument that Andeans had adhered to Christian values before 1532 sought to undermine those Spanish chroniclers who used the paganism of Andeans as a justification for the Spanish military conquest. Moreover, Guaman Poma patterned his biographies of the Inca rulers and their coyas, at least in part, after European biographies of kings and saints in order to establish both the vices and virtues of Inca rule, in a style intelligible to his intended audience. In this way he was able to make a subtle argument: despite extinguishing the moral order of the Andes and imposing idolatry, the Inca also had established ethical laws and a just social order, which he could later contrast with the disorder and corruption of Spanish colonialism.

The conquest of the Andes served as the link between both sections of Guaman Poma's work. Like El Inca Garcilaso, Guaman Poma contended that the Spaniards had not vanquished Tawantinsuyu militarily. Instead, he averred that Andean leaders (including his own father) had voluntarily submitted to Francisco Pizarro as the ambassador of Charles I. Miraculous appearances by the Virgin Mary and St. James vanquished the Inca captains and prevented subsequent indigenous resistance. In order to demonstrate the fitness of Andeans to rule, he also chronicled the steadfast loyalty of prominent Andean lords, particularly his father, Guaman Malqui, amidst the ruinous civil wars of the conquistadors. Throughout this disorder, the indigenous leaders did their best to ensure peace and tranquillity, while the Spaniards continued to squabble and to destroy everything around them. In short, the discursive strategies utilized by Guaman Poma in the El *primer nueva corónica* allowed him to rewrite history and advocate a new future for himself, his lineage, and the Andean peoples.[25]

The final two-thirds of the opus, B*uen gobierno*, purported to be a literal, factual account of the abuses perpetrated by Spanish officials and clergymen against hapless Andeans. Guaman Poma structured his account much like a Roman Catholic sermon, enumerating the sins of Spaniards and invoking divine punishment on them. By extension he hinted (like Las Casas) that such punishment might even befall King Philip III, if the monarch allowed these evils to continue.[26] The only way to impose a moral, Christian order amid the corruption and sinfulness of the colonial era was to give power to Andean elites, led by Guaman Poma's own son.

Throughout the B*uen gobierno*, Guaman Poma presented a long, repetitive litany of Spanish abuses that formed the basis for his sermon and supported his moral and political argument. While the author listed a host of Spanish crimes—such as greed, corruption, envy, and unwarranted violence—he directed some of his most scathing criticisms against the sexual immorality of the Spaniards and mixed-bloods in the Andean provinces. In describing this wanton licentiousness, Guaman Poma skillfully integrated both textual arguments and pictorial images to reinforce arguments. In figure 6, for example, he depicts a drunken banquet offered by a Spanish priest for a mestizo, an Andean, and a mulatto, all being served by a diminutive indigenous waiter. The small figure on the tray resembles the body of a headless woman, while the fruit on the priest's left resembles a phallus, with an arrow pointing to his own groin. Guaman Poma seems to suggest that the surly priest and his companions intend to seek sexual favors from "unspecified" Andean women. He continued this theme even more graphically in figure 7, which shows a corregidor and his lieutenant peering into the room of a naked, sleeping Andean woman; both men point to her exposed genitalia. Moreover, in Guaman Poma's visual presentation the woman appears to be a willing, wanton collaborator in her own sexual exploitation, which only adds to the author's outrage over the corruption accompanying Spanish rule. Finally, figure 8 demonstrates how Guaman Poma condemned the endemic lust and licentiousness among Spanish men and women. With one hand, the Spanish man makes a sign of the *figa* (a crude symbol for sexual intercourse), while the other symbolically grasps the hilt of his sword, positioned like an erect penis. For her part, the woman offers a rose, a symbol of the female sex, while her other hand rests over her pudendum. In all of these cases the text, written in Castilian and Quechua, and the drawings together communicate the author's outraged morality, reinforcing his thesis that noble Andeans were abused by a motley mixture of Spaniards, renegade indigenous accomplices, and the ignoble mixed-bloods.[27] Such graphic depictions of Spanish sins, conveyed in the text and the drawings, served to advance the author's polemical argument about the need to turn power over to the Andean elite.

Despite his carefully constructed arguments, Felipe Guaman Poma de Ayala emerged at the end of his manuscript as an aged, broken, and unsuccessful petitioner. His utopian proposal to place his son at the head of an Andean empire, ruled by Christianized indigenous ethnic lords under the Spanish King's distant supervision, remained an empty dream. He lamented a "world upside down" (*mundo al revés*), with the King residing in Castile and the Pope in Rome, leaving Andeans to be despoiled by corrupt Europeans. His monumental opus had failed to unite the histories of Europe and the Andes. Guaman Poma tried using writing to resist Spanish domination, but in the end, this did not empower the Andeans. The old, broken man could only carry his manuscript to Lima, perhaps knowing that it would probably never be read by his intended audience.[28]

The production of important written literary texts in Quechua and Spanish by Andean authors, such as the E*l primer nueva corónica y buen gobierno*, did not continue into the eighteenth century. Only the tradition of writing petitions and memorials to the Crown and viceregal authorities persisted. A number of documents, written in Castilian, to protest colonial abuses and propose concrete reforms to the Crown remain in various archival repositories, including the memorials of Vicente Morachimo and Fray Calixto de San José Tupak Inka in the mid-eighteenth century (mentioned in chapter 4).

Fig. 6. A dinner involving a priest, mestizo, mulatto, and Andean. (Guaman Poma, Nueva corónica, 603, 617)

Fig. 7. A corregidor and his lieutenant uncovering a naked, sleeping Andean woman. (Guaman Poma, Nueva corónica, 503, 507)

Fig. 8. Lust and licentiousness among Spanish men and women. (Guaman Poma, Nueva corónica, 534, 548)

The memorial of Fray Calixto even harkened back to earlier writings by Domingo de Santo Tomás and Guaman Poma, calling for self-governance by Andean ethnic leaders. In addition, communiques in Castilian from various rebel groups during the Andean insurrections in the 1780s have also been uncovered, which detailed Spanish counterinsurgency troop movements and attempted to recruit local followers.[29] There are even a very few mundane administrative documents uncovered in Quechua from the late seventeenth century, much like the sort of materials kept by indigenous officials in Nahuatl and in the various Maya dialects in Mesoamerica. While these very different texts represent evidence of literacy among some ethnic and community leaders, they nevertheless fall far short of the impressive indigenous literary productions of Guaman Poma, Santa Cruz Pachacuti Yamqui, and El Inca Garcilaso de la Vega.

Even as indigenous literacy in Castilian spread during the colonial period, traditional Andean oral and visual traditions endured. According to the dictionary of González Holguín, the Quechua word that best approximates writing, *quillka*, can also mean painting or teaching, using repetitive examples. In the Quechua-speaking world, writing, speaking, painting, and public rituals could all communicate information.[30] It is no small wonder that Andean writers, such as Guaman Poma and Santa Cruz Pachacuti Yamqui, drew on this tradition by using so many examples and mixing both Castilian and Quechua writing with pictorial images to communicate their ideas. Even after this literary awakening had ended, however, Andeans continued to value documents, pictures, and signatures, viewing them as important symbolic objects that could be stored, exhibited, or utilized in a number of special ceremonies in their communities. Throughout the colonial period Andeans continued such traditions, using royal edicts (*cédulas* and *reales provisiones*) as documents and as evidence in support of any legal claims. The King's formal signature or seal might represent the royal person or Crown authority to an Andean audience, independently of the written text's actual content. In this way Andean community leaders learned to value written documents as legal texts and ceremonial objects that transmitted a wide variety of meanings. Such customs were neither entirely Spanish nor Andean, but represented the sort of hybrid cultural practices that evolved over the course of the colonial era.[31]

Artistic Expression in the Colonial Andean World

Just as European alphabetic literacy marked a clear departure from Andean traditions, various types of indigenous artistic expression changed in distinctive ways during the colonial era in response to Spanish influences. From approximately 1000 A.D. figurative images as central motifs in Andean art virtually disappeared. Although small figurines remained present, mimetic representations of the human form, gods, and animals gave way, particularly during the Inca period, to abstract geometric forms and highly stylized animal representations in ceramics, wood carvings, textiles, paintings, and metalwork. In their monumental architecture, the Inca often used unadorned boulders and other natural rock formations as the subject of art and architecture, even carving and shaping stones into rough-hewn monuments, such as at the massive fortress of Sacsahuaman outside of Cusco.[32] After 1532, however, these indigenous artistic expressions became transformed, as European notions about the centrality of figurative art, particularly the human form, permeated all aspects of Andean artistic production during the colonial era. Over time, European motifs would appear alongside geometric and stylized designs, even on traditional indigenous art forms, such as textiles and ceremonial drinking vessels (keros).[33]

Before 1532 Andeans used abstract designs to convey meaning within an indigenous frame of reference. Within Tawantinsuyu artisans wove ceremonial tunics (uncu) with a wide variety of checkerboard geometric designs, called tucapu, arranged in distinctive patterns. As the tunic pictured in figure 9 indicates, artisans wove these uncu in elaborate and beautiful repeating patterns of tucapu, which formed an ordered iconographic system understood by ethnic groups throughout the empire. The Sapa Inca, for example, often wore tunics with specific patterns for each religious holiday (*raymi*) much as Roman Catholic priests would later wear vestments of different colors at mass during specified times in the liturgical calendar. The Sapa Inca also ordered all ethnic groups in the empire to wear clothing with distinctive abstract designs so that they could be immediately identified by their garb. Moreover, ceremonial keros were decorated with tucapu or other geometric designs for use on specific religious and secular occasions.[34]

When the Inca conquered a region, they traditionally gave leaders of newly subjugated people presents of specially designed textiles and keros as a sign of their incorporation into Tawantinsuyu. Likewise, the Sapa Inca presented gifts of textiles and keros with different designs to allied nations who had aided in the conquest. The significance of these gifts continued long after their initial presentation, because they could be later brought out and displayed to conjure up the original events leading to their production. In this way, abstract designs on textiles and drinking vessels could represent Inca historical deeds, much like a written chronicle or a realistic European painting could depict certain events.[35]

With the disruption in traditional Andean artistic patterns following the Spanish conquest, indigenous artists began to employ figurative designs to convey knowledge directly rather than using abstract, symbolic motifs. Ceremonial tunics continued to be valued by Andean ethnic lords, but after 1532 they displayed mimetic images from the natural world. As the Poli uncu pictured in figure 10 demonstrates, abstract tucapu designs were accompanied by two lions near the neck and repeated representations of human heads in the upper section of the uncu wearing the royal crown or mascapaycha. In a similar way, artisans began mixing figurative and abstract designs on *keros*. The colonial kero in figure 11, for example, is painted (rather than carved as in the Inca period) with traditional abstract designs at

Fig. 9. Inca key checkerboard tunic. (No. 91.147.
Textile Museum, Washington, D.C.)

the center, while on the upper portion, the artist also painted a more realistic depiction of the Sapa Inca and the coya.

The emergence of figurative art, in conjunction with alphabetic writing, appeared most dramatically in Guaman Poma's 398 pen and ink drawings in his El *primer nueva corónica y buen gobierno.* The European manuscript tradition tended to use pictures as mere illustrations, drawing the literate reader from the picture to the written words. Such illuminated manuscripts also allowed an illiterate person to use the picture as a partial "window" into the text. For Guaman Poma, however, the pictures and the written text formed part of a seamless whole. Apparently, in the final version of the manuscript he used the same ink source in both text and pictures, indicating that both were written simultaneously. Moreover, Guaman Poma used words to integrate his composi-tions with the written text. Each drawing, for example, had a title, which further explained its context. In addition, he frequently used captions in both Quechua and Castilian to complete the visual message, providing a deeper meaning not completely captured in the drawing. Even the lack of color in the compo-sitions tends to blur any distinction between the written and visual texts, encouraging the reader to consider both simultane-ously. Finally, Guaman Poma placed the first word or two of the following page of written text at the bottom right corner of each drawing. In figure 5 showing a quipucamayoc, for example, the word "*contador*" in the lower right is the first word in the ensuing page, "contador mayor del todo este reyno." This resembles a technique used by European manuscript publishers and may have represented an attempt by Guaman Poma to give his composition the look of a "published" book. By linking pictures and written text in this way, however, he went well beyond any European models.[36]

Andean ideas of space also inform the drawings in El *primer nueva corónica y buen gobierno.* Guaman Poma's map of the Indies, Mapamundi, has Cusco at the center and is then divided into four parts, representing the divisions of Tawantinsuyu—with Antisuyu in the north, Chinchaysuyu in the west, Cuntisuyu in the south,

Fig. 10. Poli uncu. (Poli Collection, Lima, Peru)

Fig. 11. *Figure of Inca and female under rainbow on kero (quiro),
ca. 1700, gum-based paint on wood.* (Museo Inca, Cusco)

and Collasuyu in the east (see figure 12). The northern and western divisions conformed to the upper moiety of the empire (hanan), which was associated with the sun, the masculine, and all that was dominant and superior. The southern and eastern divisions corresponded to the hurin moiety, which was tied to the moon, the feminine, and subordination. Guaman Poma used this symbolic division of space as a metaphor in approximately two-thirds of his drawings to diagram symbolically the defeat of his people and to confirm his vision of a world turned upside down. The beginnings of this catastrophe can be seen in figure 13, which shows the Inca Atahualpa meeting the Spanish conquistadors at Cajamarca. The Inca still remains at the center of the drawing, symbolizing order (much as Cusco did in the Mapamundi), while his followers occupy the superior hanan space at the upper right (viewer's left). Placed below the Andeans are the conquistadors ranked on a scale of descending honor beginning with Diego de Almagro on the left (in the hurin space) down to the least valued position on the far right, taken up by the Amerindian interpreter Felipillo. Nevertheless, the impending slaughter and the collapse of the empire following Cajamarca would lead to the chaos and disorder chronicled by Guaman Poma in the *Buen gobierno*.[37]

The union of word and image to portray symbolically Guaman Poma's vision of the social disorder can be seen most graphically in figure 14, which depicts a corregidor exchanging drinking vessels with an Andean. Here, the corregidor and his companions, a mulatto and a mestizo, occupy the superior hanan space. In an orderly world this space would rightfully belong to the Andean kuraka and the diminutive indigenous servant, who are placed instead in the inferior hurin position. The title at the top of the drawing sets the context, while the dialogue flowing down the arm of the corregidor and the Andean provide necessary details about the incident. The corregidor tells his Andean guest to drink a toast ("brindes, tomes señor curaca"), who replies in a garble of Quechua and Castilian, "I will serve you" ("apu muy señor nuqa servisqayki"). The linguistic confusion of the kuraka is only one sign of the utter collapse of order, occasioned by the presence of

Fig. 12. Mapamundi. (Guaman Poma,
Nueva corónica, 983–84, 1001–2)

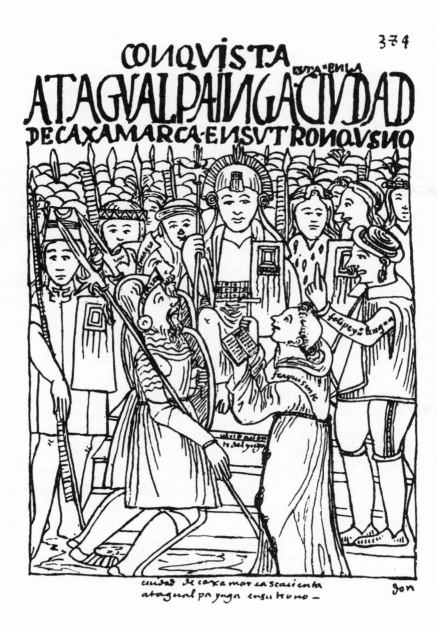

Fig. 13. Atahualpa at Cajamarca. (Guaman
Poma, Nueva corónica, 384, 386)

the mulatto and the mestizo (identified by the words on their hats), positioned between the Spaniard and the Andean. Guaman Poma saw racial mixing as the bane of the region, leading to the disappearance of the Andean peoples, along with their language and culture.[38] Words, pictures, and symbolic use of space come together in Guaman Poma to communicate his anger over a world turned upside down, but figure 14 achieves this end by mixing Andean cultural beliefs and European figurative representation.

Painting proved another artistic medium in which indigenous artists took up naturalistic figurative designs during the colonial period, while imparting some distinctly Andean stylistic motifs. According to numerous Spanish chroniclers, painting had existed as a well-developed art form in Tawantinsuyu, and the halls of the Coricancha certainly contained numerous historical paintings. According to José de Acosta, Inca paintings were crude and much inferior to their Mesoamerican counterparts, but in fact, this probably only meant that indigenous artists employed abstract and geometrical motifs, as on Andean keros and textiles, rather than mimetic, figurative images. None of these early compositions apparently survived the turbulent conquest era, and with the collapse of the Inca state, which had served as the principal patron of the arts, indigenous painting traditions became radically transformed by a European artistic ideology.

After the conquest the Catholic Church was in desperate need of skilled indigenous artists and artisans to decorate their newly built places of worship, and these people were trained to work in the European figurative tradition. Unlike Mexico, where the church organized craft schools, in the Andes most indigenous painters received their instruction in religious houses or in the private residences of European painters. One of the most prominent painters of early colonial Quito, Pedro Bedón, founded just such a church institute, the Brotherhood of the Rosary. Here Bedón trained one of the late sixteenth century's most famous indigenous painters, Andrés Sánchez Gallque, who produced the first signed (and therefore verifiable) paintings by an indigenous artist. After the arrival of Bernardo Bitti, who brought the Italian style to the Andes,

Fig. 14. A corregidor exchanging drinking vessels with an
Andean. (Guaman Poma, Nueva corónica, 505, 509)

Spanish clerical and secular authorities made more systematic efforts to establish workshops for training indigenous painters. Nevertheless, Andean painters produced works that mixed European and indigenous artistic styles.[39]

The apogee of indigenous painting in the colonial era came during the seventeenth century with the Cusco School, which flourished until approximately 1800. The former Inca capital had always been a center of Andean painting, but a devastating earthquake in 1650 led to a tremendous architectural and artistic rebirth as churchmen, public officials, and private citizens tried to reconstruct the city. The city's artists had formed guilds to control the quality, quantity, and price of artwork, but in 1688 disputes within these craft organizations led indigenous and mestizo artists to form their own separate guild. Members of this Andean-mestizo guild eventually developed their own distinctive, hybrid style.

The most famous paintings to emerge from the Cusco School dealt with the Virgin Mary, the patroness of Cusco, who had allegedly appeared in a miracle to save the city's Spanish population during the siege by Manco Inca in 1537. Many of Cusco's indigenous citizens also embraced the veneration of the Virgin, apparently because they identified her with the Andean earth mother, Pachamama, or some other female deity. Regardless of the cult's origins in the old Inca capital, the indigenous artists painting in the Cusco style ignored European notions of perspective and space. Instead, they created images of the Virgin that presented her in a flat two-dimensional style, called "statue painting." Among the many representations of the Virgin created by indigenous artists, the Virgin of Bethlehem was much favored by the local citizenry among Cusco's devotional images. As the painting in figure 15 demonstrates, artists in the Cusco school typically depicted both the Virgin and her child dressed in elaborate triangular-shaped vestments, which resembled the shape of a mountain. Visually this technique merged the image of the Virgin with the Andean landscape and also with its pre-Columbian patroness, the earth mother Pachamama. Moreover, the intricate floral brocade pattern of both gowns is composed of repetitive geometric designs, reminiscent of tucapu patterns in Inca textiles. What might appear an overly stylized, stiff, and archaic painting of the Virgin of Bethlehem, merely conveyed Andean artistic preferences in representing a European and Christian religious icon.

Many paintings produced by colonial artists (whether Andean, creole, or castas) served political, not just religious and aesthetic purposes. By the eighteenth century a tradition developed among Andean kurakas to use traditional Andean uncu, keros, and oil portraits to prove their hereditary claims to office. As late as 1780 a viceregal visitor general, Antonio de Areche, claimed that such portraits in particular "abounded in the houses of Indians who take themselves to be nobles in order to sustain their descent."[40] Some of these portraits were even admitted as evidence in court cases dealing with disputes over hereditary rights to ethnic leadership. In 1738, for example, the Marqués de Alcanizes y Oropesa attempted to remove Don Marcos Chiguan from his office as kuraka of Huayllamba and Colquepata for abusing his indigenous charges. To defend his claim to office, Don Marcos provided an oil portrait of himself dressed in the style of a Spanish royal standard bearer, wearing a mascapaycha of the Sapa Inca. As figure 16 demonstrates, his arrogant pose was supplemented by including a coat of arms originally granted by the Crown to Paullu Topa Inca, while the written text in the cartouche on the painting's lower right lists both the honors bestowed on Don Marcos by viceregal officials and his claim to be a descendant of the Inca royal family. Such portraits defiantly asserted Don Marcos Chiguan's right to his position by connecting his alleged Inca lineage with his many services to the Crown. While Don Marcos chose to dress in Spanish garb, many other members of the indigenous elite, such as the unknown Andean woman pictured in figure 17, adorned themselves with traditional Inca costumes to prove their claims to status and power in the colonial society. Ironically, colonial authorities accepted these portraits as evidence until the 1780s, when royal officials began confiscating them, fearing that any such overt links to the Inca past would only inflame the passions of indigenous people

Fig. 15. *Virgin of Bethlehem, Cusco School, eighteenth century, oil on canvas. (Museo Pedro de Osma, Lima)*

Fig. 16. Portrait of Don Marcos Chiguan, ca.
1742, oil on canvas. (Museo Inca, Cusco)

during what became known as the Great Age of Andean Rebellions.[41]

During the colonial period the artistic worlds of Europe and the Andes merged, creating dynamic new artistic practices, spanning a number of mediums—paintings, textiles, ceramics, and drawings. In each area, indigenous artists participated actively in shaping a colonial cultural and artistic order. After the downfall of the Inca state, Andean artists either went underground, stopped composing, or more often, adapted to the new European artistic ideology. Indigenous painters, writers, and weavers began producing art in the European style for churches, public buildings, and private homes. In this transformation, Andean artists continued to produce textiles and keros, often with European-style figurative images alongside more traditional designs. Even when Andean painters of the Cusco School produced images of the Virgin, they did so using a blend of European and indigenous artistic forms. Finally, this new colonial art could even be turned to political purposes, as indigenous leaders presented European-style portraits as evidence to prove their hereditary rights to office. In short, over the long colonial era, indigenous artistic expressions evolved by mixing Andean and Spanish traditions to link an imagined Andean past with the ever changing cultural present.

Changing Views of Geography and the Law

The imposition of European ideas of space, geography, private property, and written law produced long-term political and cultural consequences over the colonial period. While Andeans lacked a formal system of written law, exactly how they envisioned geographical space, set political boundaries, and determined land ownership remains unclear. According to some experts, the Inca state was jurisdictional, and ethnic identity, huacas, and local customs determined the boundaries among different groups. This argument is strengthened by the Andean custom of having ethnic groups cultivating land at different ecological levels, which made

Fig. 17. Portrait of an Unknown Female, ca. 1690,
oil on canvas. (Museo Inca, Cusco)

it difficult to establish well-defined territorial boundaries. Others emphasize that Tawantinsuyu did indeed sanction the use of territorial boundaries among the four provinces of the empire and to differentiate among ethnic groups and their ancestral lands. Despite these differences of opinion, most scholars agree that the Andean peoples did not sanction individual ownership of lands, and as a result, the spread of European ideas about private property and maintaining written legal titles proved completely alien to the peoples of the Andes.

The Inca defined religious and ceremonial space by organizing important religious shrines along lines of forty-one ritual sight lines, or ceques, radiating from the Coricancha (the Inca Temple of the Sun) in the heart of Cusco. Three of the four provinces in Tawantinsuyu—Chinchaysuyu, Antisuyu, and Collasuyu—contained nine ceques, while Cuntisuyu had fourteen ceques. There were between 328 and 400 shrines arrayed along these irregular pathways, and at least some of them were astronomically aligned with certain solar or lunar risings and settings. These ceques may even have represented a counting device for the Inca calendar (if 328 is chosen as the official number of ceques, it conforms to the number of days in their solar calendar). Given the importance of Andean religious shrines (huacas) in defining ethnic identities, the ceque system might also have been used to determine boundary lines among ayllus and with royal panacas (religious corporations to honor deceased rulers). Despite this elaborate ceremonial organization of space, there is at least some evidence that Cusco was not the only Andean site to have a ceque system. Moreover, recent archaeological excavations indicate that the sight lines may have been quite irregular, with some beginning a considerable distance outside of the Coricancha. In all likelihood, the Cusco ceque system incorporated preexisting systems of other Andean groups, and if it served as a boundary among ayllu, it was an uneven one. Like the three-field system of assigning resources to the Inca, the priesthood, and local communities, as well as the decimal organization of ethnic groups, the ceque system was probably incomplete and still evolving when the Spaniards arrived in 1532. It was an attempt to assign ritual and ceremonial space and perhaps to define ethnic boundaries, but the ceque system was apparently not fully developed and did not extend in any clear way to organize all boundaries among religious shrines and ethnic groups by the time of the European invasion.[42]

Apart from the ceques, the Inca also appear to have employed some jurisdictional and territorial boundaries in the empire. As the name Tawantinsuyu implies, the empire was divided into four unequal parts, which were partially defined by the four major roads emanating from Cusco. Moreover, no less astute an observer of Andean customs than the sixteenth-century official and entrepreneur, Juan Polo de Ondegardo, mentioned boundary markers in individual communities and between and among provinces that had some recognizable territorial definition. According to Polo,

> The Incas . . . divided the land and set up boundaries appropriate for each province according to the division they made of the livestock. Those that were dedicated to the Sun had their territory delimited where they were to graze; the livestock of the Inca had a bounded territory; and limits for the livestock of the community were also established. All of the herds were pastured without taking anything from the others. All in the same way that the boundaries and pastures were delimited within a province, the boundaries were also set between one province and another.[43]

Guaman Poma mentioned that Tupa Inca Yupanqui and Huayna Capac established boundary lines between the ethnic communities of the coast and the highlands, "so that each one would serve the royal authority in their own territory."[44] Guaman Poma also implied that there were territorial disputes in these regions, so the Inca clarified boundary lines and regularized the labor services that each group would render to the state. In addition, several chroniclers mention boundary markers on the frontiers of Tawantinsuyu, establishing the state's territorial extent.

Apart from such basic demarcations of disputed territories and community lands, it seems clear that more fluid ethnic boundaries, determined by a multiplicity of factors, also characterized Andean divisions of geographical space. In an ethnic mosaic such as the Andes, where different groups lived in dispersed settlements up and down the mountainsides, there could be no one-to-one correspondence between language, ethnicity, and clear territorial boundaries. Evidence from the colonial period indicates that indigenous groups defined their territory by toponyms, such as hills, swamps, mountains, roads, irrigation canals, deserts, or the fields of neighbors. The Inca's decimal organization of the empire and tribute assessments were also recorded on quipus according to ethnic groupings, not necessarily by bounded territories. In a region where temporary and permanent migrations to control resources were commonplace and each region contained multiethnic enclaves, this was infinitely more pragmatic than strict territorial demarcations. Moreover, the Andeans did not sanction the individual private ownership of land, and in some regions, such as the north coast of Peru, ethnic groups determined ownership by use, seeing unworked land as available to anyone capable of cultivating it productively.[45] In short, ethnic boundaries within Tawantinsuyu were unusually flexible by European standards.

Such Andean definitions of geographical space differed markedly from those employed by the European invaders after 1532. The Spaniards brought with them ideas about private property that put a premium on precisely defined geographical boundaries validated by written legal documents. Moreover, the Crown exercised control over the Andes through its political and ecclesiastical bureaucracies that demanded more clearly defined territorial jurisdictions for its various agencies. Viceroyalties, audiencias, and corregimientos, along with church divisions among bishoprics, dioceses, and parishes all depended upon more precise demarcations of the landscape than had obtained under Tawantinsuyu. As a result, King Philip II ordered his official geographer (*cronista mayor*) for the Indies, Juan López de Velasco, to conduct a geographical survey of the entire empire. This involved constructing a set of fifty questions to be distributed to every administrative district of the Indies, including the vast Andean region. These surveys, known as the *Relaciones geográficas*, were compiled in the Andes between 1579 and 1583.

As part of this massive survey, the Crown ordered (in questions ten and forty-two) local Spanish and indigenous authorities to produce European-style maps, complete with street plans, landmarks, and major geographical features. The Crown further commanded that these maps be written on paper or parchment and sent with the written responses to the remainder of the questionnaire. Despite this direct royal command, the *Relaciones geográficas* produced for the Andean region contained only five such maps, all compiled by local Spanish authorities. In contrast, the survey for New Spain consisted of ninety-two pictorial maps, mostly drawn by indigenous authorities.[46] Apparently, the lack of a formalized system of alphabetic writing, mimetic figurative art, and fluid geographical boundaries (based largely on ethnic or political considerations, rather than private property) all contributed to the failure of Andeans and colonial officials to respond to royal commands about producing maps.

Spanish ideas about maps, well-defined geographical boundaries, and private property encoded in written laws, left an enduring legacy for Andean societies. European concepts of individual ownership of lands and formalized, written legal titles proved particularly foreign and difficult to grasp for indigenous groups. In fact, problems of determining land ownership and assessing taxation forced the Crown to order a formal review of all landholdings, the venta y composición de tierras of 1591. This process required that Andeans provide legally approved written evidence to substantiate claims to their lands. Because land use was tied to local religious shrines and ethnic identities, this proved an extremely difficult but important task. By this time, however, written documents and Castilian legal principles had forced Andeans to adopt foreign ideas about what constituted a just claim to ancestral lands. As a result, identifying land parcels by toponyms and huacas gave way to written descriptions of physical boundary markers. The imposition of a formal Castilian legal ideology and ideas about ownership communicated by the written word and European-style maps symbolized new ways of thinking, of projecting political power, and of exercising dominion over the Andean peoples by the late sixteenth century.[47]

Castilian law also demanded that Andeans deal in a world of official records, written in European alphabetic script. Individual or collective memory, so precious to Andean communities before 1532, was often ruled inadmissible as evidence in courts unless supported by written documentation. Moreover, although alphabetic literacy and the Castilian legal system proved foreign mediums for the Andean peoples, they could not be circumvented easily. Written documents required a functional level of literacy, even if an individual relied on scribes to produce documentation needed in court cases. This did not mean that all Andeans could read and write Castilian, even by the eighteenth century, but it does indicate that ever increasing numbers of indigenous people had to operate in and become familiar with the literate world of colonial laws and customs. It is no small wonder that kurakas such as Don Marcos Chiguan used European-style portraits and written documents to substantiate their claims to positions of prestige and power in the Andean sphere.

Conclusions

The cultural interchange taking place between Europeans and Andeans over the colonial era is symbolized by indios ladinos such as Felipe Guaman Poma de Ayala. Given their knowledge of Castilian and indigenous tongues, these pivotal figures could serve a multiplicity of roles as interpreters, writers, church aides, petitioners, and even as the leaders of indigenous uprisings. As Guaman Poma indicated, they also stood outside both the Andean and the European social spheres as "cultural mestizos," mistrusted in both communities. At the same time, the indios ladinos were also byproducts of the complex colonial sociocultural order. For his part, Guaman Poma sought to take advantage of his ambivalent societal role by serving the church in stamping out idolatry and later as an author and reformer. He also recommended that the King place an indio ladino in every community as an overseer (*veedor*) to monitor the activities of both the European and Andean communities. Although Guaman Poma failed to get this or any of his other ideas implemented, the cultural evolution of the colonial regime ultimately gave more power to indios ladinos such as Guaman Poma or to colonial kurakas who had the skills to navigate in both worlds.[48]

The mutual exchange of cultural values during the colonial era transformed the Andean worlds. By the eighteenth century the establishment of schools for kurakas and later for the wider Andean community spread literacy in Castilian, the language of the invader, rather than traditional indigenous tongues. Along with the expansion of alphabetic writing came a more intimate knowledge of the twin pillars of Spanish colonial rule—Christianity and Castilian law. A central legal precept was the idea of private property, validated by written documentation, which fundamentally altered the ways Andeans conceptualized geographical space and rights to land, water, and other essential natural resources. Similarly, Andean artistic production changed under European influences, as figurative representations in painting, textiles, carvings, and ceramics replaced traditional Andean patterns of abstract geometrical designs. In many ways the old Andean cultural order seemed to pass slowly away during the colonial era.

Despite these cultural transformations, many Andean traditions have endured since 1532 to the present. Textile weaving remains an important art form that continues to reflect distinctive community identities and values. While indigenous weavers in the Cusco region, for example, have incorporated new forms of wool, different types of fabrics, and figurative patterns, their unique textile designs still distinguish ethnic groups from one another, symbolizing relationships within the community and its ties to the outside world and the supernatural. In this way, the old Inca custom of using dress to define ethnicity endures even to the present. Moreover, indigenous textiles continue to function at two levels, one European and the other distinctly Andean: they are sold in marketplaces (first brought to the Andes by the Spaniards) to tourists and other outsiders, but through their distinctive traditional designs they retain definite links to the Andean past. From the early colonial period onwards, it became pointless to speak of authentic European or Andean cultural values; these had become completely commingled, producing new hybrid forms of cultural meaning, which each colonial social group interpreted over time in its own way.

6

Religious Conversion and the Imposition of Orthodoxy

A common error [among Andeans] is their tendency to carry water on both shoulders, to have recourse to both religions at once. . . . Most of the Indians have not yet had their huacas and conopas taken away from them, their festivals disturbed, nor their abuses and superstitions punished, and so they think their lies compatible with our truth and their idolatry with our faith.

Pablo José de Arriaga, 1621[1]

I found a variety of opinions about this when I arrived in Lima; and among the serious and most important men there were those who told me there was much idolatry. . . . [O]thers told me that it [idolatry] was the invention and [a product of the] greed of the visitadores who used their titles to enrich themselves, and that this did serious injustice to the Indians. . . . [O]thers said that there was some idolatry, but not as much as was claimed.

Archbishop Gonzalo de Campo, 1625[2]

THE SPANISH INVADERS justified their overthrow of Tawantinsuyu in 1532 by vowing to reap a harvest of indigenous souls for the Roman Catholic faith. In later years Spanish jurists would echo and refine such arguments to defend their continued occupation and colonization of the region. Initially, the Andean peoples seemed enthusiastic converts as thousands accepted baptism, exchanging their adherence to official Inca rites for Roman Catholicism. As the first priests introduced the rituals of their faith, indigenous converts eagerly embraced outward displays of Catholic worship—the veneration of the cross and colorful devotional objects, ornate churches, cults of the saints, and the ritual use of music, dances, and prayer. Over time, however, many churchmen suspected Andeans of putting these Christian rites to their own uses. Whereas clergymen demanded that converts abandon their beliefs for Christianity, Andeans often incorporated Catholic ritual and dogma into their own religious framework, much as they had done with the official religion of the Inca generations earlier. Just as European and Andean cultures became commingled into new hybrid forms of meaning, so too did Catholicism and indigenous religious practices become "mutually entangled," producing a constantly evolving mixture during three hundred years of colonial rule. Nevertheless, as the first quotation above by the Jesuit Pablo José de Arriaga indicates, this situation produced periodic tensions between Andeans and local clergymen. By the seventeenth century Arriaga and others promoted efforts to stamp out or extirpate all "deviant" indigenous religious practices by force. Indeed, Arriaga wrote a widely used manual for Catholic inspectors on how to identify and obliterate such forms of "idolatry" in 1621.

While clerical authorities experienced frustration over the incomplete "spiritual conquest" of the Andes, they differed sharply about the problem's severity and how to deal with it. For most advocates of forcible conversion, such as Arriaga, the issue was a relatively simple one: after baptism the Andeans either renounced all "pagan" beliefs or they were apostates. Anyone who continued worshipping traditional deities or huacas merely served the Devil, and churchmen had the responsibility to eradicate such idolatry by formal Church campaigns of extirpation. This led to legal trials of suspected idolaters, the destruction of Andean religious icons, and the imposition of punishments, followed by instruction in Catholicism. As the second quotation above by Archbishop Gonzalo de Campo indicates, however, not all churchmen shared this viewpoint. Indeed, for significant numbers of clergymen the survival of ancient religious practices merely indicated the persistence of religious "error," which could be combated most effectively by persuasion and education, not forceful extirpation.

Like Church officials, Andeans differed in their responses to conversion efforts. Some traditionalists favored resisting Catholicism, which by the 1560s culminated in nativist movements, such as Taqui Onqoy in Huamanga. More often, however, communities adapted and transformed their religious practices, drawing spiritual power from a mixture of traditional and Roman Catholic beliefs. These Andeans continued favoring their own religious specialists, shamans, and healers, while still supporting local priests and taking part in Christian religious rituals. Although Christianity continued making steady inroads within Andean communities in the former Tawantinsuyu over time, elements of indigenous religious practices endured alongside Christianity, as they do to the present day.

The historical sources dealing with the processes of conversion and imposing orthodox Catholicism in cities, towns, and villages scattered throughout the rugged Andean landscape are both limited and fraught with interpretative difficulties. Since Andeans did not utilize alphabetic writing before 1532, only limited written evidence about traditional religious practices remains. Moreover, much of the early documentation compiled by Spanish priests and laymen concerns the state cults of the Inca, not the more localized network of gods, shrines, and rites among the multiplicity of ethnic groups in the Andes. During the late sixteenth and seventeenth centuries, clergymen and church inspectors attempting to extirpate idolatry produced voluminous documentation, but this too must be utilized with care. Spanish clergy and lay observers interpreted Andean religious practices from their own biased Christian viewpoint, often misunderstanding or misrepresenting indigenous beliefs in their reports and letters.

The particular religious concerns of each judge and his assistants also influenced their notions of what constituted idolatry or merely represented "religious error." Even when Europeans recorded the testimony of Andeans verbatim, translators had to turn expressions in Quechua, Aymara, or a host of other indigenous languages into Castilian, which led to serious distortions. A Quechua word such as *supay*, for example, usually signified an unpredictable spirit with malevolent or more benign qualities, yet most scribes in idolatry trials rendered it as Satan, which grossly misrepresented the meaning. Indigenous defendants or witnesses also mixed both Christian and traditional religious symbols and images in ways that represented the spiritual changes and mixture that had occurred by the seventeenth century. Moreover, Andeans under interrogation by priests or inspectors at idolatry trials often lied to protect themselves or to deflect blame on others, particularly local enemies within the ayllu.

Finally, many Andean communities endured multiple visitations by extirpators, and residents grew experienced in how to give details or suppress vital information, depending on their needs. When the extirpation trials lost momentum by the 1750s, however, clerical and lay officials expressed less interest in the persistence of Andean religious practices, and any written evidence about indigenous popular piety becomes much scarcer during the remainder of the colonial period. It is no small wonder that contemporaries and modern-day scholars alike have expressed widely different interpretations about the process of religious change in the Andes. Nevertheless, the topic is central to understanding the evolution of Andean societies under Spanish rule, and scholars from several disciplines—such as anthropology, history, and literary or cultural studies—have written voluminously on the subject.

The World of Andean Popular Religion

Within a generation of Tawantinsuyu's collapse, popular adherence to the state religious cults of the Inca faded, except in the ethnic heartland surrounding Cusco and in the remote mountain exile kingdom of Vilcabamba, until its capture by the Spanish in June 1572.[3] The whole nexus of personal, community, local, and regional religious traditions, however, proved more difficult for Spanish priests and friars to uproot. The Andean peoples believed that the sacred penetrated every aspect of their world, profoundly influencing daily life experiences. Mountains, streams, trees, boulders, and even mundane objects, such as small stones, could represent or evoke the divine. Religious specialists, healers, and even ordinary folk summoned these spiritual forces, spoke with them, and prayed for their continued support of human activities. The identification of divine powers with the material world also linked Andean men and women to specific geographical locations, where their gods, shines, and holy places could protect them from human enemies and arbitrary forces of nature. Religious myths and practices united people with their land, their god, and their past.

The principal centers of divine power in Andean religions, known as huacas, could reside in a variety of objects in the natural landscape. According to most religious traditions, the huacas had once been god-like men or women endowed with supernatural powers who roamed the earth and intervened in the affairs of other deities and human beings. This legendary past had been a time filled with uncertainty, when good and evil were pitted against each other with varied and unpredictable outcomes. A particular huaca often supported the efforts of one or more ethnic groups, who sometimes saw themselves as progeny of the god. Once the huaca had accomplished its destiny, it commonly turned into a mountain, a stone, or some other object. The powers of each huaca remained invested in this particular portion of the Andean landscape, and people associated with the deity, called *llacta*, would continue to worship the place, tying the community spiritually to the land itself. Myths about huacas recalled the origins of ethnic groups and helped to make sense of their history and customs. Andeans also prayed to their huacas for advice about sowing, land fertility, access to water, and a host of other human problems. For their part, huacas communicated through Andean priests or religious specialists. Nevertheless, these huacas could be benevolent, vengeful, or even capricious, and they required constant prayers, sacrifices, and offerings of coca leaves or maize beer (chicha). In this way Andean peoples were wedded to cults of particular deities who helped them deal with the vagaries of drought, pestilence, crop failure, disease, pain, defeat, and even death in an uncertain world.[4]

While most huacas exercised influence in only a limited domain in the world, some exceptional deities had regional or supraregional followings, such as Paria Caca and his sister Chaupi Ñamca. According to myths set down in the Huarochirí Manuscript, Paria Caca first appeared as five eggs that hatched into falcons and then became men who founded the ethnic group that ultimately settled in the province of Huarochirí.[5] Paria Caca was a wise and immensely powerful being of the highlands who performed wondrous deeds, vanquishing other huacas and their human worshipers while advancing the cause of his favored people. During these struggles he gained control over an awe-inspiring landscape of mountains and lakes that became the seat of his spiritual power.

According to Andean legend, Paria Caca was closely associated with his sister, Chaupi Ñamca, whose power centered in the lowland region surrounding the Rimac River. Again, the myths compiled in the Huarochirí Manuscript indicate that the power of these two siblings complemented each other in a perfect male-female symmetry atop the hierarchy of huacas. To augment their already considerable spiritual power, Paria Caca arranged his sister's marriage to another commanding coastal huaca, Pacha Camac. In this way the dominant highland deity forged kinship alliances with the two most influential male and female huacas of the coast, giving them all an identity and supernatural powers that transcended any immediate locality or ethnic group. Moreover, by pairing male and female deities, the Andean cosmology created a gendered hierarchy of spiritual power, in which gods tended to control traditionally male activities and goddesses female activities.[6]

Despite the extensive domain of powerful huacas such as Paria Caca, most manifestations of divine power were more localized. Special lineage gods (*chancas*), for example, operated within the spiritual orbit of more powerful huacas. Whereas most huacas resided in features of the natural world, chancas were usually more humble figures of stone, sometimes adorned with coins, wax, or other commonplace items. Christian priests often found it hard to distinguish between lesser huacas and chancas, but the latter belonged to smaller lineage groups or extended families entrusted with their care, whereas huacas pertained to larger groupings, such as an ayllu. The small, moveable chancas exercised spiritual power over a host of household tasks, and according to custom, these gods might be consulted before approaching the local huaca. The care and worship of a chanca was usually entrusted to a member of the lineage group, and like more powerful deities, chancas required prayers, sacrifices, and ritual chicha.

Less powerful household or personal deities, called *conopas*, were usually small stones, often shaped like an animal (usually an alpaca or llama) or a food crop (such as corn or a potato), which had a direct connection with fecundity. Conopas were numerous and in 1617 three Jesuit priests claimed to have confiscated over 2,500 of them in the Chancay region alone. Andeans prayed and made offerings to these deities to control the care and health of livestock, agricultural crops, and even to heal the sick. Whereas entire communities worshipped huacas on given feast days, individuals made entreaties to their own personal conopas, which were passed on from one generation to the next. Sometimes Andeans carried a pair of male and female conopas, which continued the tradition of gender complementarity and also contributed to the symbolic connection of these deities with fertility.[7]

An extremely important aspect of Andean religion was ancestor veneration, and communities preserved the bones or mummies of important relatives, called mallquis. A separate set of priests made offerings to the mummies of deceased Incas and other prominent figures, providing ritual meals of chicha and other foodstuffs, surrounding them with utensils used in life (such as textiles, hoes, or weapons), and conveying them to community religious celebrations. It is unlikely that less prominent families maintained mallquis for most deceased relatives, but the practice was widespread. According to Andean religious traditions, by performing specific rituals and mummification, the dead could reach their final destination or resting place, called *pacarina*. This term also referred to the community's birthplace or point of origin; in this way the dead returned to their ayllu's roots. The recently deceased mallquis formed a link with the community's ancient and sacred ancestors, the huacas. Even after arriving in pacarina, the mallquis would become angry if their living relatives did not venerate them properly at important rituals and on the anniversary of their death, which reinforced the ongoing need to maintain a relationship between the living and the dead.[8]

The entire indigenous panoply of huacas, chancas, conopas, and mallquis formed an essential part of the cultural and religious identity of different ethnic groups throughout the Andean region. As successive waves of conquerors (culminating in the rise of Tawantinsuyu) exercised dominion over different ethnic groups, the invaders appreciated these ties between local peoples and their deities. As a result, the Inca forced subject peoples to worship their gods, but they still respected local religious practices. This relationship was symbolized by the Quechua word *mañay*, which can be translated as a compromise, a demand, or an alteration in traditional behavior. This new religious compromise evolved constantly, incorporating old and new belief systems that recognized the dominance of the Inca's spiritual power, without abandoning local traditions. For this reason, regardless of the brutality of conquest wars, the Inca and their subject peoples recognized the new mañay with an exchange of gifts (particularly textiles and keros) that symbolized the acceptance of the new relationship by both parties. For Andean peoples, abandoning their deities and shrines meant forsaking their culture, traditions, and history. When the Spanish arrived in the Andes, they neither understood nor accepted such a spiritual compromise; conversion required a complete acceptance of Christian precepts, leaving behind any and all aspects of the "pagan" Andean past. Andeans, on the other hand, saw conversion to Catholicism as the establishment of a new and continuously evolving religious pact or mañay, which allowed them to draw on both the spiritual power of Christianity and traditional indigenous deities. Moreover, individuals or groups might even make choices about which Christian or Andean religious concepts to incorporate, only to reverse or alter them later. Such fundamental tensions characterized early efforts by Spanish clerics to convert Andeans and later to impose orthodox Catholicism in the region.[9]

Early Efforts at Religious Conversion

Given the traditional missionary zeal of Christianity, clergymen accompanied all major military expeditions in the Andes, but the process of evangelization proceeded slowly. The Dominican Fray Vicente de Valverde accompanied Pizarro's army to Cajamarca, and later became the first bishop of Cusco in 1537. Along with members of the secular clergy, between 1533 and 1540 the Franciscans, Mercedarians, and Dominicans sent missionaries to the Andes. In 1543 the first bishop of Lima, Fray Jerónimo de Loayza entered the viceregal capital, and by the time that the Society of Jesus began sending missionaries in 1568, the other orders already had established monasteries in all principal towns. Both the friars and secular priests also had begun ministering in rural areas. Despite these impressive beginnings, however, the process of evangelization in the Andes was thwarted in many areas by divisions within the church over how to approach the conversion process, the apathy of many encomenderos (who were more often concerned with gaining wealth than saving souls), bitter civil wars among the early Spanish settlers, a shortage of suitable priests, and attitudes among the Andean peoples themselves.[10]

By the sixteenth century divisions had surfaced within the Roman Catholic Church over the proper means of converting the Andean peoples. Since the early days of the Church, evangelization had involved reaching out to nonbelievers, often by finding broadly similar religious symbols and practices that would facilitate conversion.[11] For some Church authorities, converting Andeans involved little more than using approaches that mixed both Christian and Andean concepts of the sacred, along with reasoned arguments, to turn indigenous peoples from "darkness" to the "light" of Christianity. Among the most vocal and articulate advocates of conversion by persuasion were the Dominicans, Fray Bartolomé de Las Casas and his disciple in the Andes, Fray Domingo de Santo Tomás. Las Casas argued that only by evangelizing the indigenous peoples could the Spaniards justify their presence in the New World. Moreover, according to Las Casas, the Church had to rely on peaceful conversion methods that would allow Andeans to accept Christianity of their own free will. Las Casas also favored using Andean religious imagery of the sun to adorn churches, uniting indigenous iconography with Roman Catholic tradition. Following this reasoning, the Augustinians in Guamachuco (in north-central Peru) even employed indigenous textiles to decorate Christian churches and buildings, and Fray Domingo de Santo Tomás compiled his Quechua-Castilian dictionary and grammar in the early 1560s to promote conversion efforts in that language. While Las Casas firmly believed that Satan had led the Andeans into religious error, he also thought that demonic influence could be countered with gentle persuasion and indoctrination. Las Casas insisted that Andean religion was merely an erroneous reflection of Christianity, and that some elements of the old ways could be salvaged and used in conversion efforts. Later churchmen and indigenous authors, such as Guaman Poma and Santa Cruz Pachacuti Yamqui, even proposed that Christian saints had brought their faith to the Andes before 1532, in order to assert that conversion by persuasion would promote a natural transition from paganism back to the true faith.

Disagreements among churchmen over the proper way to evangelize the indigenous peoples abounded in this early period. Some members of both the regular and the secular clergy, for example, argued that syncretism and education were inadequate conversion tools without the use of force. The Jesuit José de Acosta articulated this position forcefully in his influential 1588 treatise on conversion, *De Procuranda Indorum Salute*. According to Acosta, the simple-minded nature of Andeans and their barbaric religious customs (inspired by the Devil) made most syncretic methods dangerously ineffective. Acosta believed that conversion by persuasion only worked with more civilized pagans, such as the gentiles of the Mediterranean basin, whom St. Paul and his disciples had converted using persuasive methods during the early years of the Church. As a result, Acosta called for using stronger tactics—forceful destruction of idols and pagan rituals, followed by the imposition of rigid Roman Catholic orthodoxy. Acosta even found Quechua too unsophisticated a language for conveying Christian doctrine effectively. Acosta did temper his position, however, by placing most of the blame for the problems of evangelization on corrupt or inadequately trained clergymen. Nevertheless, the political efforts of Francisco de Toledo to uproot Andean communities from their traditional lands and huacas clearly reflected more hard-line approaches. Such ideas also influenced the manuals and sermons of extirpators such as Pablo José de Arriaga. This debate within the church never fully ended, but it raged with particular vehemence in the second half of the sixteenth century and during the periodic extirpation campaigns between 1609 and 1750.[12]

The hierarchy within the colonial church attempted to resolve tensions over appropriate methods of indigenous conversion in the three Lima Provincial Councils in 1551–52, 1567–68, and 1582–83, but they achieved only limited success. The First Provincial Council called for dispatching regular and secular clergy to found parishes (*doctrinas*) throughout the Andes, extending the sacraments of penance and communion to converts and encouraging priests to learn indigenous languages. In addition, the council demanded that priests destroy pagan idols, discourage the work of indigenous religious specialists, and repress any lingering Andean religious practices. The Second Provincial Council advanced these same points, and further urged priests to take great care in stamping out all signs of ancestor veneration and the use of Christian festivals for clandestine pagan rituals. It also encouraged priests to let Andeans pray in their own tongues and to utilize interpreters for confessions, whenever local clergyman lacked suitable training in indigenous languages. The Third Provincial Council in 1582–83 reflected reforms emanating from the Council of Trent (1545–63), and its resolutions attempted to steer a moderate course in debates over conversion. On the one hand, the council demanded that Andeans reject totally their religious traditions, but it also emphasized the "timid" and "childlike" nature of the indigenous people, recommending only moderate punishments for religious error. In addition, churchmen also called for instruction and confessions to take place in indigenous languages and published a standard doctrinal manual and a trilingual edition of thirty-one sermons (in Castilian, Quechua, and Aymara) to ease this process. Nevertheless, by steering a middle course between advocates of voluntary conversion and those favoring the use of force, the Third Council did little to resolve the ongoing tensions within the colonial Church.[13]

Quite apart from these clerical divisions over appropriate conversion strategies, apathy among the conquistadors and political turbulence during the first forty years following the Spanish invasion also inhibited evangelization in the Andes. Encomenderos had the responsibility of supporting priests to oversee conversion efforts in their jurisdictions, but all too many conquistadors cared only about enriching themselves, not spreading the faith. According to Fray Domingo de Santo Tomás in 1563,

> Until now there has been great and extraordinary disorder
> in this land, and it is that the encomenderos provide in their
> encomiendas the priest that they want, for the instruction
> of the Indians . . . because they merely name those that help
> them extract the most in tributes . . . and the churchmen
> can do nothing to get rid of them and put in these parishes
> anyone but those favored by the encomenderos.[14]

Such problems only worsened during episodes of civil strife
among the Spanish settlers. These conflicts led to the forced
impressment of Andeans into various marauding armies of conquistadors and to widespread death and destruction. All impeded
any systematic efforts at evangelization, at least until the final
defeat of the rebellion of the encomenderos under Francisco
Hernández Girón in 1554. Even after the wars had ended, their
interest in exploiting silver deposits led many encomenderos to
focus on mobilizing Andean laborers for the mines at the expense
of sponsoring evangelization. In a joint letter to the Crown from
the provincials of the Franciscan, Dominican, and Augustinian
orders complained as late as 1562: "[W]ith the past tumults and
disturbances . . . we have not been able to do much fruitful work
in the conversion of them."[15]

When Francisco de Toledo arrived in Peru in 1569, he began
exerting pressure on both secular clergy and the religious orders,
such as the Franciscans, to undertake the massive job of evangelization. In Europe, the Franciscans and other monastic orders
traditionally lived in monasteries, and papal decrees strictly
forbade them from administering parishes. This was the work of
the secular clergy. As a result, the first Franciscans to arrive in the
Andes in 1533 had little experience in evangelization and virtually
no training in parish work, if they had not worked elsewhere in the
Indies. Members of the order did not establish their first
monastery until 1548, and the friars only agreed to found parishes
in indigenous towns when Toledo ordered them to undertake the
task. In the central Andean province of Jauja, for example, the
Franciscans had arrived in 1534 and established their monastery

at Concepción fourteen years later. But, it was not until Toledo's visita in 1570 that they agreed to set up eleven doctrinas in the province. Even then, the parishes were badly understaffed. The friar responsible for the doctrinas in Jauja initially had only nine priests to tend to the spiritual needs of 21,894 Andeans, making administration of the sacraments impossible, let alone any meaningful religious instruction. Over time the friars learned local languages, utilized the sermons and catechisms circulated after the Third Provincial Council in 1582–83, established schools, and administered the sacraments, but the task remained enormous and the numbers of well-prepared, dedicated clergy insufficient.[16]

Compounding the problems caused by shortages of priests and friars were sinister charges of clerical arrogance, inefficiency, and even corruption. Royal inspectors found the Dominicans, who administered the parishes among the Lupaka peoples in the rich province of Chucuito, guilty of wide-ranging abuses. The order began preaching in the region in 1542, but civil strife delayed their evangelization efforts until 1547, when the friars established seven parishes to propagate the faith. After twenty years of effort, however, local Lupaka leaders complained that friars seldom left their doctrinas to minister in the surrounding rural areas, leaving over fifteen thousand people unbaptized. Moreover, because few Dominicans knew Aymara, the most widely spoken indigenous language, religious instruction became a farce; most of the Lupaka questioned by Church inspectors in 1567 did not know even the rudiments of Catholic doctrine and few had received the sacraments regularly, especially penance. Even more disturbing were the constant complaints by Andeans of financial corruption. Drawing on the immense prestige that the order initially enjoyed in the region, the Dominicans allegedly extorted excessive amounts in salaries, extraordinary donations, fees, and fines. All this money went to enrich the friars and the order, which managed to build seven churches and residences in the provinces and renovated several others. Local residents also complained of having to donate unpaid labor to construct these buildings. The Dominicans apparently also demanded lands from the Lupaka, laborers to work them, personal servants, and porters to carry goods for sale in Cusco, Arequipa, and La Paz. These complaints about the Dominicans eventually led Viceroy Toledo to expel the order from Chucuito in November 1572. Responsibility for ministering to the Lupaka then fell to the secular clergy, the Augustinians, and later to the Jesuits, who established missions in Juli along the shores of Lake Titicaca.[17]

Cultural difference also played a role in thwarting the complete acceptance of Christianity by Andeans, and nowhere was this more apparent than in the sacrament of penance. Because many early friars and priests did not know indigenous languages, hearing meaningful confessions was virtually impossible, despite clear Church requirements that baptized Andeans confess at least once annually between Septuagésima Sunday and the eighth day of Corpus Christi. One of the principal complaints levied against the Dominicans in Chucuito, for example, was their failure to fulfill this duty, except for indios ladinos, who obviously knew Castilian or Latin. To facilitate the task, Church leaders at the Third Provincial Council commissioned confessional manuals in Quechua and later Aymara, which listed detailed questions for priests to ask each penitent. Nevertheless, the task remained complex. Words conveying Christian concepts such as sin or Satan did not have exact equivalents in most indigenous languages. Moreover, the notion of what constituted sin differed in European and Andean societies. Fornication, for example, was viewed as a serious offense by clergymen, while many Andean males apparently did not prize virginity in women and tended to favor spouses with sexual experience and proven erotic appetites. Couples often lived together for extended periods as a form of trial marriage (sirvinacuy), a practice that the Spanish clergy abhorred, viewing it as little more than a pretext for licentiousness. In short, religion reflected deeply embedded cultural beliefs and practices, and Andeans and Spanish priests took many years to understand each other. As a result, Christian penance became a common locus for cultural misunderstanding and contestation during the early colonial era.[18]

Given the many problems in converting Andeans to orthodox Roman Catholicism, it is hardly surprising that traditional Andean religious practices and hybrid forms of religious expression persisted, even permeating Christian rituals such as the Corpus Christi celebrations in Cusco. Although the old capital of Tawantinsuyu, with its wealthy and powerful old Inca nobility still intact, was hardly typical of most provinces, the Corpus Christi celebrations did embody the mixture of indigenous and Christian religious practices existing throughout the Andes. The feast of Corpus Christi from late May to mid-June roughly coincided with the ancient Inca ritual of Inti Raymi, commemorating the Sun and the harvest season. Inti Raymi was last celebrated by Manco Inca in 1535, but Corpus Christi celebrations in Cusco began as early as the 1550s. From the outset important indigenous dignitaries continued coming to Cusco for the festival, wearing traditional clothing and carrying emblems of their places of origin, much as they had done for Inti Raymi. The religious processions past Christian churches—often built atop Inca shrines—and the carrying of religious figures, particularly the saints, also resonated with Andeans accustomed to similar processions with their gods and mallquis. Such continuities between the Corpus Christi celebrations and the feast of Inti Raymi provide eloquent testimony to the ways that Andeans drew on the sacred powers of their traditional beliefs and the new faith, Christianity.[19] For them, one did not exclude the other.

Taqui Onqoy: The Return of the Huacas

Amidst these early efforts to convert Andeans to Christianity, Luis de Olvera, a Spanish priest in Parincocha (in the province of Huamanga) discovered alarming news of an apparently millenarian, nativist movement called Taqui Onqoy in 1564. According to leaders of the movement, the Andean huacas were no longer confined to mountains, streams, and rocks, and instead possessed human beings, called *taquiongos*. According to testimonies of

Christian observers, those chosen by the huacas would "dance and tremble and move in a circle, and in the dance they called on the Devil and on their huacas and idols, at the same time abjuring . . . the true faith of Jesus Christ and all the teaching they had received from Christian Priests."[20] The word *taqui* (signifying in Quechua a historical dance) and *onqoy* (a feast to prevent disease or disasters) together conveyed the idea of a "dancing sickness" that would purge the taquiongos of Spanish-Christian impurities, leaving them free to embrace their traditional deities. The huacas also spoke through these taquiongos, complaining that they were starving for sacrifices and chicha. Moreover, the vengeful huacas warned of a convulsive struggle in which they would vanquish the Spaniards and their God—which only looked after Europeans, not Andeans. According to the taquiongos, indigenous peoples would also perish in this struggle if they did not renounce Christianity for the old ways, repudiate tribute payments, and refuse mita service. The most prominent of these huacas were not Inca deities, but regional gods, such as Tiahuanaco, Pacha Camac, Titicaca, and Chimborazo, and there is no direct evidence that the taquiongos attempted to join forces with the Inca rebels at Vilcabamba. Instead, the movement was confined to the provinces of Parincocha, Lucanas, Chocorbos, Vilcashuamán, and Andahuaylas (all in southern Huamanga), where it nonetheless attracted over 8,000 people in a region with no more than 150,000 inhabitants.[21]

The Taqui Onqoy movement emerged during a period of political and economic crisis in the Viceroyalty of Peru. In Lima, the fractious members of the audiencia and its weak-willed president, Lope García de Castro, attempted to rule a kingdom racked by thirty years of civil war among the conquistadors and the omnipresent Inca rebellion in Vilcabamba. Moreover, the silver economy centered in Potosí had reached a crisis, as labor shortages and inadequate refining methods slowed production. Meanwhile, a group of royal commissioners oversaw an acrimonious debate beginning in 1561 between advocates of making encomienda grants hereditary and influential clergymen urging their abolition, led by the Dominican Domingo de Santo Tomás.

Powerful indigenous lords, represented by the sympathetic mestizo lawyer, Francisco Falcón, also presented a plan to pay the Crown to end the encomienda system and return political power to Andean leaders, making the situation even more politically charged. Moreover, regional economic crises and epidemic diseases weighed heavily on poorer regions, such as southern Huamanga where the mita for the Huancavelica mercury mines already had produced hardships. In short, the years before the arrival of Francisco de Toledo in 1569 were difficult ones for the Spanish colonizers and the Andean peoples. Indeed, Taqui Onqoy was only the most visible and prominent of several religious movements and rebellions to erupt during these years of crisis in the 1560s.[22]

Spanish authorities responded quickly and decisively to the threat of Taqui Onqoy, dispatching a dedicated and morally upright priest, Cristóbal de Albornoz, to capture and punish the taquiongos. In an anti-idolatry campaign that lasted two years, Albornoz arrested over eight thousand participants and meted out punishments ranging from permanent exile for leaders to requiring that lesser participants serve local priests or receive mandatory religious instruction. Once Albornoz began his legal proceedings, Taqui Onqoy also started to crumble from within, as many participants soon denounced the movement, begged forgiveness, and returned to the Church. In a public ceremony in Cusco, the principal leaders even confessed that they had deceived their followers because, "they did not know anything but to be poor and to acquire food through the offerings [to the huacas]."[23] The available records indicate that few ethnic leaders openly became taquiongos, and this brief popular outburst quickly dissipated.

The radical message of Taqui Onqoy, calling for a pan-Andean alliance of huacas and their human cohorts to expel the invaders, had limited appeal outside of southern Huamanga. By the 1560s most Andeans had already begun to accept some basic European cultural and religious precepts and to incorporate them into their own lives. That process could not easily be reversed. In fact, some of Taqui Onqoy's basic premises were impregnated with European and even Christian ideas. In calling for pan-ethnic unity, for example, the taquiongos referred to their followers as Indians (indios), a homogenizing concept introduced by the Spaniards for the multiplicity of indigenous ethnic groups in the Andes. The leaders also rallied their disciples on a large multiethnic encomienda in southern Huamanga, ignoring traditional Andean ethnic categories. Many of the leaders were also baptized Christians, with names such as Juan Chocne and María Magdalena. Finally, despite their complete rejection of Christianity, the taquiongos preached that the old gods would initiate a new order purged of past impurities. This messianic message certainly drew upon Andean religious traditions about cycles of cosmic cataclysm and renewal, but it also resembled Catholic symbolism concerning apocalyptic death and resurrection. In short, Taqui Onqoy was itself a cultural and religious hybrid. By 1565 Christianity could not be excised from the Andes; it was a growing part of the new religious understanding that was emerging in the Andes since the overthrow of Tawantinsuyu.[24]

The First Campaigns to Extirpate Idolatry, 1609–27

Graphic and deeply troubling evidence about the persistence of Andean religious practices in 1608 set in motion events leading to the first systematic campaign to extirpate idolatry in the Viceroyalty of Peru. The news came first from Francisco de Avila, a priest who had served since 1597 in the parish of San Damián de Checa (southeast of Lima in the province of Huarochirí). Avila was an ambitious churchman from Cusco of dubious parentage, who ran afoul of his parishioners in San Damián in 1600 and again in 1607 for allegedly exploiting indigenous labor, taking long absences from his parish, charging exorbitant clerical fees, trading in agricultural goods, and engaging in scandalous sexual relationships with local women. All of these charges contravened the directives of the Third Provincial Council, and clerical investigators removed Avila from his parish and incarcerated him in a Lima jail, pending the outcome of a church investigation. While in jail Francisco de Avila rallied supporters, who began collecting information systematically on the existence of "pagan" religious rituals in Huarochirí, which prompted church leaders to release him from custody. Avila then dramatized these discoveries by relating an incident in August 1608 at a feast of the Assumption from a nearby doctrina in Huarochirí, where he alleged that Andean parishioners used Christian rituals to mask traditional rites for the huacas, Paria Caca and Chaupi Ñamca. Avila presented all of this information, along with a large cache of conopas, chancas, mallquis, and a local priest of the Chaupi Ñamca cult (Hernando Pauccar), to the new archbishop of Lima, Bartolomé Lobo Guerrero. Such evidence of widespread idolatry convinced many hard-line clerics to demand immediate action to obliterate any residue of Andean religious practices.[25]

Quite apart from the apparently mixed motives for Avila's revelations, the persistence of Andean religious practices produced little surprise among most knowledgeable clergymen. The Lima Archdiocese administered a vast area with 162 parishes, presided over by 108 secular clergymen and 67 friars (35 Dominicans, 16 Mercederians, 15 Franciscans, and 1 Jesuit). According to the dictates of the Council of Trent, each of these parishes should have served no more than two hundred to three hundred families, an ideal that was never achieved, even in Lima. In more remote areas of the viceroyalty such as Chucuito, the number of families seldom fell below four hundred to five hundred per priest. Even after secular clergy, the Augustinians, and the Jesuits had replaced the Dominicans in Chucuito by 1572, the large numbers of indigenous parishioners scattered throughout each doctrina forced the often ill-prepared clergymen to hire assistants for administering the sacraments. Most clerics and their assistants knew only rudimentary Aymara, and when they tried reading prepared sermons in that language, the bored, confused parishioners apparently found it difficult to understand anything more than the most basic topics covered. Moreover, church manuals required each priest to ask a battery of questions in Aymara to each penitent at confession, a task that took at least fifteen minutes for someone fluent in the language. For the overburdened priests, hearing confessions once annually for Easter was a gargantuan task that took months to do properly. Systematic religious instruction and efforts to root out idolatry were virtually impossible. Under these circumstances, clergymen in Chucuito, Lima, and elsewhere must have known that the mixtures of Andean and Christian practices uncovered so dramatically by Francisco de Avila in Huarochirí were actually commonplace and understandable occurrences.[26]

Nevertheless, Avila's revelations made an immediate impression on Archbishop Lobo Guerrero, who was already sympathetic to advocates of forceful evangelization and the extirpation of Andean religious practices. The viceroy, the Marqués de Montesclaros, and the provincial of the Jesuits shared the archbishop's enthusiasm, providing a strong group of advocates for a legal campaign to extirpate idolatry in the archdiocese. As a result, Lobo Guerrero permitted Francisco de Avila to give a formal public sermon in Latin in the cathedral dealing with the problem of idolatry before an assemblage of the major clerical and secular officials on 13 December 1609. The priest used the occasion to denounce indigenous religious practices, praising the archbishop for emulating the Catholic zeal of early Church evangelizers.

The sermon was a complete success for Francisco de Avila. Along with the viceroyalty's key political and religious figures, the now famous priest presided over a public act of faith (*auto de fe*) in the central square of Lima on 20 December, where he gave a public sermon in Quechua and Castilian, condemning idolatry. Then, the various idols and mallquis collected by Avila in Huarochirí were publicly burned. For serving as a priest of the indigenous Chaupi Ñamca cult, Hernando Pauccar was given two hundred lashes, had his hair shorn, and was sentenced to exile in a Jesuit college in Chile to receive Catholic instruction. Four days after this spectacle, Francisco de Avila was cleared of all charges of wrongdoing in San Damián.[27]

Archbishop Lobo Guerrero built on the momentum created by the auto de fe to name the ambitious Francisco de Avila judge-inspector of idolatry (*juez visitador de idolatrías*) for the Lima Archdiocese in early January 1610, with the authority to begin a campaign against idolatry. In 1612 the archbishop granted this same title to two fellow enthusiasts of extirpation, Diego Ramírez and Fernando de Avendaño. Avila's first inspections in Huarochirí and later Yauyos were improvised affairs, with the judge usually accompanied by a notary, a representative of the viceroy, and two or three Jesuits to instruct the Andeans on reforming their idolatrous ways. Avila himself strongly favored Jesuit participation, and several members of the order, such as Arriaga, even became zealous proponents and theoreticians of extirpation. The procedures employed in the trials, however, relied heavily on the earlier campaigns of Cristóbal de Albornoz against Taqui Onqoy and rules laid down by the Holy Office of the Inquisition, which by this time had no authority over indigenous people. Avila and his cohorts conducted inquiries in each village, destroyed major Andean religious shrines, and built a bonfire to burn all idols and mummies, followed by punishments and religious instruction.

Over time, the visitations acquired a more definite set of legal and religious policies governing their conduct, which culminated in the publication of Arriaga's manual for extirpators in 1621. The archbishop delegated his extensive powers over matters of religious discipline to the judge-inspectors, who had jurisdiction over all ecclesiastical authorities, the right to inspect any doctrina, examine the competency of local priests and dismiss them, and discipline all convicted idolaters. Because the judge-inspectors could not travel to every parish in the archdiocese, they named teams of extirpators to fan out across the region and assist their efforts. The "ideal" teams typically consisted of a clergyman (*visitador*), accompanied by an attorney (*fiscal*), a notary, a scribe, and two or three Jesuit priests. Over time, the numbers involved in the visitations became less predictable, particularly as the Jesuits began to lose enthusiasm for the campaigns by mid-century. Nevertheless, upon entering a doctrina, the visitor issued an edict of grace, giving everyone in the community three days to come forward with evidence about idolatry. Each day the visitor or the parish priest celebrated mass in the vernacular, explaining the sources of religious error and demeaning all forms of idolatry. Once they had acquired the names of likely idolaters and the location of Andean shrines and religious icons, the visitor and his team would begin interrogations, using torture whenever deemed necessary. All accused parties could retain defense attorneys or prepare their own cases. Visitations lasted from only a few days to many months, depending on the problems encountered, but in all cases, the local community had to lodge, feed, and support the needs of the visitors and their retinues. Punishments for those found guilty depended on the severity of the crime and degree of repentance displayed. For grave offenses, the visitors could impose the death penalty, severe public lashings, or exile. After its construction in 1617, judges sentenced the most grievous idolaters to confinement in the Santa Cruz prison in Callao. Less serious crimes could merit public humiliation, terms serving local priests, or mandatory religious instruction. All forms of discipline during the inspections were public, and usually accompanied the destruction of any huacas, chancas, conopas, or mummies found during the inquiry. Finally, the visitor and the Jesuits would preach and provide other forms of religious instruction in Andean tongues to members of the parish. Although the exact procedures followed in each idolatry trial varied, all reflected this mixture of detection, punishment, and religious education.[28]

The extirpators sought a complete reform of indigenous religious practices, which involved both enforcing the established rules of Roman Catholicism and sponsoring religious education in the parishes. The judges viewed the Andean communities as a breeding ground for all types of offenses. Too often the indigenous converts to Catholicism lapsed into idolatry, worship of "false gods," immorality, and failure to heed the Ten Commandments and the doctrines of Roman Catholicism. At the same time, the extirpators assumed that the Andeans had an inferior capacity for understanding, which largely explained their religious

shortcomings and their failure to respect the sacred. The extirpators aimed to uncover all cases of idolatry and to make examples
of egregious offenders before the entire parish. The task of the
trials was to enforce Christian doctrine and ritual practices, morality, and respect for the true faith. Moreover, the visitors expected
that proper religious instruction would elevate the capacity of the
Andeans to understand and to live a proper Catholic life. Nonetheless, the balance between the coercive and the educational
components of the trials varied with each different group of
inspectors.[29]

Despite its passionate supporters and mounting evidence of
religious error in Andean communities, extirpation campaigns
remained unpopular with many in the viceroyalty. A chorus of complaints from indigenous communities decried the heavy financial
costs and greed of the visitors and their retinues. They also
complained about injustices committed in the legal proceedings
and the overly severe punishments. Even within the clergy, many
opposed forceful extirpation on humanitarian and ideological
grounds. Bishops in Arequipa, Huamanga, Cusco, and Trujillo
opposed extending the process to their dioceses, arguing that
idolatry did not exist. They contended that Andeans were guilty
only of religious error and superstition, which could be handled
effectively with education rather than forceful methods. The
provincial of the Augustinians, Francisco de la Serna, echoed these
sentiments, and so did the head of the Mercedarians. Given this
level of opposition, most of the idolatry campaigns between 1610
and 1627 were confined to the Lima Archdiocese. Even here,
however, clerical and lay opponents of extirpation bided their time
until 1621, when the departure of the hard-line viceroy, Francisco
de Borja y Aragón, the prince of Esquilache, and the death of
Archbishop Bartolomé Lobo Guerrero, emboldened the cathedral
chapter of Lima to suspend all idolatry investigations just one day
after the bishop's death. The investigations were not renewed in
any systematic way until 1625 under the sponsorship once again
of an enthusiastic advocate of extirpation, Archbishop Gonzalo de
Campo. Nevertheless, the campaigns ended just as abruptly with

his death (possibly by poisoning) in 1626. In short, extirpation only flourished with the support of strong clerical and lay patrons, such as Lobo Guerrero, Campo, the Marqués de Montesclaros, or the prince of Esquilache.[30]

The Villagómez Era and the Apogee of Extirpation, 1641–71

Campaigns to extirpate Andean idolatry began anew with the appointment of Pedro de Villagómez as archbishop of Lima in 1641. Villagómez was born in 1589 in Castroverde de Campos in northern Spain into a prominent family with a long history of bureaucratic and clerical service. As a young man, Villagómez proved himself both pious and scholarly, and after taking his vows he went to Seville as a canon of the cathedral in 1612, receiving his doctorate in law and canonical law from the local university in 1624. The rising young churchman went to the Viceroyalty of Peru in 1632 to complete a royal inspection (visita general) of all government tribunals in Lima. Although Villagómez ran afoul of most of the influential politicians in the capital during his investigations, he righteously portrayed himself as a humble servant of his King and Pope, while depicting his enemies as corrupt and self-serving. Villagómez became exposed to Andean religious practices after the Crown named him bishop of Arequipa in 1635. During a prolonged inspection of the diocese, the new bishop found shocking evidence of "idolatrous superstitions" among the indigenous communities. In 1638, Bishop Villagómez convened a synod, and among his pressing concerns was devising more systematic means of eliminating Andean religious practices. This synod established the legal framework and procedures for his later efforts to mount a full-scale campaign against Andean religious practices in the Lima Archdiocese.

After promotion to the Lima metropolitan see in 1641, Archbishop Villagómez began rallying support for a renewed crusade to extirpate idolatry, which began in earnest with the publication of his pastoral letter of 1649. Borrowing heavily from Arriaga's earlier manual of 1621, the archbishop's letter was a passionate exhortation, which relied on carefully chosen biblical references to justify a new idolatry campaign. He then named a new crop of visitadores de idolatrías, including several aged veterans of earlier campaigns, such as Fernando de Avendaño, Alonso Osorio, and Francisco Gamarra; Francisco de Avila had died earlier in the year. Most were ambitious, experienced (and indeed, quite aged), and well-educated creole clergymen, dedicated to imposing Roman Catholic orthodoxy. Villagómez timed the departure of his idolatry inspectors to coincide with the installation of a holy relic, a piece of the true cross sent as a present from Pope Urban VIII. Before departing from Lima, the inspectors marched in procession to the cathedral, where Villagómez blessed their white ceremonial banners, which contained a green cross and the motto written in red, "Behold the cross of the Lord uniting adverse factions."[31]

Once in the provinces idolatry inspectors uncovered incontrovertible evidence that Andeans often practiced a curious and unpredictable mixture of indigenous and Christian rites. When inspector Bernardo de Novoa entered the village of San Pedro de Acas (in Cajatambo) in 1657, for example, he found that Andean religious specialists, whom the inspectors termed dogmatizers, exercised a strong hold over community affairs. According to local Christian witnesses, the feast of St. Peter (the village patron) coincided with the Andean agricultural rite of Vecosina. In the days preceding the Christian feast, the religious head of the community, Hernando Hacas Poma, and his fellow dogmatizers made offerings of guinea pigs, llama blood, chicha, and coca leaves to the huacas and mallquis, asking their permission to take part in the Christian festival. On the day of the feast of St. Peter, these dogmatizers poured chicha on the ground and spread out coca leaves to honor the indigenous deities before commencing traditional dances to celebrate Vecosina. In the evening, indigenous ministers and selected villagers typically met at the home of the bearer of St. Peter's image in the celebration, where they celebrated by drinking and making offerings, apparently to the saint and to their Andean huacas and mallquis. The ritual probably represented an effort by the Andeans to incorporate their Christian patron saint into their own traditional panoply of religious symbols, but to Novoa and the inspectors, it represented blatant idolatry.[32]

Novoa and his assistants found that confession was another locus of religious confusion and conflict among the indigenous citizens of San Pedro de Acas. Andeans in Cajatambo had practiced purification rites before holidays that resembled the sacrament of penance. The villagers confessed to Andean religious specialists any wrongdoing such as adultery, failing to make offerings to Andean deities and mummies, and neglecting to fast or abstain from sexual activity during ritual periods. At the same time, Catholic priests and friars fluent in Quechua had established the practice of annual confessions in the town to repent Christian sins. Hernando Hacas Poma and his cohorts urged people to make a distinction between Andean transgressions and Catholic sins (*pecados*). Hacas Poma then instructed the parishioners to confess indigenous trespasses to Andean ministers and pecados to the priest. In effect, Hacas Poma and the other dogmatizers offered local Andeans a religious compromise, dividing responsibility with the priests over rites of purification, depending on the transgressions involved. For Novoa and the idolatry inspectors, however, Andean forms of penance merely represented the Devil's work, which had to be punished and replaced with orthodox Catholic rites.[33]

Another source of tension within Andean communities involved folk healers (*curanderos*), whom Spanish religious authorities often viewed as servants of the Devil. The Andeans traditionally relied on local healers to cure sickness, concoct love potions, or cast spells on enemies. These healers claimed to draw their powers from local Andean deities, which some idolatry inspectors viewed as constituting a pact with Satan. Using threats of punishment and torture, idolatry inspector Antonio de Cáceres extracted a confession from an Andean faith healer, Juana Icha, that she had engaged in a demonic pact involving sexual intercourse with a mountain spirit or supay named Apu Parato. According to Juana Icha, Apu Parato visited her in a series of dreams, taking the form of her late husband and then of an Andean in a black cape. Later, after some badgering by her interrogators, Juana Icha added that in exchange for granting her the powers of a curandera, Apu Parato demanded food and then sexual intercourse, "inserting his member inside her and ejaculating a cold yellow liquid."[34] For Andeans, the tale of Apu Parato giving curative powers to Juana Icha in exchange for traditional sacrificial foods, such as coca leaves and animal blood, probably symbolized the establishment of a reciprocal relationship between deities and humans. Antonio de Cáceres, however, interpreted the story as clear evidence of witchcraft, involving an explicit demonic pact.[35]

While the attitudes and biases of the inspectors could influence the testimony of witnesses, so too could local political imbroglios within indigenous communities. In the village of Santo Domingo de Ocros, for example, the enemies of Francisco Vergara denounced him for idolatry in 1665, apparently to unseat him as kuraka. Vergara's chief rival for the post, Francisca Flores, and her supporters entered into an alliance with the idolatry inspector, Fernando de Arce, and the local priest, Gabriel Menéndez de Coca, to prove the kuraka guilty of idolatry. Flores claimed hereditary rights to Vergara's post, while both Coca and Arce were involved in court cases involving land disputes with the kuraka. The idolatry trial was simply one more act of litigation to depose Vergara and ensnare him. In a similar manner, the investigations of Bernardo de Novoa in Acas involved a power struggle among dogmatizers, including Hernando Hacas Poma, the local priest, and the priest's indigenous lay assistant, Francisco Poma y Altas Caldeas. The priest's aide provided some of the most damning evidence against the dogmatizers, claiming that the formidable old Hacas Poma had cast a near-fatal spell on him after Poma forced him to attend mass. Local idolatry inspectors all too frequently became enmeshed in such triangular power struggles involving Andean religious leaders, the priest, and kurakas over political and religious control in indigenous communities.[36]

The mixture of fear, political intrigue, and religious zeal surrounding the idolatry trials, prompted many indigenous communities to resist the inspectors with every means at their disposal. Local dogmatizers often hid huacas, chancas, conopas, and mallquis from the idolatry inspectors until the proceedings had ended. Even when Andean religious icons were destroyed, indigenous ministers continued to worship the locations where they had been, or they recreated representations of the shrines and deities. Local community leaders also defended themselves by utilizing Spanish courts to bring suit against inspectors, alleging a wide array of abuses. The intrepid and zealous visitor Bernardo de Novoa, for example, had four villages charge him with extracting false evidence about idolatry by using threats and torture. The parishioners of San Pedro de Acas even alleged that Novoa's abuses had caused the death of elderly citizens, including Hernando Hacas Poma. Moreover, the litigants complained that excessive financial exactions by Novoa during the two-year idolatry proceedings had bankrupted the parish. Although the courts cleared Novoa of any wrongdoing in his investigation, similar legal cases throughout the Lima Archdiocese cast doubts on the wisdom of idolatry trials and did much to weaken the movement, particularly after the death of the zealous and powerful Archbishop Pedro de Villagómez in 1671.[37]

Powerful civil and ecclesiastical authorities continued raising concerns about the vigorous, centralized campaigns of extirpation waged by Villagómez. The archbishop remained unpopular with most politicians, especially within the Audiencia of Lima, and a criminal court judge (*alcalde del crimen*), Juan de Padilla, wrote a series of condemnations to the King between 1654 and 1657. Padilla blamed the persistence of Andean religious practices on the incompetence and idleness of the clergy, arguing that idolatry trials failed to strike at the root cause of the problem. Influential clerics, such as the bishop of Quito, Alonso de la Peña Montenegro (1653–87), also undermined the trials by classifying

most forms of indigenous religious practices as merely superstition, not formal idolatry. These lesser offenses required better
religious instruction, not severe punishment. Even the Jesuits,
who had proven such staunch supporters of the early idolatry
campaigns, also began to waver in their backing by the 1650s,
refusing to dispatch members of the order to accompany the
expeditions and to provide religious instruction following trials.
Although some Jesuits still teamed up with the investigators without official sanction, the society's official withdrawal undermined
the prestige of the campaigns and highlighted the coercive over
the educational components of the proceedings. In the end,
although idolatry trials continued, without the support of their
powerful patron, Pedro de Villagómez, the proceedings became
more sporadic and were closely supervised by authorities in Lima.

The Final Stages of Extirpation, 1671–1750

After the heyday of extirpation during the tenure of Pedro de
Villagómez, clerical efforts to eradicate Andean religious practices
slowly shifted in emphasis. Apart from a brief flurry of activity
between 1690 and 1701 when eighteen trials took place, efforts to
prosecute idolatry became less frequent. None of the archbishops
of Lima succeeding Villagómez shared his intense passion for
extirpation. These more intermittent idolatry inspections continued to uncover and punish Andean religious practices much as in
earlier campaigns. Nevertheless, the inspectors lacked the
sweeping authority granted by Lobo Guerrero and Villagómez,
until Archbishop Diego Morcillo Rubio de Auñón appointed
Pedro de Celís as inspector-general of extirpation in 1725. Even
the broad powers granted to Celís, however, were more circum-
scribed than in earlier investigations. By the late seventeenth
century, clerical authorities began shifting idolatry cases to the
central ecclesiastical court in Lima, where they could be most
easily monitored. This was probably a response to complaints by
Andeans and the political and clerical opponents of these earlier

campaigns. Moreover, indigenous defendants relied more heavily on experienced Spanish trial lawyers in Lima, who proved quite adept at securing acquittals or minimizing punishments. Finally, the inspections of Pedro de Celís remained confined to the province of Cajatambo, and with the death of his patron, Archbishop Morcillo, in 1730, even this wave of extirpation ended abruptly. Very sporadic, local idolatry trials continued thereafter, but by 1750 the main campaigns had ended.[38]

The subtle changes in these later extirpation investigations are most visible in the detailed legal case presented in 1723 against two Andean religious specialists from Santiago de Carampoma, Huarochirí—Juan de Rojas and Francisco Libiac Condor. According to testimony in the case, Juan de Rojas kept a chapel in his house. There, he held public rituals to a venerable village chanca, which began by sounding a seashell trumpet. Likewise, Francisco Libiac Condor had inherited the right to keep important village chancas and conopas, and he led local people in prayers, orations, and ritual sacrifices. Indeed, Libiac Condor was widely revered in the region for his skills as a religious specialist. Despite being uncovered as Andean religious leaders, both men received the services of judge advocate in Lima, Melchor de Carvajal, who mounted a skillful defense. He argued that both men were victims of ignorance. Moreover, both had repented and cooperated fully with the idolatry inquiry. According to Carvajal, Rojas and Libiac Condor were also relatively new converts to Christianity, entitled to mercy and further instruction in the faith. In the end, these arguments managed to lessen the punishment. Francisco Libiac Condor, the more notorious dogmatizer of the two, received only a public flogging and a fine of twenty-five pesos. Although the issues involved in these later extirpation trials were similar to earlier cases, the proceedings in Lima were conducted with greater care, and judges showed more willingness to accept religious error as a legitimate defense. Apparently, by the eighteenth century clergymen had begun to reach a compromise about how to deal with persistent Andean religious practices; they would continue to root out idolatry, but the guilty were seldom viewed as apostates, and thus did not merit the most severe forms of discipline.

These later extirpation cases also reveal much about the resiliency of Andean religion after nearly two hundred years of Catholic evangelization. Despite their outward displays of Christian devotion, many Andeans in Carampoma and elsewhere still publicly attended traditional religious rites. In fact, seven years before extirpators prosecuted Juan de Rojas and Francisco Libiac Condor, an extirpator visiting the parish had arrested and later convicted another dogmatizer, Francisco de la Cruz.[39] Even repeated visits by extirpators apparently could not eliminate the community's ongoing need for traditional religious specialists, shamans, and healers.

Late Colonial Popular Religion, 1750–1825

Although enthusiasm for the extirpation of idolatry had waned by the 1750s, Christianity continued making slow and steady inroads within Andean communities during the second half of the century. Andeans continued flocking to local religious festivals, which became larger and more ostentatious ceremonial occasions. The familiar festivals, saints' holidays, and devotional objects associated with Catholic worship gave indigenous communities the opportunity to celebrate, to evoke the divine, and to share a sense of common purpose and mutual obligation. In addition, as church leaders moved away from forcible extirpation, they began emphasizing Christian concepts of love and charity, which along with popular rituals appealed to Andeans. Occasional extirpation trials persisted, but over time priests and the church hierarchy generally ignored or downplayed evidence of recurring indigenous religious practices or subterranean ties between traditional Andean rituals and Christian festivals and icons. The miracles associated with popular religious icons, such as the Virgin of Copacabana, for example, certainly had links to pre-Columbian deities in the Lake Titicaca region. By the eighteenth century, however, most churchmen exploited these connections to increase popular expressions of faith, instead of viewing them with intense suspicion. Indeed, the popularity of devotions to the Virgin of Copacabana or the Virgin of Chiquinquirá in the North Andes actually reached new heights during the century. By the time he wrote his memorial to the Crown, Fray Calixto de San José Tupak Inca confidently justified his complaints about Spanish abuses against his people by arguing that Andeans were by then all "good Christians." Popular piety in its many different forms served to lure Andeans to the churches, despite their tendency to continue mixing Catholicism with enduring traditional religious beliefs.[40]

During the political and economic tumult of the second half of the eighteenth century, the spiritual and ritual life of Roman Catholicism also provided unity and security for many Andean communities. In the seventeenth century, widespread indigenous migration and the rise of the forastero population led to a reformulation of community social, cultural, and religious practices. This process of ethnogenesis broke down traditional ethnic boundaries and the Andean religious practices associated with them. In addition, competition among indigenous groups and Spaniards for limited landholdings intensified in many regions, producing conflict and hardship. The dramatic increase in tax and labor obligations arising from the Bourbon Reforms also put additional pressure on Andeans during the century. Such economic burdens only worsened in 1751 when the Crown legalized the forced distribution of goods (repartimiento de comercio or *mercancías*) by local corregidores. In short, during the changing colonial world of the late eighteenth century, the Roman Catholic Church provided at least some sense of security and cohesion in the daily lives of the Andean peoples.

Relations between priests and their indigenous parishioners were complex and most often depended on local conditions and the personalities involved. Some clergymen were popular and caring community leaders, but widespread complaints about the moral laxity, ineptitude, and dishonesty of other priests and friars persisted. In his famous memorial, the Andean kuraka, Vicente Morachimo, provided a stunning catalog of abuses by clergymen and colonial bureaucrats alike. Morachimo claimed that both regular and secular clergymen forced Andeans to work for meager wages repairing churches, tending the land of priests and religious sodalities (*cofradías*), and carrying their produce to distant markets. The kuraka even told the case of the Dominican Fray Félix de Moncada, who allegedly forced his indigenous parishioners in Santa María Magdalena de Cao (outside of Trujillo) to work on his sugar plantation without pay. The friar also redirected water from irrigation canals to his own fields and grazed his goats on community pasture lands.[41] The Spanish naval officers, Jorge Juan and Antonio de Ulloa, echoed these reports of pervasive clerical corruption. Juan and Ulloa related the particularly salacious example of a friar in Cuenca (in the southern part of the Audiencia of Quito) who tried unsuccessfully to seduce the daughter of a prominent local kuraka, even asking for her hand in marriage. When the kuraka complained that priests could not marry, the wily friar forged a patent ostensibly giving his provincial's permission to marry the girl, and that evening a sham wedding took place.[42] Reports of poorly trained or lazy parish priests and friars also abounded. In 1766, for example, a clerical inspector in Chucuito reported that five of eighteen priests in the region knew only the rudiments of Aymara, making religious instruction and hearing confessions in the parishes nearly impossible. As late as 1793 a church investigation found that only 5 to 10 percent of the Andeans in some portions of the Lupaka parishes of Chucuito met their annual Easter obligation to confess and receive communion.[43] Under these circumstances, the persistence of Andean religious practices was inevitable. Over time, however, most parish priests, regardless of their honesty and effectiveness, came to understand or ignore evidence of idolatry, particularly when parishioners paid their salaries and came to mass periodically.

During the reign of King Charles III (1759–88), political and religious reformers began attacking clerical abuses and also expressions of popular religious piety, which they regarded as little more than superstition bordering on idolatry. These reformers, called Jansenists, often favored expanding royal control within Spain and the empire at the expense of papal jurisdiction and the powers wielded by local parish priests and the religious orders, particularly the influential Society of Jesus. Jansenists and their political allies in Spain finally gained enough power in 1767 to have the order expelled from the empire. Given the popularity and leverage exerted by the Jesuits within many indigenous communities, the expulsion order removed a major force for evangelization, particularly in frontier zones where the order operated large missionary operations. Efforts by Jansenists to attack popular piety and local religious devotions in the Andes, however, met with more limited success. The Church normally made only halfhearted efforts to reform what Jansenists called the "excesses" and "superstitions" embedded in local religious practices. Any effort to curb Andean expressions of popular piety and channel them into more sedate churches and cloisters was doomed to fail by the late eighteenth century.[44]

Instead, reformers in the Viceroyalty of Peru generally concentrated on limiting the political and economic power of the Church on the local level, which often provoked suspicions, dissension, and even confrontations between clerical and lay authorities. Many influential politicians believed the Church had gained too much power early in the century, when the Crown had appointed archbishops of Lima to serve as interim viceroys during the years 1710–16 and 1720–24. Royal authorities avoided this practice later in the century and began curtailing the power of the viceregal church, even at the level of indigenous doctrinas. Local priests traditionally had served as power brokers between viceregal authorities and indigenous communities, providing information to the state, interpreting laws to their parishioners, and even assisting in compiling population counts needed for tribute collection. Reformers imposed a number of changes in these power-broker relationships to curtail the strong local influence of clergymen in the doctrinas. Viceregal officials sponsored new censuses to catch tribute frauds, increased tax rates, and in the 1750s enforced the repartimiento de comercio. All of these policies dramatically extended the power of local magistrates at the expense of clergymen. They also provoked competition between corregidores and parish clergy for economic and political control over Andean communities. By giving priority to collecting state levies and meeting repartimiento quotas, the viceregal government effectively limited the resources available to pay clerical salaries, fees, and taxes. In short, the process of political centralization and imposing heavier fiscal exactions on the Andean communities undercut the role of clergymen as political and economic forces at the local level.

The growing tensions among churchmen, colonial officials, and Andean communities were vividly apparent in a series of disputes over tribute payments and surreptitious ancestor veneration in Andagua (near Arequipa) between 1748 and 1754. One of the principal innovations of the Bourbon Reforms was to increase tribute revenues, but the indigenous peoples of Andagua stubbornly resisted paying the higher taxes. The leader of the anti-tax faction was Gregorio Taco, a petty merchant in the local wool trade, whom Spanish residents of Andagua also accused of practicing witchcraft and idolatry. Apparently, Gregorio Taco was a respected local religious specialist, who argued that making sacrifices to local mallquis, conopas, and chancas protected the town and its prosperous regional commerce with Arequipa and highland mining towns. Despite his reputation as a dogmatizer, Taco enjoyed the support and friendship of the local parish priest, Joseph Delgado, who proved tolerant of local religious customs. Despite their resistance to increased tribute payments, Taco and the other citizens of the parish faithfully paid the salary and fees owed to Delgado, whom they considered a legitimate local leader. After several failed attempts to capture Taco, in 1751 the region's corregidor, Joseph de Arana, sent a force of 150 men to arrest him, to collect all tax arrears, and to destroy any idols found in the area. The force drew the ire of Reverend Delgado, who denied the presence of idolatry and even threatened the Spanish expedition's leader with excommunication. Nevertheless, the Spanish force rounded up Taco and his cohorts, exacted confessions (sometimes using torture), and destroyed a host of local mummies, chancas, and conopas.

At this point, the entire affair became mired in a series of petty jurisdictional conflicts. The Church hierarchy in Arequipa heard about the arrests, protested that idolatry fell under its purview, and sent its own idolatry inspectors to Andagua. When Arana refused to remand the prisoners to clerical authority, the bishop threatened him with excommunication. The imbroglio then came to the attention of judges in the Audiencia of Lima, who claimed jurisdiction over the affair in Andagua. Amidst these internecine disputes, Gregorio Taco and most of his allies secured their release from jail and even lodged formal complaints against excessive tribute rates and the destruction of local religious objects. Such divisions also allowed local Andean dogmatizers, such as Taco, to practice their own mix of Christianity and local indigenous rites with impunity and to defy local authorities over their right to tax the indigenous peoples.[45]

The Church-state conflicts occasioned by the Bourbon Reforms further weakened royal authority in the years from 1780 to 1825. The rebellions of Tupac Amaru in the Cusco region and Tomás Katari and Tupac Katari in Upper Peru shook the foundations of royal authority in the Andes. After their suppression by viceregal authorities, hostility to the colonial regime continued in many Andean communities. Even the imposition of the intendancy system in the 1780s throughout much of the Andes could not revitalize state control over regional indigenous populations. During Spain's political crisis following the French invasion of the Iberian peninsula in 1808, even the symbolic unity provided by the monarchy had crumbled. By this time Andean peoples had witnessed the slow decline in the power and prestige of the twin pillars of colonial rule—the Church and the monarchy. By attempting to clear away the customs, traditions, and popular rituals that proved such an important bond between the indigenous peoples and Roman Catholicism, the Crown ultimately managed to undermine its own power and legitimacy in the Andes. After all, the monarchy and the Church were intimately bound together in the indigenous popular imagination, and as the colonial state began its slow-motion collapse between 1808 and 1825, the loyalty of Andeans to the Crown continued to weaken. After the long process of evangelization begun in 1532, the indigenous peoples now faced an increasingly secularized creole leadership in most of the newly independent nations carved out of the former Tawantinsuyu. Despite the ongoing influence of Roman Catholicism, a weaker church structure allowed the convergence of Andean and Christian religious practices to continue throughout the eighteenth century, persisting even to the present day.

Conclusions

Although the spiritual conquest of the Andean world remained incomplete, the effects of three hundred years of evangelization and over a century of campaigns to extirpate idolatry produced immense cultural and religious changes. The state religious cults of the Inca fell to the official rituals and dogma of Roman Catholicism. Andeans quickly embraced the ritual festivals, cere-monies, music, dances, prayers, and devotional objects of Christianity. On the other hand, they stubbornly clung to tradi-tional rites associated with their huacas, chancas, mallquis, and conopas, a problem that bedeviled generations of churchmen in the Viceroyalty of Peru. Supporters of forcible conversion, such as Archbishop Pedro de Villagómez, utilized systematic legal campaigns to extirpate idolatry, while many other clerics favored a more moderate stance, viewing continued Andean religious practices as signs of religious error that could be combated by education. The problem of convincing Andeans to renounce their own beliefs in favor of Christianity proved more complex than either the extirpators or their critics envisaged. Traditional Andean religious beliefs united the spiritual and materials worlds; turning away from these traditions involved rejecting their identities and their past. Instead, most indigenous peoples incorporated Roman Catholic ritual and doctrine into their own religious framework, producing a complex, evolving mixture that differed over time in each region of the Andean world. This ever changing set of spiritual compromises or mañay began slowly incorporating more Christian precepts by the eighteenth century, but complaints about clerical corruption, and the divisiveness and tumult produced by the Bourbon Reforms weakened the church and the spread of Catholic orthodox beliefs during the waning years of the colonial order. As a result, traditional indigenous religious practices continue to have meaning today, as Andeans still revere their conopas and mix Christian and traditional religious beliefs into their own brand of Catholicism.

The history of religious conversion and the imposition of Catholic orthodoxy often involved a tragic mixture of idealism, intolerance, persecution, misunderstanding, and even brutality. What extirpators viewed as apostasy, Andeans often perceived as preserving their own cultural and spiritual identity. Throughout the colonial era, the universalizing dogma of Christianity came into conflict with Andean notions of mañay. The tale of Cristóbal Choque Casa in the Huarochirí Manuscript indicates the profound dilemma faced even by stalwart Andean converts to Christianity. Sometime after his conversion, Cristóbal Choque Casa related that in a dream, he had engaged a powerful local huaca in mortal combat vanquishing him. Despite this apparent victory, however, different huacas returned to Choque Casa's dreams for combat each night, repeating an endless cycle of nightmarish struggles against his old faith. Apparently, even those who rejected past beliefs during their waking hours could attain no peace in sleep. The persistence of Andean religious practices indicates that most indigenous converts were unwilling to face the nightmares of Cristóbal Choque Casa.[46] Instead, they attempted a spiritual accommodation between the old and the new, Christianity and the old deities. The spiritual conquest of the Andes ended not in complete victory, but in a compromise between Christianity and native Andean beliefs—a constantly evolving mañay.

7

RESISTANCE, REBELLION, AND CONSCIOUSNESS

ON 24 SEPTEMBER 1572 the last Sapa Inca, Tupac Amaru I, left a cell in Colcampata prison to face his executioner in the main square of Cusco. The last remnant of the once proud Inca state, the remote fortress at Vilcabamba, had fallen in June to an expeditionary force dispatched by Viceroy Francisco de Toledo. After the capture of Tupac Amaru and a hasty three-day trial, a Spanish judge condemned the young Inca to death. Despite the efforts of leading churchmen and Cusco's prominent Spanish and Andean families to secure a pardon for Tupac Amaru, Toledo remained determined to carry out the court's sentence. The execution itself was a carefully orchestrated ritual. The Inca emerged from prison in a black robe of mourning, seated on a mule, with his hands tied and a rope at his neck. The procession from Colcampata to the Plaza de Armas included important clerical and lay authorities, a troop of four hundred Cañari warriors, and members of the viceroy's personal bodyguard. Even the choice of Cañari soldiers to accompany the Inca was calculated. These people had remained restive under Inca rule since their defeat and resettlement from the

North Andes to Cusco, and they had been among the most loyal indigenous allies of Francisco Pizarro.[1] Crowds of Andeans thronged the streets and surrounding buildings to witness and mourn the impending death of their ruler. Once he mounted the scaffold, Tupac Amaru raised his hands to silence the crowd. Then, he delivered a short speech renouncing the Inca state religion and declaring his own conversion to Christianity. At that point, the Inca's Cañari executioner came forward, blindfolded the prisoner, and placed the young ruler's neck on the block. With a single blow the executioner severed Tupac Amaru's head, holding it aloft to the assembled crowd. Within a scant few seconds the bells of the cathedral tolled, and many among the assembled crowd of Andeans began wailing in sorrow.

Although the Inca's body was taken for burial in the city cathedral, Toledo ordered that his head should be displayed publicly, hoisted on a pole. Because so many Andeans had gathered to worship and give homage to their dead ruler, however, the viceroy ordered the head taken down and buried with the body after only two days. Toledo had designed the public execution to symbolize the final defeat and humiliation of the Inca, and the viceroy would not tolerate having the Andeans honor their ruler in death. To Francisco de Toledo, the stroke that decapitated Tupac Amaru I completed the Spanish overthrow of Tawantinsuyu, begun at Cajamarca in 1532.[2]

Over two hundred years later on 18 May 1781, the main plaza of Cusco served as the scene of another grisly public spectacle, the execution of the rebel José Gabriel Condorcanqui, called Tupac Amaru II after the last Inca ruler. Tupac Amaru II, who claimed descent from the Inca royal family, had led a rebellion against the colonial regime that threatened to expel the Spaniards from the Andean highlands and establish a new Inca empire. On the day of execution, Spanish authorities bound Tupac Amaru and his fellow prisoners in handcuffs and leg irons, tied them to the tails of horses, and dragged them along the ground to the Plaza de Armas. Before his own death, Tupac Amaru was forced to watch the brutal execution of his key followers and family members, including his wife, Micaela Bastidas, and their twenty-year-old son, Hipólito. After these gruesome affairs, Tupac Amaru was led to the center of the plaza, where the executioner cut out his tongue and threw him face down on the cobblestones. He then tied the rebel's hands and feet to four horses, which were driven in separate directions literally to pull him apart. The horses apparently lacked the strength for the task, and instead, the poor man remained suspended in air moaning pitifully. Finally, his executioners decided to behead Tupac Amaru. Afterward, they dismembered his body along with those of his wife, son, and uncle. Their remains were sent later to the principal centers of the revolt as a grim reminder of the stakes involved in rising up against Spanish authority. The rebel's nine-year-old son Fernando was forced to watch the entire ordeal of his family's execution before his expulsion from the Andes to serve a sentence of permanent exile in Africa.[3]

Between the fall of Vilcabamba and the rebellion of Tupac Amaru II, numerous indigenous revolts and insurrections broke out against abuses of Spanish colonial rule. Some of these revolts were only small-scale, spontaneous outbreaks of violence, while others encompassed entire provinces. During the eighteenth century these uprisings became more frequent, as the Spanish colonial regime attempted to heighten fiscal pressures, exercise closer administrative control over the Andean communities, and impose trade restrictions. All of these policies exacerbated persistent social and economic tensions present in the Andes during the colonial era, ultimately erupting into the rebellions of Tomás Katari, Tupac Amaru II, and Tupac Katari. Between 1780 and 1783 these massive insurrections inflamed much of Peru and Upper Peru, serving as the greatest challenge to Spanish rule since the sixteenth-century revolt of Manco Inca.

During the late colonial period indigenous rebels independently began developing more sophisticated political and social agendas. Sometimes this involved a vigorous assertion of community rights and a greater measure of political autonomy. In other cases, rebels promised to establish a completely new political order to replace the Spanish colonial regime. Tupac Amaru II, for example, vowed to fulfill messianic prophecies about the return of the Inca, who would expel all corrupt Spanish authorities and found a new kingdom free from oppression and misery. Although these bloody rebellions in the 1780s failed, violent outbursts against Spanish rule continued throughout the colonial era. Later, indigenous soldiers fought actively in the wars for independence, again seeking to advance their own political and social objectives.

Each uprising during the colonial period prompted the production of differing quantities of official documentation, as authorities tried to learn the causes of this unrest and to punish rebel leaders. The quantity and quality of the documentation produced in each upheaval varied, however, depending on the severity of the violence, its geographical extent, and the magnitude of the judicial proceedings in its aftermath. The voluminous documentation produced by the rebellion of Tupac Amaru II (1780–81), for example, provides a wealth of information about topics such as the colonial regime's abuses against indigenous peoples, the stated aims and motives of rebel groups, and the judgments rendered by colonial authorities. Because the Spanish legal system often obliged defendants to answer a series of broad, open-ended questions, trial records can reveal much about daily life, ethnic divisions and rivalries, and Andean concepts of justice. Historians, anthropologists, and specialists in cultural studies have also begun to see violent uprisings as "ritual or cultural episodes," examining patterns of violence, the degree of planning and organization, the use of Christian and traditional Andean religious symbols or icons, and messianic visions of a revived Inca past that may have emerged. In short, these moments of armed revolt provide scholars with unique opportunities to witness patterns of resistance, rebellion, and the evolution of an indigenous political consciousness over time.

Inca Resistance: From Manco Inca's Rebellion to the Fall of Vilcabamba

The establishment of the Inca state-in-exile at Vilcabamba had its origins in the rebellion of Manco Inca in May 1536.[4] Within weeks after taking Cusco in 1533, Francisco Pizarro arranged the coronation of Manco as the Sapa Inca to aid the Spaniards in consolidating their hold over Tawantinsuyu. Manco Inca remained a dutiful and loyal puppet-ruler until he grew weary of his allies' greed and arrogance. At that point, the Inca slipped away from Cusco, raised an army of a hundred thousand, and besieged the former capital city. His generals also defeated and destroyed several relief expeditions, swept the Spaniards from most highland centers between Cusco and Lima and attacked the viceregal capital in August 1536. With the arrival of reinforcements from other areas of the Spanish Indies, however, Francisco Pizarro broke the siege of Lima and gained the military advantage over Manco and his armies. Despite renewing his assaults on Spaniards in the highlands over the next three years, victory eluded the Sapa Inca, and by 1540 he had set up his exile kingdom in Vilcabamba (northwest of Cusco). From there, his troops waged guerrilla attacks on Spanish settlements. Finally, four years later two Spaniards assassinated Manco Inca, and the throne passed to his young son, Sayri-Tupac.[5]

Distracted by periodic civil wars among the conquistadors, Spanish authorities abandoned attempts to invade Vilcabamba, opting instead to negotiate a peace treaty with the Inca kingdom. In 1557 the viceroy, the Marqués de Cañete, reached an accord with Sayri-Tupac, who agreed to leave his stronghold and reside in Cusco in exchange for a full pardon and the right to maintain his remote fortress-city. The Sapa Inca also received extensive rural and urban properties and rights to tax revenues. After a visit to the viceroy in Lima, Sayri-Tupac and his large entourage of followers set up residence in Cusco, where he and his coya were baptized as Roman Catholics in 1558 by the bishop. In 1561, however, this compromise unraveled when Sayri-Tupac died unexpectedly during a visit to his rural estates in Yucay.[6] The throne then passed to his elder brother, Titu Cusi, residing in Vilcabamba.

Unlike his predecessor, Titu Cusi was not inclined to cooperate with the Spanish authorities, and he renewed guerrilla operations from Vilcabamba, harassing commerce, raiding settlements, and plundering rural estates. Although little is known about socioeconomic organization in the exile community, Titu Cusi's more aggressive policies apparently reflected the ascendancy of a more militantly anti-Spanish faction in Vilcabamba, wedded to earlier militaristic and religious traditions of Tawantinsuyu.

Despite this resumption of hostilities, colonial officials continued trying to negotiate a settlement that would put an end to the independent Inca kingdom. Spanish persistence finally paid off when Titu Cusi agreed to sign the Treaty of Acobamba in 1567. The Inca probably feared provoking a Spanish punitive expedition, so he negotiated highly favorable terms—an annual income, estates and tax revenues, and the right to remain in Vilcabamba. In exchange, Titu Cusi agreed to end hostilities, to accept baptism into the Catholic Church, and to recognize the sovereignty of the Spanish King. Although Spanish authorities continually urged the Inca to leave Vilcabamba, he remained ensconced there until his death in 1571. Then he was succeeded by his more militant brother, Tupac Amaru I, an Andean religious leader who rejected both Christianity and the prospect of peace with Spaniards.[7]

The task of negotiating with Tupac Amaru I fell to Francisco de Toledo, the stern and determined viceroy who viewed Tawantinsuyu as a corrupt, tyrannical, and illegitimate empire.[8] When his negotiator Atilano de Anaya was killed while on a mission to the Sapa Inca in Vilcabamba, Toledo decided to end negotiations and mount a military force to destroy the indigenous state. Command of the expedition went to a seasoned veteran of the civil wars, Martín Hurtado de Arbieto, who had 250 well-equipped Spanish soldiers in his army. After vanquishing the Inca's troops at the Battle of Coyao-Chaca, Hurtado de Arbieto occupied Vilcabamba on 24 June 1572. Although Tupac Amaru initially managed to escape the invaders, they eventually captured him trying to flee to the lowland jungles. The victorious army reached Cusco on 21 September, where the Sapa Inca was hastily tried and executed. With the fall of Vilcabamba and the death of Tupac Amaru, the threat of armed indigenous insurrection diminished. In fact, despite several potentially dangerous conspiracies and some relatively isolated revolts by indigenous groups, no large-scale Andean insurrections erupted until the eighteenth century.[9]

Juan Santos Atahualpa and Messianic Rebellion

The first such major uprising against Spanish rule was launched in 1742 by Juan Santos Atahualpa in the jungle zone bordering the central Andean provinces of Tarma and Jauja. This lowland region remained on the frontier of Spanish Peru, where the Franciscan order had begun establishing missions in the late seventeenth century. While some indigenous groups gravitated to the missions, many others rejected Franciscan efforts to convert, acculturate, and discipline local ethnic groups. Juan Santos Atahualpa, who apparently took his name from the Inca captured by Pizarro at Cajamarca, united these disaffected jungle peoples and some highland migrants into a formidable guerrilla force that repeatedly defeated Spanish efforts to quell the insurrection between 1742 and 1752.

Although Toledo may have thought the execution of Tupac Amaru I ended the last vestiges of Inca power, Juan Santos Atahualpa utilized the residual appeal of the "lost glory" of Tawantinsuyu by proclaiming himself "Apu Inca" (Inca Lord). Juan Santos, apparently a highlander from Cusco, had received a Christian education from the Jesuits and claimed descent from the Inca royal family. Although his Franciscan critics claimed that Juan Santos was actually a lowborn impostor, his true background remains a mystery. Nevertheless, upon arriving in the jungle settlement of Quisopango in May 1742, Juan Santos initiated a revolt, ostensibly to reclaim his ancestral kingdom and to reestablish the cosmic order disrupted by the Spanish invasion in 1532. Juan Santos ordered the expulsion of all hostile Spaniards, blacks, and mestizos, proclaiming that his new order would bring prosperity and peace from the jungle to the highlands and then to the coast. He promised that the revolt would culminate with his own coronation as Sapa Inca in Lima. Juan Santos Atahualpa mixed this nativist-messianic appeal with strong doses of Christian doctrine. Franciscan and Jesuit visitors to his camp remarked how the Inca prayed daily in Castilian, Latin, and indigenous tongues. Although the details of the rebel leader's ideas remain sketchy (largely drawn from hostile Franciscan accounts), they apparently appealed to discontented jungle peoples and some highlanders, and the Inca quickly gained supporters throughout the lowland region known as the Cerro de la Sal.

As the rebellion expanded, Spanish commerce with the lowlands dwindled and Franciscan missionary activities were disrupted, forcing Spanish authorities in Tarma and Jauja to take military action. When a series of local militia expeditions either failed to locate the indigenous rebels or met defeat, Juan Santos became emboldened enough to expel the Franciscan missionaries from lands under his control. Given these stunning reversals, the viceroy in Lima dispatched a veteran military commander, General José de Llamas, with 850 regulars from the Callao garrison to stamp out the insurrection. Although Llamas had gained a considerable reputation defending the coast against a threatened English invasion, his soldiers experienced repeated defeats against the indigenous forces. By 1747 the Franciscans decided to attempt an ill-fated pacification of the region by simply reoccupying their mission parishes. In March three friars and their escort of ten Spanish soldiers were massacred by local indigenous troops. Another group of three missionaries failed to arrange a truce in the hostilities after meeting with the Inca.

In 1752, Juan Santos Atahualpa decided to launch a bold invasion of the highlands, hoping to spread his messianic message. His troops had made earlier forays into highland regions, but this time the Inca apparently decided to mount an audacious full-scale assault on the Comas region of Jauja. When his forces quickly took the mountain city of Andamarca on 3 August 1752, local indigenous citizens proclaimed loyalty to "our Inca," rushing forward to kiss his hands and feet. Despite this early success, no huge levy of highlanders rushed to join the Inca's army, and within three days he retreated to his lowland base of operations. Although he would never mount another serious invasion of the highlands, Juan Santos remained firmly in control of the Cerro de la Sal.

After the Inca's unsuccessful attack on Jauja, the viceroy turned jurisdiction of these highland provinces bordering the Cerro de la Sal over to military governors, who established a defensive ring of fortresses to contain the rebellion in the lowlands. After Juan Santos Atahualpa died of unknown causes sometime between 1755 and 1756, the rebellion remained confined to the jungle provinces. Nevertheless, Spanish authorities could not reassert their authority until the 1780s, when missionaries and merchants began returning to the lowland region.

Despite the obvious successes of the insurrection in the Cerro de la Sal, the messianic movement of Juan Santos Atahualpa never garnered widespread support in the densely populated central sierra, the heartland of the former Tawantinsuyu. Several daunting obstacles to a pan-Andean rebellion confronted the Inca. Unlike the loosely governed jungle frontier regions, Spanish authorities had consolidated their political and military power in the sierra, which impeded any widespread revolt. In addition, omnipresent ethnic divisions in the Andes inhibited the possibility of any indigenous alliances made across regional boundaries. Powerful indigenous and mestizo kin networks, such as the Astocuri, the Apoalaya, and the Limaylla, also had a vested interest in maintaining the status quo, rather than acknowledging the leadership of Juan Santos Atahualpa, an unknown outsider. Finally, the messianic image of the Inca's return apparently failed to captivate the indigenous popular imagination during this period. For many Andean ethnic groups and their leaders, the prospect of crowning an Inca king failed to generate much enthusiasm. Indeed, the return of some version of Tawantinsuyu probably promised more of a threat than an imagined utopia.[10]

The insurrection of Juan Santos Atahualpa had repercussions even in the viceregal capital, where indigenous leaders conspired in 1750 to rebel, capture the viceregal palace, and gain control of the city. This plot also had messianic overtones. According to one organizer, the seventeenth-century creole mystic, St. Rose of Lima, had foretold of the Inca's return in 1750, making the planned revolt the fulfillment of divine prophecy. Some plotters also favored contacting Juan Santo Atahualpa, offering to crown him Sapa Inca. Others, however, argued for an interim government of local Andean leaders, followed by the selection of a new Inca. Nevertheless, Spanish authorities discovered the plans and on 26 June 1750, they arrested all major conspirators. The only ringleader to escape capture was Francisco Jiménez Inca, who had returned earlier to his home in Huarochirí.[11] When Jiménez Inca heard of the arrests, he rallied kinsmen and allies in the province. Within a week, he and his followers had expelled Spanish authorities from all but the provincial mining centers. Twenty days later, however, the rebellion collapsed when a large Spanish military expedition from the mining town of Yuli recaptured Huarochirí and arrested rebel leaders. The short-lived uprising never fulfilled the prophecy of St. Rose, nor had the rebels managed to link forces with Juan Santos Atahualpa. Still, the Cerro de la Sal remained unpacified and simmering discontent in the highlands erupted into periodic small-scale riots and revolts for the next several decades.[12]

The Repartimiento de Comercio and the Spread of Discontent, 1750–80

One of the principal catalysts for discontent in Andean communities before the outbreak of the Great Rebellions of the 1780s was the viceregal government's legalization of the repartimiento de comercio (or *reparto*) in 1751.[13] Conflicts over land distribution, tribute rates, mita allocations, the succession to ethnic leadership posts, and abuses by local priests and corregidores frequently disturbed local indigenous communities during the eighteenth century. The spread of the reparto often exacerbated such local tensions, leading to an escalation of violence. The principal aim of the forced distribution of European and American goods and mules was to compel Andean participation in the internal market, as the highland mining economy began its resurgence by the 1740s. Nonetheless, indigenous communities had little control over the types of goods in each allocation and prices were invariably inflated, often making it difficult for communities to meet both their tribute and reparto quotas.

While the legislation of 1751 imposed substantial economic burdens on Andean communities under its jurisdiction, it also provided advantages to at least some colonial interest groups.[14] Before legalization, the repartimiento de comercio had operated informally, but by the 1720s corregidores and merchants began expanding it throughout most of highland Peru and Upper Peru to offset the overall decline in internal commerce. In 1720 the Crown also abolished the mita for all but the mines at Huancavelica and Potosí, which curtailed the profits of hacendados, textile mill owners, and most miners who had benefited from cheap state laborers. By this time expanding imports of European wares also were undermining the price for local textiles and other commodities. These trends depressed many local markets, which hurt both regional elites and the Lima merchant community who had controlled the supply of most commodities to the interior provinces. Expansion of the reparto, however, revitalized the economic prospects of these groups by promoting the circulation of local commodities such as rough woolen textiles, yerba maté (Paraguayan tea), coca, aguardiente, and foodstuffs; the systematic distribution of mules even guaranteed the transport of goods throughout internal trade routes, particularly to the new mining centers of Huantajaya, Hualgayoc, Huallanca, Condoroma, and Pasco. Moreover, as Andeans fell behind in their reparto quotas, they were forced to sell their labor in mines, textile mills, and on Spanish estates, which eased labor shortages occasioned by restrictions on the mita. The repartimiento de comercio also strengthened the local political and economic power of corregidores, at the expense of parish priests and local Andean kurakas, an outcome that dovetailed with the plans of political reformers in Lima, anxious to restrict the influences of religious and community leaders. Nevertheless, creole, mestizo, and Andean producers gained no tangible benefits if they were not involved in supplying commodities for the repartos, because regional markets were often saturated by the forced distributions.[15]

The repartimiento de comercio weighed most heavily on indigenous communities already disrupted by a wide array of problems, particularly strife over ethnic leadership. From the mid-seventeenth century the prestige and influence of traditional kurakas (most often called *caciques* by this period) came under attack from groups of entrepreneurial Andean commoners who began challenging hereditary leaders for community leadership. Many of these indigenous businessmen had made considerable sums in commerce, mining, or landholding activities. Their fortunes often eclipsed the sources of wealth available to traditional caciques. As a result, litigation in the courts over who had the right to communal leadership positions proliferated. During such local power struggles, local corregidores often put added pressure on caciques to collect tribute and ensure reparto quotas. Weakened by such internal strife, ethnic lords seldom mounted effective resistance to these powerful Spanish officials, regardless of the consequences for their communities. When they did resist or failed to meet tax and reparto assessments, the corregidores usually replaced them with more pliable caciques. Frequently these "intruder" caciques were outsiders—Andeans, mestizos, creoles, or even Spaniards—who merely served as henchmen of the corregidor.

This trend toward replacing hereditary leaders with intruders not only damaged ties of loyalty between caciques and their people; it also dramatically weakened and even destabilized the entire indigenous political order. In one particularly egregious case, Florencio Lupa, cacique of the Moscari people in Chayanta, north of Potosí, used his political influence with the local corregidor to gain ethnic leadership over two rival ethnic groups, the Panacachi and the Pocoata. Such a multiethnic union or *cacicazgo* was unprecedented and deeply resented by the Panacachi and the Pocoata. Moreover, Florencio Lupa was an unscrupulous and ambitious cacique who used intimidation and even violence to impose tribute and reparto allocations on his unwilling subjects. Over time, Lupa became powerful enough to challenge local priests, Spanish landowners, and even government officials. In this way, political pressures accompanying the expansion of the reparto system allowed unscrupulous intruder caciques, such as Florencio Lupa, to use their unprecedented political powers to violate traditional indigenous political rights throughout many regions of Peru and Upper Peru.[16]

The resulting crisis of political legitimacy prompted a groundswell of litigation before local courts and the audiencias, but when legal recourse failed, many Andeans began turning to violent solutions. Such uprisings were usually small-scale affairs directed against abusive corregidores, corrupt local priests, exploitative Spanish entrepreneurs (land owners, miners, or *obrajeros*), and even some caciques. Over time, however, these revolts spread over wider areas, becoming more serious challenges to Spanish authority. One particularly bloody indigenous uprising in Chulumani (in Sicasica province, near La Paz) in 1771, for example, arose to protest the exploitative administration of the reparto by a ruthless corregidor, the Marqués de Villahermosa. Since the local cacique was a mestizo ally of Villahermosa, leadership in the revolt passed to two indigenous commoners, Juan Tapia and Mateo Puma. Both solicited funds for the uprising from community members, proclaiming that "it was time to free themselves from the oppression of the Spaniards."[17] These leaders of Chulumani first tried to petition the audiencia, but when the corregidor refused to comply with the tribunal's order to suspend reparto debts for the region, Tapia and Puma convinced an assembly of community members to take violent action. The indigenous peoples took up arms and besieged the corregidor in the regional center of Chulumani, erecting a gallows outside the town and promising to punish any "thieves and scoundrels" for their crimes. The rebels also demanded the release of some indigenous prisoners and the withdrawal of Villahermosa and his lieutenant from the province. During the siege of Chulumani, indigenous leaders even organized a shadow government, granting military and political titles to subordinate leaders. When the corregidor's deputy arrived with a small detachment of reinforcements, however, Villahermosa launched a daring counterattack that scattered the indigenous rebels and ended the uprising.[18]

As the rising tide of revolts in Peru and Upper Peru demonstrated, Andeans were increasingly willing to seek violent solutions to abuses of the colonial regime. The breakdown of traditional ethnic political structures, with the introduction of intruders (whether Andean, mestizo, creole, or Spanish) as caciques, only heightened the danger of an uprising. Communities could no longer rely on powerful, respected community leaders to resolve their grievances, particularly when local officials, such as the Marqués de Villahermosa in Chulumani, refused to abide by the decisions of Spanish courts. Violence seemed the only solution. Although these uprisings seldom challenged the Crown, rebels did begin articulating a political agenda that moved from ending oppression to advancing some tentative designs for self-government. It was an ominous portent of things to come in the 1780s.

The Great Age of Andean Rebellions, 1780–83

Bourbon reform policies during the 1770s—particularly changes in trade and mining policies, military organization, patterns of colonial administration, and heightened fiscal pressures—led to an escalation of existing political and social tensions in many regions of Peru and Upper Peru. In 1772, for example, the Crown ordered an increase in the sales tax (alcabala) from 2 percent to 4 percent on both colonial and European goods, and a scant four years later raised the rate to 6 percent, making it the highest in the empire. In order to collect these levies more effectively, the viceregal government established customs houses (aduanas) in the key cities and placed suboffices along major trade routes. The Crown also disturbed regional trade patterns by removing Upper Peru from the Viceroyalty of Peru in 1776, placing it instead under the jurisdiction of the newly created Viceroyalty of the Río de la Plata, with its capital in Buenos Aires. During this same period colonial officials started taking more accurate censuses of the colonial population, carefully recording the numbers of Andeans to ensure that tribute and other levies were collected efficiently. The net result was a dramatic upsurge in tax revenues, accompanied by regional economic downturns that heightened fear and discontent. In some areas, hacendados, textile mill owners, miners, merchants, muleteers, petty traders, artisans, and Andeans living in urban and rural areas found their economic interests seriously undermined by these reforms. Regional unrest among a wide array of social groups set the stage for a series of revolts between 1777 and 1780 in La Paz, Arequipa, and even Cusco. The most serious threats to Spanish authority, however, came from the oppressed indigenous communities of Peru and Upper Peru.[19]

Tomás Katari and Unrest in Chayanta

The first phase of the massive Andean rebellions of the 1780s began inauspiciously as a series of legal protests by the Aymara peoples of Macha (in Chayanta province, north of Potosí) seeking redress over abuses in tribute collection and reparto allocations. The leader of this movement was Tomás Katari, an illiterate Andean peasant in his early thirties who spoke no Spanish. Despite his relative youth and humble origins, Katari would inaugurate a remarkable struggle leading to unprecedented claims for indigenous autonomy and political power in the region. Between 1777 and 1780 Tomás Katari led the ten ethnic communities of Macha in a series of legal confrontations with the corregidor, Joaquín Alós, and his allies among local caciques, parish priests, and the judges of the Audiencia of Charcas. These disputes led ultimately to the expulsion of Spanish authorities from the region, the assumption of power by Katari, and then to a widespread insurrection of the Aymara peoples against the Spanish colonial regime.

The catalyst for the struggles in Chayanta was the repartimiento de comercio, which imposed especially onerous burdens on the Aymara peoples. Ethnic leaders had long controlled the communal assignment of lands, herds, and all tax and labor burdens. In recent decades, however, local corregidores such as Joaquín Alós had imposed abusive reparto quotas and replaced uncooperative community leaders with their own henchmen who seldom had any ties or responsibilities to local indigenous communities. Given the extensive powers wielded by caciques, these intruders threatened the entire political and economic operation of local Aymara communities. To curtail such abuses, in 1764 the Crown had granted the Audiencia of Charcas full authority to resolve complaints brought by Andean communities against their corregidores, but this measure brought little relief. Instead, the move promoted the establishment of informal political alliances between local corregidores and those audiencia judges seeking to share in illicit profits from tributes and reparto allocations.

This cozy arrangement received a potential setback, however, when the Crown transferred Upper Peru to the new Viceroyalty of the Río de la Plata in 1776. Unlike their counterparts in Lima, who were often tied to merchants involved in the repartimiento de comercio, bureaucrats in Buenos Aires had little interest in promoting the forced distributions, which only fostered corruption, indigenous unrest, and the accretion of excessive powers by highland corregidores. Nevertheless, the viceroy and the Audiencia of Buenos Aires lacked the power to redress indigenous complaints, especially when they stood opposed to the interests of corregidores and judges in the Audiencia of Charcas. Instead, the new administrative boundaries created the circumstances for endless jurisdictional disputes between the government in Buenos Aires and local courts and magistrates in Upper Peru.

Tomás Katari and the Aymara peoples of Macha used widespread fraud in the tribute system to contest the stranglehold over power exercised by local Spanish magistrates. For the people of Macha, tribute assessments and the mita became a powerful political vehicle, because they represented the symbolic link between the Spanish King and indigenous communities throughout the Andes. To the Aymara peasants, meeting these tax and labor obligations guaranteed their control over lands, crops, herds, and the entire body of corporate rights then threatened by Alós and his cronies. Moreover, colonial legislation demanded the immediate removal of any Spanish official cheating on tribute and mita assessments. As a result, the Aymara protesters concentrated their political counterattack on taking Alós and his political allies to court for defrauding the Crown of tribute receipts. In this way, Katari and the other protesters undoubtedly hoped to dislodge the abusive local officials, regain their "rightful" control over community resources, and reestablish a more balanced reciprocal relationship with the Spanish Crown.[20]

In 1777 and 1778 Tomás Katari and his fellow protesters presented evidence of tribute fraud against Alós before the Audiencia of Charcas and the royal treasury of Potosí. Both bodies initially ordered the corregidor to suspend all intruder caciques and to appoint Katari the tax collector. When Tomás Katari tried to deliver these decrees to Alós in June 1778, however, the corregidor confiscated his documents and had him publicly whipped by the mestizo cacique, Blas Bernal. According to Katari, Alós then stated before the assembled citizens that "he was their absolute corregidor and visitador, and that there were no audiencia or royal officials, and if they complained again [before these courts], he would hang them from the stirrups of his horse."[21] The Charcas and Potosí officials did nothing to challenge Alós and enforce their own rulings.

The protesters at Macha responded to this affront by dispatching Katari on a long, arduous 2,100-mile journey to

Buenos Aires (which lasted nearly three months), where he could register their complaints with the viceroy. After hearing about the outrages in Chayanta, the viceroy ordered the Audiencia of Charcas to appoint a special prosecutor to verify Katari's story and settle the matter according to the law. Nevertheless, when Katari returned to Macha in 1779, the audiencia steadfastly refused to enact the viceroy's order. After suffering arrest by corregidor Joaquín de Alós once again, Katari tried to assume the responsibility for delivering the rightful amounts of tribute to the treasury in Potosí. He hoped this would both assert his loyalty and prove that the lesser amounts of tribute sent by Alós during his tenure had defrauded the Crown. Upon his arrival in Potosí on 10 June 1780, however, Spanish authorities arrested Tomás Katari yet again.

This last detention of Katari triggered an explosion of mass violence throughout Chayanta, as the Aymara peasants took matters into their own hands. When Alós and a local militia contingent came to the town of Pocoata to review the assembly of workers for the annual mita quota to Potosí on 26 August 1780, Katari's supporters attacked and captured the corregidor. The rebels then exchanged Alós for Tomás Katari.

After the bloodshed at Pocoata, the frightened members of the Audiencia of Charcas named Katari cacique of the region. Within three months he had expelled Alós and the magistrate's handpicked caciques, taking complete control over local governance in Chayanta. Katari used his new authority to lower tribute rates, and to abolish both the mita and the repartimiento de comercio. At the same time, Katari ordered all the indigenous towns in Chayanta to remain loyal to the Crown and continue delivering their tribute payments. Nonetheless, as the uprising spread, many communities refused to meet their state obligations. Instead, the rebels took vengeance on local leaders who had been loyal to Alós, executing Florencio Lupa (the controversial and powerful cacique of the multiethnic union of Moscari, Pocoata, and Panacachi) and Blas Bernal, who had whipped Katari in June 1778.[22]

The viceroy in Buenos Aires became so alarmed by affairs in Macha that he removed jurisdiction over the region from the Audiencia of Charcas and appointed a military governor, Ignacio Flores, to settle the uprising. Nevertheless, before Flores could take command, the audiencia sent troops to ambush and capture Katari in December 1780. En route to his incarceration in La Plata, his Spanish escort apparently murdered Tomás Katari, pushing him off a cliff.[23]

With the death of Tomás Katari, rebellion engulfed Chayanta and the surrounding provinces. Led by Katari's brothers Dámaso and Nicolás, the rebels assaulted towns throughout the region, executing anyone who had participated in their brother's murder or who had abused Andeans. In 1781 the Aymara army even attempted an unsuccessful siege of the city of La Plata, but within a year, Spanish troops had defeated them. Crown officials then executed the leaders and scattered the remaining rebel troops. Nonetheless, what had begun as a series of legal protests about tribute and abuses of the repartimiento de comercio ended in a full-scale armed insurrection to overthrow Spanish authority north of Potosí. The rebels' defeat, however, did not lead to the pacification of Peru and Upper Peru.

Tupac Amaru and the Rebellion in the Cusco Region

Amidst the unrest in Chayanta, an even more violent and serious insurrection arose southeast of Cusco in Tinta (also called Canas y Canchis). Its leader was José Gabriel Condorcanqui, who took the name Tupac Amaru II after the Sapa Inca executed in 1572. The Bourbon Reforms had provoked considerable economic hardship in Tinta, exacerbating both ethnic tensions among Andean communities and conflicts over leadership positions. The corregidor, Antonio de Arriaga, added to these problems through his heavy-handed administration of tribute and reparto assessments, earning the enmity of many indigenous communities. He had even run afoul of the bishop of Cusco, Juan Manuel Moscoso y Peralta, in a series of jurisdictional disputes with clergymen, leading the prelate to excommunicate Arriaga on 27 July 1780. Condemned by the church and hated by many in Tinta, Arriaga continued his abusive and tyrannical rule until Tupac Amaru's followers captured him on 4 November. The rebel leader then intimidated the frightened magistrate into handing over twenty-five thousand pesos in tribute receipts and a cache of arms. On 10 November 1780, before approximately four thousand onlookers, Tupac Amaru declared that he had orders from King Charles III condemning the corregidor. Tupac Amaru commanded that Arriaga be stripped of his sash, sword, and his staff of office, and then sentenced him to death. After hearing this verdict, Arriaga ascended the gallows in the main square in Tungasuca (Tinta's capital), dressed in a penitential robe, to meet his end. Within a few weeks a massive uprising began, which spread from Tinta to Lake Titicaca and later joined with the Aymara rebels in Upper Peru.[24]

The leader of this insurrection, José Gabriel Condorcanqui, was the son of a prominent cacique in Tinta who claimed descent from the Inca royal family. As a young man José Gabriel had received his education in Cusco at the prestigious Jesuit school of San Francisco de Borja, established for the sons of indigenous leaders. He was also related to many of the prominent families in the region, which was not uncommon in the old Inca heartland, where creole, mestizo, and Andean lineages often intermarried or served as godparents for each other's children. José Gabriel Condorcanqui married the mestiza, Micaela Bastidas Puyucahua, with whom he had three sons. After his marriage, Condorcanqui inherited over 350 mules from his father, which he used to ply the trade route from Cusco to Potosí. This allowed José Gabriel to extend his web of business and personal connections well beyond Tinta. In addition, he owned modest mining interests and some coca fields in Carabaya to the south. Despite acquiring wealth from his varied enterprises, Condorcanqui remained frustrated by his failure to obtain viceregal recognition of his hereditary right to become cacique in Tinta. He even ventured to Lima pleading his case, but to no avail. José Gabriel nurtured a particular hatred for

Antonio de Arriaga, who had sided with Condorcanqui's rivals for ethnic leadership in Tinta, such as Eugenio Sinanyuca. By 1780 José Gabriel Condorcanqui had sufficient cause to oppose Spanish officials, particularly Arriaga, the family lineage to claim ethnic leadership, and the contacts needed to mobilize a mass rebellion.

Hostilities ensued shortly after Arriaga's death. Utilizing the money and weapons extorted from the corregidor before his execution, Tupac Amaru quickly mobilized an army of several thousand and occupied neighboring Quispicanchis. To counter this threat, Spanish authorities in Cusco raised an army of creole militiamen and then added over eight hundred Andeans, mobilized by the loyal caciques Pedro Sahuaraura and Ambrosio Chillitupa. These troops pursued the rebels to the town of Sangarará, where the Spanish commander, Tiburcio Landa, billeted his troops in the town church to seek refuge from an impending snowstorm on 17 November 1780. The soldiers posted no sentinels, and at four in the morning they awoke to find themselves surrounded by Tupac Amaru's indigenous army. The rebel leader ordered all creoles, women, children, and clergymen to leave before his troops attacked, but Landa apparently prevented anyone from evacuating the building. The indigenous soldiers then mounted an assault on the church. During the attack, the Spaniards' gunpowder caught fire and exploded. In the fire and the melee that followed at least 576 of Landa's troops lost their lives, including twenty Spaniards. As a sign of goodwill, Tupac Amaru ordered the twenty-eight captured creoles treated for their wounds and released. After this overwhelming victory, thousands more flocked to Tupac Amaru's army, swelling his ranks to over fifty thousand by December. Nevertheless, the bloodbath at Sangarará also frightened potentially sympathetic creoles and prompted Bishop Moscoso to excommunicate his former friend, José Gabriel Condorcanqui-Tupac Amaru.[25]

Tupac Amaru II used a diverse set of Andean and Christian symbols in forging an ideology designed to attract a broad-based coalition against the colonial regime. He played on the widespread discontent against local authorities by promising a new political order free of corregidores, Spaniards, and anyone else guilty of exploitation. Tupac Amaru widely invoked the image of the King of Spain, a powerful symbol of unity in the Andes, by declaring that he had executed Arriaga on the monarch's orders and by using the rallying cry of "Long live the king, down with bad government." Like Juan Santos Atahualpa, he also took the title of Sapa Inca, even dressing in traditional royal tunics decorated with the golden sun image and commissioning a painting of Micaela Bastidas and himself dressed like an Inca royal couple. Moreover, the rebel leader self-consciously drew upon popular messianic beliefs, such as the Inkarrí myth, which foretold that Tupac Amaru I would have his decapitated head united with his body under-ground. Once united in body, the Inca would rise up and return to power, bringing order and social justice to the Andes. By the 1780s such resurrection myths appealed to a wide range of social groups. Many creole and Andean elites, for example, avidly read Garcilaso de la Vega's *Comentarios reales*, which presented a favorable view of Tawantinsuyu. Even the Jesuits, in the Colegio de San Francisco de Borja, where Tupac Amaru received his schooling, displayed portraits of the Inca kings, establishing a linkage for generations of indigenous students between Christian education and a romanticized vision of the indigenous past. Just as Mexican creoles laid claim to an invented tradition that linked the Aztec empire to the founding of a new nation of Anáhuac (divorced from the colonial regime), so too did different ethnic groups in the Andes seize upon the Inca past to imagine a new political future.[26]

Since the Inca was a religious as well as a secular leader, Tupac Amaru mixed both Christian and Andean religious symbols to bolster his legitimacy. He styled himself "protector of the faith" and "God's chosen instrument on earth," proclaiming that Christianity would be the only religion practiced in his new political order. Tupac Amaru also invoked the prophecies of Saint Rose of Lima predicting a return of the kingdom to its "former rulers." In addition, he utilized traditional Andean rituals, such as holding religious ceremonies on the site of huacas and calling on recruits to fight for the memories of their dead ancestors. Tupac Amaru clearly envisaged a new multiethnic kingdom, and so he formulated a political ideology designed to attract churchmen, creoles, mestizos, indigenous elites, and Andean peasants to his cause.

To implement this eclectic ideology, Tupac Amaru devised his own concrete political agenda. The Inca called for ending the repartimiento de comercio and the hated mita, slashing tribute by 50 percent, stopping restrictions and taxes on trade, and granting liberty to all slaves. Each of these reforms appealed to a slightly different constituency, but taken together they provided a powerful program for a new state headed by the Inca to replace the "morally bankrupt" colonial regime.[27]

Apart from relying on his messianic ideology, Tupac Amaru used kinship, personal, and business connections to forge the rebel army. The Inca's family members—his cousin, Diego Cristóbal Tupac Amaru, his brother-in-law, Antonio Bastidas, his son Hipólito, and of course, his wife Micaela Bastidas—formed his inner circle of advisors. According to contemporaries, the Inca's wife took charge of all logistics in the rebel camp, and she issued orders freely in the commander's name. Tupac Amaru also relied heavily on his family and personal connections throughout Tinta, where he recruited the bulk of his army. Most local caciques supported the rebel cause with varying degrees of enthusiasm, except those few, such as Eugenio Sinanyuca, who were sworn enemies of the Inca and his family. The rebel leader also used his kinship and godparentage (*compadrazgo*) connections to extend his web of followers from Tinta to Quispicanchis. Finally, Tupac Amaru used sympathetic muleteers to recruit followers and spread news of the revolt along the trade route from Cusco to Potosí, where he had worked for so long. Indeed, once the rebellion spread beyond this network of connections in Tinta and Quispicanchis, Tupac Amaru found it much harder to recruit enthusiastic supporters.[28]

The command structure of the rebel army generally reflected the hierarchies of Cusco's diverse regional society. Among those leaders later prosecuted by colonial authorities, there were nineteen Spaniards and creoles, twenty-nine mestizos, seventeen Andeans, and four blacks or mulattos. Apart from a few large landowners, the bulk of these rebel leaders were members of the colonial middle class—farmers, scribes, urban tradesmen and artisans, muleteers, caciques, and a few school teachers. Moreover, Tupac Amaru organized his army along the lines of the colonial militia, with the highest command positions going to creoles, prominent mestizos, and caciques. Mestizos or Andeans usually held intermediate ranks, while the overwhelming bulk of the army's rank and file were indigenous tributaries or forasteros. Most noncombatant staff positions went to creoles, Spaniards, and close family members. In short, the army was essentially an elitist rather than a populist organization, following the Inca's political program of attracting a broad-based social coalition.[29]

Despite Tupac Amaru's efforts to fashion an ideology and a military structure capable of uniting regional society against the colonial regime, his support among the creole upper classes quickly eroded. After the bloodbath at Sangarará, most creoles shrank from the reality of facing a new political order backed by large numbers of bloodthirsty indigenous soldiers intent on taking revenge against the Spaniards, whom they called *puka kunkas* (red necks). These fears turned to panic as reports of atrocities against all "white" men, women, and children—creoles and puka kunkas—poured into Cusco. The indigenous hordes allegedly beheaded adult Spaniards and creoles, drank their blood, cut out and consumed their hearts, ripped out tongues, pierced eyes, removed genitals, dismembered bodies, raped women, and murdered babies. Although some ritual mutilations had deep roots in Andean warfare, all such actions clearly contravened the orders of Tupac Amaru and his commanders to spare innocent citizens, especially creoles. The available evidence, however, indicates that the Inca's poorly disciplined troops most often directed their rage against those most guilty of oppressing the indigenous peoples: corregidores, puka kunkas, and those creoles associated with reparto and tribute abuses. Nonetheless, rebel soldiers also killed many innocent victims during the bloody conflict. Whether acts of violence represented more radical efforts among the rebel army to turn the conflict into a race war, or merely the excesses of battle-hardened troops, such atrocities undermined the Inca's efforts to build a broad coalition by pushing frightened creoles to support the royalists.[30]

After his decisive victory at Sangarará, Tupac Amaru moved the bulk of his army to the Lake Titicaca region, hoping to consolidate his gains and prevent any royalist attacks from Puno and Arequipa. He also sought to swell his ranks with recruits among the Colla peoples, where he had political and family connections. Meanwhile, his wife and chief advisor Micaela Bastidas tried to collect basic supplies and arms in Tinta for the final assault on Cusco. By 6 December, however, Micaela Bastidas scolded the Inca for delaying too long, warning that his rebel troops were getting restless. She urged him to attack Cusco immediately before the royalist forces could organize properly, adding ominously: "I see your lack of enthusiasm about such a grave affair is putting everyone's life in danger."[31]

Upon his return from the south on 16 December, Tupac Amaru belatedly heeded his wife's advice and prepared for an attack on Cusco. By that point, however, rebel defeats in Quispicanchis had already eroded the aura of invincibility surrounding the Inca and encouraged the Spaniards defending the city. Moreover, Tupac Amaru's siege plans quickly went awry, as Spanish troops prevented his army from surrounding Cusco. Efforts to negotiate the city's surrender further delayed any military action. Finally, on 8 January 1781 the Inca attacked with a force of thirty thousand from the north, trying to cut the defenders off from grain-producing valleys supplying the city and from the road to Lima. When Spanish defenders impeded his advance, the Inca suddenly decided to withdraw two days later. Apparently, Tupac Amaru had hoped to take the city without major bloodshed, and with his troops dangerously short on food and arms, he decided against attempting a protracted siege. After this major setback, the military momentum shifted to the colonial forces, as the rebels limited themselves largely to guerrilla operations.

With the failure to take Cusco, the political and military fortunes of Tupac Amaru plummeted. The class and ethnic tensions within the movement began surfacing with greater intensity. Apart from the loss of creole support, many Andean leaders from outside Tinta rallied to the royalist cause. Large indigenous forces under the command of powerful caciques hostile to Tupac Amaru, such as Mateo García Pumacahua (from Chincheros, north of Cusco) and Diego Choqueguanca (from Azángaro) joined with Spanish and creole reinforcements from Lima and neighboring provinces. By February, Tupac Amaru's forces had retreated to his command center in Tinta, where a Spanish army from Cusco, under the command of José del Valle, surrounded the rebels. When his troops failed to break out of this encirclement, the Inca and his family fled to the town of Langui. With a 20,000-peso bounty on his head, Tupac Amaru was captured on 6 April 1781. He was then taken to Cusco and executed, leaving what remained of his army under the command of his cousin, Diego Cristóbal Tupac Amaru.

Julián Apasa-Tupac Katari and the Aymara Rebellion

After the defeat and capture of the Inca, Diego Cristóbal led his rebel forces into Upper Peru, where they took Puno in May 1781 and established connections with Aymara rebel forces in Chayanta and La Paz. After Tomás Katari's death in January, command of the revolt in Chayanta had passed to his brothers, but in March another large rebel force operating in the La Paz region fell under the control of an illiterate Aymara-speaking forastero, Julián Apasa. The ascendancy of Apasa was assured when Spanish authorities captured and executed Dámaso Katari in late April, and then just over a week later his brother, Nicolás Katari, was killed in the battle of Chuquisaca. Although Julián Apasa always acknowledged the superior authority of Diego Cristóbal and the Cusco faction, he generally maintained his own independent sphere of authority among the Aymara-speaking troops around La Paz. Apasa even began calling himself the "viceroy" Julián Tupac Katari, which roused the ire of the Cusco leaders.[32] Nevertheless, after Tupac Amaru's death, the primary military theater of the Great Rebellion had shifted from Cusco to Upper Peru.

Although born of very humble origins in Sicasica, Julián Apasa moved boldly and forcefully to head the Aymara rebellion in La Paz. According to his wife, Bartolina Sisa, he had been active organizing an indigenous rebellion in the region at least two years before the outbreak of Tupac Amaru's revolt. Apasa was a small-scale trader in coca and rough woolens, and by 1780 he had established a network of family and business connections throughout the region. With the outbreak of hostilities in Chayanta and Cusco, Julián Apasa apparently attempted to identify himself with both Tomás Katari and Tupac Amaru to legitimize further his claims to leadership. He took the name Tupac (meaning brilliant in Quechua) from the Cusco leader and Katari (indicating serpent or snake in Aymara) from the influential Chayanta rebel. Indeed, some reports claimed that when he arrived in the La Paz area, Julián Apasa even wore a veil or mask to cover his face, pretending to be the reincarnation of Tomás Katari. Apasa also claimed to have letters from Tupac Amaru and even a royal edict from the King giving him command of the La Paz forces. His efforts were further aided by the absence of any rival creole or indigenous leaders. Unlike Tupac Amaru's uprising, the Aymara revolt in Upper Peru always remained a peasant movement, giving strong, charismatic men from humble origins, such as Apasa and Katari, a greater opportunity to assume leadership roles.[33]

Julián Tupac Katari epitomized qualities associated with a traditional Aymara warrior, which helped him maintain a tenuous hold over his poorly disciplined peasant soldiers. This was important because he lacked the commanding physical presence of Tupac Amaru; the Aymara leader was apparently of medium stature, with twisted arms and legs (probably resulting from a childhood disease or malnutrition). Despite this deformity, like Aymara warrior-leaders from the mythical past, Tupac Katari displayed unpredictable outbursts of violence, bouts of drunkenness, legendary carnal appetites, and an excessive concern with the trappings of honor and respect. According to the Quechua commander, Miguel Bastidas (also called Miguel Tupac Amaru), Apasa displayed a "fury and desire to kill all whites and Spaniards," and he even directed his fearsome anger against his own troops, who "looked upon him with terror because of the liberty with which he . . . dispatched so many Indians when they opposed him."[34] Despite the disapproval of Bastidas, such behavior fit the image of a strong indigenous leader, attempting to whip up a blood lust against the enemy and seeking to maintain discipline among poorly trained troops. Even Tupac Katari's propensity for drunkenness and lustful behavior probably increased his standing with the rank-and-file soldiers. Among Aymara peasants, drinking was part of indigenous religious ritual (often used to connect with sacred powers), while proving his sexual virility also demonstrated Tupac Katari's physical power, which resembled that of impulsive deities from Andean mythology. Their leader's concern with wearing fine clothes, keeping a large store of coca and chicha, and taking numerous honorific titles such as viceroy, also conjured up popular notions of a proud but fearsome warrior. Moreover, when Apasa dressed in the trappings of the Sapa Inca, like Tupac Amaru, he sought to reinforce his messianic appeal and legitimacy.[35]

Tupac Katari also promoted a curious mixture of Christian and Andean rituals to bolster his leadership of the movement in La Paz. At his camp in El Alto, he supported a coterie of priests to celebrate mass, lead processions, and administer the sacraments. Nevertheless, many Christian observers ridiculed Katari's declarations that he was sent from God and that his followers would rise to life after dying in battle. These same critics mocked Tupac Katari's penchant for consulting a "silver box" during mass and for making faces into a small mirror, which he claimed allowed him to predict the future. While these acts confounded Spaniards, creoles, and Tupac Katari's more hispanicized indigenous observers, they probably made more sense to his peasant soldiers. Many Aymara peoples believed that mirrors represented "eyes" that allowed holy men to communicate with divinities and predict the future. Likewise, his silver box apparently contained small ritual objects (called *champi* in Aymara or conopas in Quechua). To his peasant troops, performing these traditional Andean rituals during mass (when Jesus was said to be present in the consecrated host) merely demonstrated Tupac Katari's ability to draw on spiritual powers from both Christian and Andean religious traditions. Like most of his soldiers, Tupac Katari felt free to mix these rituals, while still asserting sincerely that "I am as Christian as anyone else."[36]

Despite his supposed "hatred for all whites," Tupac Katari apparently wanted his troops to avoid a bloody race war and forbade using arbitrary and indiscriminate violence. According to Gregoria Apasa, the sister of Julián Tupac Katari, "it is certain that they killed Spaniards, because the Indians overstepped themselves, Julián only ordered that they kill some."[37] There is also evidence that the Aymara soldiers imposed their own limits on the bloodshed. They most often directed their anger selectively, against those Crown officials, peninsulars, and creoles deemed guilty of oppressing the people. They also targeted mestizos, caciques, and Andeans if they dressed in Spanish clothing or had collaborated with the royalists. When Quechua and Aymara troops took the provincial capital of Sorata, for example, they first ordered all males who had fought against them put to death. Nevertheless, the rebels named a creole as town magistrate and then ordered all Spanish, creole, and mestizo women and children to change into Andean garb and chew coca. Symbolically this act of transformed these "outsiders" into legitimate members of the indigenous community. In other cases, however, Aymara soldiers killed all the rich and powerful in a captured community, while sparing poorer citizens, which gave the rebellion the character of a class war. Like the uprising in Cusco, both loyalist and rebel soldiers committed numerous atrocities against their opponents and even innocent civilians. The widespread bloodshed reflected the bitterness of what can best be viewed as a civil war in the La Paz region, which pitted supporters of the colonial order against an Aymara peasant army dedicated to destroying it.

Cases of atrocities committed by Aymara soldiers also stemmed from the fragile control exercised by Tupac Katari over his army. The Aymara peasant army was more decentralized than either the Quechua army (of Tupac Amaru and his successors) or loyalist forces, which intensified the problem of maintaining discipline. Katari tried to rely on kin, friends, and business allies to fill leadership positions, but his movement attracted few among the traditional ethnic leadership. Instead, Katari felt compelled to consult large, representative war councils to gain support for his military plans during the siege of La Paz. In all likelihood, this lack of discipline and organization probably prompted many of Tupac Katari's well-documented outbursts of temper against his troops and his use of floggings and capital punishment against disobedient commanders, subalterns, and rank-and-file soldiers. In short, the Aymara movement was always more loosely organized, democratic, diverse, and difficult to control.[38]

Although the kinsmen of Tupac Amaru nominally led the rebellion, relations between the Quechua and Aymara commanders were often strained. The Cusco leaders and Tupac Katari had to speak through interpreters, and disparaging comments directed by Miguel Bastidas-Tupac Amaru and the others from Cusco against Tupac Katari indicate the suspicion and friction felt on both sides. In May 1781, Diego Cristóbal, Miguel, and Andrés Tupac Amaru operated largely from their base in Puno, while Tupac Katari busied himself with attempts to take La Paz. The first siege of the city lasted 109 days until July 1781, when a loyalist army commanded by Ignacio Flores arrived to relieve the city. In mid-August, however, a mixed Quechua and Aymara army under the joint command of Tupac Katari and Andrés Tupac Amaru laid siege a second time. This effort too failed after seventy-five days, when a large Spanish force under José Reseguín arrived. After the failed sieges of La Paz, the war turned against the rebels and the Quechua and Aymara commanders barely consulted with each other. Relations soured further as Tupac Katari began emphasizing racial solidarity among his Aymara followers, which damaged the Cusco leader's efforts to forge a broader-based ethnic coalition.

With the war nearly lost and the two camps divided, leading members of the Tupac Amaru clan decided to abandon their Aymara allies. Andrés transferred command of his army to Miguel Bastidas, while he and Diego Cristóbal opened negotiations in Azángaro with the Spanish authorities to arrange a pardon for their entire family. By 3 November 1781, these efforts led Bastidas to surrender the entire Quechua army and accept the government's terms for a pardon, which Diego Cristóbal pointedly emphasized, "did not include Julián Katari, who is independent of this family line."[39]

Tupac Katari was unaware of this betrayal, and he kept his troops in the field, hoping to unite forces with the Quechua army and continue the revolt. When he received word of the pardon and surrender of his allies, Tupac Katari stubbornly urged his followers to persist alone. A few days later, however, the Aymara leader was lured into a trap and captured. On 14 November 1781 in the town of Peñas, Julián Apasa-Tupac Katari was tied by heavy ropes to four horses that pulled in separate directions, ripping his body apart. Like Tupac Amaru before him, the Aymara leader was then decapitated, with his head displayed in La Paz and his remaining body parts sent to several centers of the revolt to dampen enthusiasm for any further uprisings against the colonial order.

Enduring Rebellions from 1783 to Independence

In the wake of the three great Andean rebellions, colonial authorities implemented wide-ranging reforms to pacify the rebellious provinces, to heal local divisions, and also to eradicate any vestiges of the upheavals. In a conciliatory gesture, the Crown abolished the repartimiento de comercio in 1780 and three years later issued a general pardon to all but the rebel leaders. Viceregal authorities next moved against anyone suspected of plotting revolt, even arresting those members of Tupac Amaru's family who had surrendered to gain a royal pardon. In 1783, for example, Diego Cristóbal Tupac Amaru was arrested for conspiring to foment rebellion, tortured, and executed. Over ninety kinsmen of Tupac Amaru were taken to Lima in chains and sent to exile in Spain, only to be shipwrecked in route. The visitor general of the viceroyalty, José Antonio de Areche, and his chief advisor, Benito de Mata Linares, also attempted to stamp out any signs of Inca revivalism. They ordered all paintings that invoked images of Tawantinsuyu destroyed, including those displayed in the Jesuit school of San Francisco de Borja in Cusco. They also banned the circulation of Garcilaso de la Vega's *Comentarios reales*. Both men then tried unsuccessfully to have the Crown abolish the traditional office of cacique, fearing that these indigenous leaders might foment new revolts.

At the same time, the Crown imposed a series of administrative reforms to regain effective political control, and ordered viceregal officials to overhaul the tribute system to raise more tax revenues for the depleted royal treasuries in Peru and Spain. In 1784 royal authorities imposed the intendancy system throughout the Viceroyalty of Peru and transferred the Puno district to the Río de la Plata, where the system had been in force since that viceroyalty's creation in 1776. As part of this administrative renovation, reformers abolished the network of corregidores, replacing them with subdelegates (*subdelegados*) responsible directly to the intendant. The Crown also created a new audiencia in Cusco in 1787, hoping to provide an avenue for legal redress and to diffuse any tensions that might balloon into violent revolt. Finally, the colonial regime undertook a thoroughgoing reform of the tribute system to ease the fiscal exigencies of the nearly bankrupt viceregal treasury. Local officials took ever more accurate census records of the tributary population, closed legal loopholes, and raised tax rates. The net result was a striking upsurge in tribute revenues, particularly in the intendancy of Cusco, already hurt by economic recession worsened by the devastation following the rebellions.[40]

These reforms in the 1780s continued the overall process of weakening indigenous political institutions. Although the Crown finally decided to eliminate the office of cacique only in those communities that had supported the rebellions, uncertainty about the position's future damaged the prestige and power of ethnic leaders. Following the lead of their predecessors, the subdelegates often summarily replaced caciques incapable of meeting tribute quotas, often with their mestizo and creole allies, which only aggravated the crisis of indigenous authority. The problem became so obvious that the Audiencia of Cusco eventually prohibited subdelegates from naming caciques in their district in 1798, but the practice continued anyway. Viceregal authorities also deprived caciques of the right to make tribute collections, a task that gradually fell to indigenous mayors (*alcaldes de varayoks*), further dividing and weakening the structure of local authority. Even powerful loyalist caciques frequently found their positions undermined.

Because the Crown never provided them with adequate salaries, many subdelegates and their allies took advantage of political crises within indigenous communities by engaging in corrupt and monopolistic business practices, even imposing outlawed reparto quotas. Subdelegates, intruder caciques, parish priests, and local businessmen often formed alliances to profit from abusing indigenous communities. Controlling the tribute system gave the subdelegates and their allies access to tax revenue, unpaid indigenous labor, and communal and privately owned lands set aside for the needs of the cacique and his ayllu. Without strong ethnic leadership to oppose such economic plundering, Andean communities suffered, particularly when trying to meet ever higher tribute assessments. The devastation of the recent rebellions also undermined local trade, agriculture, and manufacturing, which only worsened the economic distress caused by heavy taxes and rapacious local officials.[41]

The exploitation and political turmoil afflicting indigenous communities provoked a rising tide of litigation brought by indigenous plaintiffs before subdelegates, intendants, and the Audiencia of Cusco. These Andeans protested a wide range of abuses, such as the usurpation of land, tribute fraud, coerced labor, illegal repartos, wrongful imprisonment of Andeans by local authorities, disputes over succession to cacique positions, and jurisdictional conflicts among local authorities. In all too many cases, however, the courts failed to resolve these nagging local problems.

When recourse to the courts failed or seemed impractical, protests and even small-scale rebellions erupted, usually directed against abusive local authority figures—particularly subdelegates, caciques, and priests. In 1790, for example, a two-day riot broke out in Asillo (Azángaro province) over the appointment of Tomás Mango Turpo as cacique. Although General Ignacio Flores appointed him cacique to reward his loyalty during the Tupac Amaru rebellion, Mango Turpo was very unpopular in Asillo. Before the rebellion Mango Turpo had grown wealthy by forging alliances with former corregidores of Azángaro and had shared in substantial profits from abuses of the repartimiento de comercio. A rival for the post, Manuel Ramos Guaguacondori, fomented rebellion among local community members to prevent Mango Turpo from taking office. Although Spanish authorities quickly crushed the revolt in Asillo, similar outbursts of violence erupted in Andean communities throughout Peru and Upper Peru during the late colonial period.[42]

These undercurrents of social and political alienation only worsened with the political turmoil in the Andean provinces provoked by the Napoleon Bonaparte's invasion of Spain in 1808. When the French forced King Charles IV and his son Ferdinand to renounce the throne, a crisis of political authority emerged within the Andean provinces. Several creole groups formed local governments (juntas) in Quito, La Paz, and other Andean regional capitals, claiming to rule until the resumption of legitimate royal authority in Spain. Although viceregal troops stamped out most juntas, the powerful symbol of the King as a unifying element in colonial society had been seriously compromised.

Matters became even more confused when the Spanish Liberal constitutional government in Cádiz in 1812 proposed wide-ranging reforms within the empire. Among the most controversial were granting representation in the Spanish legislature to Americans, awarding full citizenship for Amerindians, abolishing indigenous tribute levies, and holding local elections for municipal offices throughout the empire. Andean communities differed in their responses to these innovations. The reforms effectively ended the corporate status of indigenous communities, making them subject to losing communal lands and to paying new colonial taxes, such as the alcabala. On balance, in those provinces more isolated from market forces the abolition of the head tax appeared to be a boon, because meeting the new burdens would not have amounted to the sums sent in tribute. For communities that participated actively in market exchanges, however, the prospect of paying the full array of sale taxes, tithes, and other duties carried a much stiffer price tag and threatened future economic prospects. Ending Amerindian tribute also imperiled the nearly bankrupt royal treasury. The Viceroy of Peru, José Fernando Abascal, simply refused to abide by this abolition order. Finally, the return to Spain of King Ferdinand VI brought an end to all Liberal experiments in representative government and social reform, as the Crown tried to reestablish the old absolutist colonial order.

During this confused and turbulent era, a serious threat to royal authority erupted in Cusco with the Pumacahua Rebellion of 1814. Unrest in Cusco focused on the dispute between the creole-controlled *cabildo* and the audiencia, which represented Spanish interests. Conflicts arose over whether Andeans should vote in local municipal elections, a process that creole factions supported and the peninsulars opposed. After the city council members protested efforts by the audiencia to suppress a popular riot in the city in October 1814, the judges ordered the arrest of several members of the cabildo. This sparked an uprising of the city's middle and lower classes led by José Angulo, who demanded immediate implementation of the Liberal reforms of 1812. Angulo also called for an end to corruption, bad government, and the heavy taxes levied by Viceroy Abascal to support the suppression of the rebels in Peru and Upper Peru. To broaden his base of support, Angulo recruited the wealthy, seventy-year-old former royalist cacique, Mateo García Pumacahua, who remained popular in many local indigenous communities. The aging cacique had served a short term as interim president of the Audiencia of Cusco, but his abrupt dismissal by Crown authorities left Pumacahua embittered and susceptible to Angulo's appeals for help.

Given Pumacahua's military reputation and experience, Angulo made him commander of the rebel army, and the cacique soon raised a largely indigenous force of twenty thousand men. The rebels struck quickly and enjoyed some initial successes, capturing several key cities, including La Paz where Pumacahua tried unsuccessfully to link up with a rebel army from Buenos Aires besieging Potosí. At the same time, largely independent indigenous rebellions broke out in the towns of Ocongate and Marcapata (in Quispicanchis). By late 1814, however, the tide began to turn against the insurgents. A mixed Spanish and Andean army under General Juan Ramírez recaptured La Paz and then in March 1815, he decisively defeated Pumacahua's forces. Ramírez had Pumacahua executed on the battlefield before his vanquished troops, and later ordered Angulo and the other rebel leaders hanged for treason.[43]

Despite the collapse of the Cusco revolt of 1814, indigenous troops continued to fight in the wars for independence in both royalist and rebel armies. Most often, like the troops of Pumacahua, they did so out of loyalty to ethnic leaders or to advance their particular political agendas. As the colonial order finally crumbled, Andeans also sought a place in the emerging nation-states. Nevertheless, independence and the advent of creole-dominated governments yielded few tangible benefits for the embattled indigenous communities. Despite their struggles in the courts and on the battlefield, Andeans failed to realize their hopes for freedom and liberty.

Conclusions

After capturing Cusco in 1533, the Spanish invaders slowly attempted to stamp out indigenous resistance in Tawantinsuyu. The eruption of Manco Inca's revolt in 1536 began four years of warfare culminating in the retreat of the Sapa Inca to his fortress at Vilcabamba. Despite progress in negotiations with Manco's successors, Sayri Tupac and later Titu Cusi, the rebel state at Vilcabamba remained a potent threat, especially during the periodic civil wars among the conquistadors. For this reason, Viceroy Francisco de Toledo launched a punitive expedition to capture Vilcabamba, which succeeded in taking the fortress, capturing Tupac Amaru I, and extinguishing the last center of Inca resistance. The execution of the Sapa Inca in 1572 effectively ended the Spanish conquest of the Andes. While periodic, small-scale protests and revolts erupted in the seventeenth century, none of these outbursts threatened the foundations of Spanish rule. With the onset of the Bourbon Reforms during the eighteenth century, however, a rising tide of dangerously violent rebellions swept across the Andes.

These reform efforts by the Bourbon dynasty often provoked this violence by exacerbating political and social tensions in Andean communities, particularly the move to legalize the abusive repartimiento de comercio. Although tribute assessments, mita service, and clerical fees might impose hardships, most indigenous peoples accepted them as long-standing obligations to the Crown. When these assessments became too burdensome, Andeans resorted to litigation, protests, and occasionally even revolts to gain redress. The repartimiento de comercio, however, fell outside the traditional pact of reciprocity with the colonial state, and it seriously disrupted local political and social relationships. Enforcing reparto quotas led many corregidores to quarrel with priests and to replace recalcitrant caciques with intruders—especially mestizos and creoles having no loyalty to local ayllus. Antonio de Arriaga, for example, managed to alienate Tupac Amaru II by refusing to recognize his claim to hereditary leadership. The corregidor of Tinta also fought with local clerics, leading to his excommunication by Bishop Moscoso. These ill-conceived policies damaged two pillars of local authority and stability—the ethnic caciques and the Church.

The Bourbon Reforms not only undermined local sources of political and moral power, they also promoted jurisdictional disputes within the colonial bureaucracy, impeding the ability of community leaders and the courts to resolve local disputes peacefully. When viceregal authorities, the Audiencia of Charcas, local magistrates, and caciques failed to resolve indigenous complaints in Chayanta, for example, a new breed of community activists, led by a commoner, Tomás Katari, saw no viable alternatives to violent rebellion. The destabilization of community political institutions and the failure of judicial options throughout the central and southern Andes also allowed these rebellions to expand well beyond their home provinces, encompassing much of Peru and Upper Peru. The principal restraint to the spread of Tupac Amaru's rebellion was his failure to recruit several strong regional ethnic leaders outside Tinta, such as Mateo García Pumacahua. In areas where the ethnic leadership had been weakened or discredited (as in much of Upper Peru), however, rebellion engulfed the landscape.

The move from resistance to violent rebellion demonstrated the emergence of a new Andean political consciousness by the 1780s. In Chayanta, Tomás Katari and his supporters fought for community rights, demanding that the Crown fulfill its reciprocal political compact with the Aymara peoples of Macha in return for indigenous loyalty, tribute payments, and mita obligations. Whenever civil authorities violated these norms of reciprocity, the Andeans felt compelled to rebel. In other regions, however, an even more coherent political consciousness emerged. The Inkarrí myth, predicting a return of the Inca to establish a new political order and replace the "bankrupt" colonial regime, exercised a strong hold over many of Tupac Amaru's followers in the Cusco region. These beliefs also resonated in Upper Peru during the rebellion of Tupac Katari. Whereas the messianic appeal of Juan

Santos Atahualpa remained confined to his followers in the Cerro de la Sal, forty years later this idea reverberated among creoles, castas, and Andeans, particularly in regions where colonial policies had caused serious political, social, and economic disruptions.

Although the restoration of a new Inca dynasty represented a heightened Andean political consciousness, the idea also meant different things to the various groups caught up in rebellion. For some creole, mestizo, and Andean elites, returning to a romanticized "classical" past endowed their people with an ancient national history, divorced from the Spanish colonial regime. For many of the Andean rank and file, however, a restored Inca dynasty apparently involved realizing more concrete political goals: an end to tribute, repartos, and mita obligations, and the expulsion of abusive puka kunkas. While some leaders envisaged a new order loosely affiliated with the Spanish Crown, others wanted a completely independent Inca monarchy. Finally, Tupac Amaru wanted to establish a stratified social order headed by the Inca, but many other Andean rebels wanted to alter or even smash these hierarchical remnants of the old colonial heritage.

Despite these differences in political outlook and the failure of the Great Rebellions by 1783, Spanish authorities could never exterminate this Andean political consciousness. Litigiousness, protests, and rebellions continued from the 1780s through the independence era, even flaring up into periodic regional uprisings, such as the Pumacahua Revolt of 1814. Andeans also fought on both sides of the independence struggles though the 1820s. Assertions of indigenous political rights varied over time, yet they persisted. Indigenous rebels attempted to shape the formation of nineteenth-century nation-states in the Andes, and modern-day revolutionary movements still continue presenting different visions of political and social justice.

Not all forms of indigenous resistance and consciousness manifest themselves in protest movements or violent rebellions. Some take more subtle forms. Popular theater presentations, for example, such as the Quechua play *Tragedy of the Death of Atahualpa*

(*Atau Wallpaj P'uchukakuyninpa Wankan*), continue to express resistance by retaining links to the Andean past. Early versions of this drama may have been performed in the 1550s, but the most famous version of the play dates from the nineteenth century in Chayanta, the site of Tomás Katari's rebellion. Usually performed entirely in Quechua, the play depicts the first encounter between Pizarro and Atahualpa and the sequence of events leading to the Sapa Inca's execution by the conquistadors. It ends with the King of Spain rebuking Pizarro for killing the Inca; the conquistador then falls dead himself in retribution for the crime. The events depicted in the *Tragedy of the Death of Atahualpa* signal the end of a historical cycle or *pachacuti* in Quechua, a time when the world was turned upside down and power passed to the European invaders. Yet in Andean terms, this play also gives hope for a new revival, when the world will be righted (as promised in myths such as Inkarrí) and the indigenous peoples empowered once again. The "hidden messages" contained in popular theater performances or in more overt acts of political resistance allow Andeans to continue asserting their own vision of the past, present, and future.[44]

8
CONCLUSION

WHEN ATAHUALPA ENTERED CAJAMARCA on 16 November 1532, he ruled the largest and most sophisticated indigenous empire in the Americas, but within a few hours he was a captive of foreign invaders who would ultimately destroy Tawantinsuyu. The once-powerful Sapa Inca had ruled a massive domain extending from his capital in Cusco through the patchwork of Andean highland valleys and across coastal tropical zones and desert plains. This empire also encompassed a kaleidoscope of ethnic groups, languages, and cultures, and its citizens had attained amazing achievements in art, technology, military sciences, and social organization. After the carnage at Cajamarca, however, this diverse Andean world underwent dramatic and irreversible transfor-mations, which neither Atahualpa nor the Spanish invaders could have imagined. Over the course of three centuries, large numbers of European emigrants arrived in the Andes and initiated profound alterations in traditional Andean modes of production, technology, politics, religion, culture, and social hierarchies. At the same time, the indigenous peoples merged these changes with their own traditional political, socioeconomic, cultural, and religious ideas. In this way European and indigenous lifeways became intertwined, producing a new and constantly evolving hybrid colonial order in the Andes. The precise chronology for these changes varied, with politics, society, economic life, culture, and religion often moving at a different pace. Nevertheless, even after three hundred years of colonial domination, recognizable elements of Atahualpa's world endured.

The first great turning point in the political life of the Andes after 1532 was the viceregency of Francisco de Toledo (1569–81). In the years following the events at Cajamarca, the Spanish conquistadors consolidated their tenuous hold over the former Inca domain by dividing up the indigenous communities into encomienda grants, which allowed them to extract taxes and labor from their Andean charges. Within a generation, however, endemic civil wars among the settlers, the onset of epidemic diseases, and Andean resistance to oppression from the conquistadors, all disrupted the fragile indigenous system of vertical exchanges and undermined the encomienda system. At the same time, the silver-mining industry experienced disturbing declines in production, largely caused by labor shortages, inefficient smelting techniques, and the exhaustion of easily accessible high-grade silver ores. Moreover, the threat of a widespread Andean rebellion, emanating from the Inca state in Vilcabamba and the millenarian Taqui Onqoy movement also loomed large. Indeed, by the 1560s the colonial socioeconomic order had reached a crisis that threatened Spanish power in the Andes.

Upon his arrival, Toledo decided to deal with these challenges by constructing a strong state apparatus capable of siphoning the immense wealth of the Andes to meet the economic needs of Spain. After visiting most parts of the realm, this energetic viceroy developed a system of forced resettlement to facilitate supervising and taxing indigenous communities. Toledo also established regularized tax rates and assessed tribute levies in silver, which encouraged Andeans to participate as producers and consumers in the emerging market economy to gain the specie for these fiscal obligations. Finally, Toledo completely reorganized and extended the system of corvée labor to keep the mercury and silver mines operating. These reforms remained the mainstay of the colonial regime until the eighteenth century. This vigorous assertion of royal authority took power from the initial Spanish settlers, and it completely excluded the Andean peoples from participating in colonial governance.

The strength and unity of the colonial state created by Toledo began to erode by the early seventeenth century in the Andes. Although the law prohibited creoles from holding many high-ranking bureaucratic posts, local citizens often forged economic and social alliances with colonial bureaucrats to influence policy decisions. At first, bribery, corruption, and influence peddling became tools for colonial officials and their creole allies to make the regime responsive to local rather than just metropolitan needs. Later, the sale of key public offices accelerated this process of local empowerment by allowing colonial interest groups to gain possession of many bureaucratic positions themselves. Most Andeans, however, were excluded from this form of power broker-ing. A few important leaders, such as Bartolomé Tupa Hallicalla of Azángaro, managed to prosper and to attain both power and influence in the colonial government, but as the downfall of this kuraka indicates, even their position was inherently insecure. In fact, the only way for most Andeans to gain some measure of influence was to resist oppressive colonial policies. Some fled their communities to escape dishonest corregidores, high taxes, and the dreaded mita service. Others remained and fought injus-tice by utilizing the courts to defend themselves—Andeans regularly pressed legal cases to ameliorate their lot.

The second watershed in the political history of the Viceroyalty of Peru came with escalation of Bourbon administrative reforms during the eighteenth century. Rampant corruption, administrative inefficiency, indigenous resistance, and declining tax revenues led to a maj r effort at rejuvenating royal authority. Crown officials broke up he massive Viceroyalty of Peru (in 1739 and then again in 1776) and by 1750 ended the sale of most high-level appointments to the colonial bureaucracy. After 1765 the Crown escalated efforts to raise taxes and regulate trade, and by the 1780s it imposed the new system of intendants throughout many of the Andean provinces. In the end, these innovations provoked a groundswell of local opposition from most social and ethnic groups, including the Andean population. By the early nineteenth century, however, royal authority had begun to decline once again, leaving only higher taxes and new forms of oppression for the indigenous peoples. Francisco de Toledo had created a strong colonial state apparatus, but he failed to place it squarely under the control of the metropolis. Efforts by the Bourbon reformers to reverse this trend toward local control ultimately also failed, culminating in the successful independence movements between 1808 and 1825.

Socioeconomic changes followed a chronology that diverged in certain key ways from political developments. After decades of civil war and confusion, the Toledan reforms again played an important role in the structure of the emerging colonial society and economy. Between 1569 and 1620, Toledo and his successors established the foundations of a lucrative export economy revolving around the extraction of massive quantities of silver from highland mining centers, particularly the legendary "red mountain" of Potosí. The nexus of trunk and feeder lines in this colonial economic order, however, grew increasingly complex, and as silver production began to decline, a more diversified market system emerged from the 1620s. Although mining remained an important sector, silver extraction and the transatlantic trade no longer attracted so much of the available capital, which could now flow to more vibrant sectors—agropastoral enterprises, manufacturing, artisan activities, and intercolonial trade links. Whereas peninsular merchants had dominated the international trade in silver through the Lima *consulado*, these newer productive enterprises also benefited regional creoles and even some indigenous elites, such as Bartolomé Tupa Hallicalla, the wealthy indigenous entrepreneur from Azángaro. For most Andeans, however, the colonial market economy offered exploitation rather than opportunities for enrichment. Still, they resisted oppressive colonial policies. To escape forced labor drafts in the seventeenth century, many Andeans paid miners for an exemption from the mita, becoming indios de faltriquera. Moreover, when mita quotas, high taxes, and the abuses of corrupt colonial officials became intolerable, ever larger numbers of Andeans abandoned their traditional communities to work in urban centers or in Spanish rural enterprises. Nevertheless, as migration proceeded apace in the Andes, through the process of ethnogenesis Andeans formed new communities and ethnic identities.

Whereas creoles continued wielding considerable political power until the Bourbon Reforms, their socioeconomic gains suffered severe setbacks between 1687 and 1730, when this more expansive colonial economic order suffered a series of devastating shocks by the late seventeenth century—primarily epidemics and natural disasters. Nevertheless, after 1730 a more buoyant period of growth took hold. Mining and the transatlantic trade enjoyed a slow but steady resurgence, internal commercial linkages expanded, and despite cyclical ups and downs, the entire nexus of colonial markets began to enjoy renewed prosperity. Indeed, the wide-ranging political, fiscal, and commercial reforms of the Bourbons after 1765 attempted to take account of these new socioeconomic realignments by exercising greater control to siphon off the resources produced by the increasingly complex network of the colonial market economies. In this case, political reforms followed socioeconomic developments.

After the shock of the conquest, Andean cultural and artistic production began to change slowly, reflecting European influences. The chronology of these mutations, however, is less precise than political or even socioeconomic transformations. The downfall of the Inca state removed the principal patron for the arts, and both colonists and missionaries began introducing European concepts of alphabetic writing. Nonetheless, by the early seventeenth century a new colonial culture began to flower, mixing European and Andean patterns. The friars and secular clergymen had opened schools to teach Castilian, and the first complete dictionaries and grammars had appeared in Quechua (1607–8) and Aymara (1612), the two most common indigenous languages. Both of these enterprises coincided with a brief but impressive output of literary works written by mestizo and Andean authors, such as *El primer nueva corónica y buen gobierno* of Felipe Guaman Poma de Ayala. While Guaman Poma wrote using a mixture of Castilian and Quechua, Spanish priests managed to compile a series of local Andean religious traditions, written entirely in that indigenous language, the *Ritos y tradiciones de Huarochirí*. Although this literary outpouring quickly receded, the tradition of Andeans writing petitions and memorials to royal authorities in Castilian persisted, as indigenous literacy in that language spread. Andean communities also kept and revered written documents as texts, transmitting a wide variety of meanings for legal and ceremonial purposes.

During the seventeenth century other types of indigenous artistic representation (painting, wood carving, ceramics, and textiles) also merged European conceptions of figurative art with indigenous abstract, geometric modes of expression. Along with these cultural changes came Castilian ideas about written laws and private property, which transformed Andean conceptions of geographical space and rights to land, water, and other natural resources. In short, by the seventeenth century the European and Andean peoples had influenced each other in a multiplicity of ways to produce a hybrid colonial culture.

Just as political, socioeconomic, and cultural practices reached maturity during the seventeenth century, so too did efforts at religious evangelization. The Spanish invaders justified their colonization of the Andes by spreading Christianity among the indigenous peoples. At first, large numbers Andeans converted, embracing baptism and a host of Catholic rituals and practices—including the panoply of saints, veneration of the cross and devotional objects, ornate churches, and elaborate church rituals and festivals, using music, dances, and prayers. As a result, when more regular and secular clergymen began arriving to spread their faith among the Andean communities, state religious cults of the Inca gave way to the official rituals and dogma of Spanish Catholicism.

To ease this process, Church councils developed confessional manuals, sermons, and instructional guides for priests. In 1564 the millenarian Taqui Onqoy movement posed a threat to the establishment of this new Christian order, but the campaign of Cristóbal de Albornoz suppressed this movement in Huamanga within two years. By the time Toledo left the Viceroyalty of Peru in 1581, both the political and the "spiritual conquest" of the Andes seemed to be complete.

By the seventeenth century these feelings of optimism about evangelization had passed, as many churchmen found evidence that Andeans continued practicing traditional religious rites. While clergymen expected indigenous converts to abandon their beliefs entirely in favor of the "true faith," it became clear that many Andeans simply incorporated Catholic beliefs and practices into their own religious framework, much as they had done with the state cults of the Inca. This Andean notion of spiritual compromise, or mañay, proved unacceptable to Catholic authorities, but churchmen remained deeply divided over how to deal with it. When Francisco de Avila, the parish priest of San Damián de Checa (Huarochirí), provided abundant evidence of persistent Andean religious practices, however, advocates of campaigns to "extirpate" idolatry through force gained the support of key political and religious leaders, including Lima Archbishop Bartolomé Lobo Guerrero. The archbishop dispatched inspectors throughout the archdiocese of Lima, who destroyed Andean religious icons, held clerical trials of suspected idolaters, and imposed rigorous punishments, followed by religious instruction in orthodox Catholic beliefs. By 1627, however, the death of Archbishop Lobo Guerrero allowed more moderate churchmen to end the extirpation campaigns, arguing that the survival of Andean religious rites merely indicated the persistence of religious error, which could be combated most effectively by persuasion and education, not legal trials and punishments.

The appointment of another enthusiastic advocate of forceful extirpation, Pedro de Villagómez, as archbishop of Lima in 1641 led to a renewal of expanded idolatry campaigns, lasting until his death in 1671. These more extensive campaigns represented the apogee of clerical efforts to root out and destroy any vestiges of Andean religious practices, and the trials provoked widespread opposition in the viceroyalty. Andeans protested the excesses of the idolatry inspectors, government officials condemned this extension of clerical authority, and many churchmen continued to maintain that persistent Andean religious practices represented merely superstition, not idolatry. In fact, before the death of Villagómez, the Jesuits, staunch former participants in the campaigns, withdrew their support. As a result, with the archbishop's passing in 1671, the momentum of the extirpation campaigns abated. Idolatry trials continued but at a much reduced pace, and by the eighteenth century clerical authorities held extirpation trials in the central ecclesiastical court in Lima, where the proceedings could be monitored more easily. By 1750 enthusiasm for the movement clearly had waned.

During the eighteenth century, Christian rituals, festivals, and religious icons became increasingly embedded in the Andean religious consciousness. Local priests generally tolerated a modicum of traditional indigenous religious rites, as long as parishioners paid their clerical dues, went to mass periodically, and displayed proper Christian piety at festivals. Apart from periodic complaints and tensions about clerical corruption, by the eighteenth century Andeans began incorporating more Christian precepts into their spiritual life, while more obvious forms of indigenous religion began to recede. The tumult and divisiveness provoked by the Bourbon Reforms, however, provoked new conflicts among the Church, the state, and the Andean communities. Just as the reforms led to widespread political unrest, so too did they weaken the Church and the spread of orthodox Catholic beliefs during the final decades of colonial rule. In the end, Christianity became the predominant religion in the Andes, but it always remained permeated with many diverse forms of traditional indigenous beliefs, rites, and practices. As with cultural changes, Andeans generally opted for compromise over confrontation in spiritual matters.

The first epoch of violent resistance to Spanish authority occurred between the Spanish invasion in 1532 and the execution of Tupac Amaru I. Although the rebellion of Manco Inca in 1536 failed to capture Cusco and expel the invaders from the Andes, it did lead to the establishment of an Inca state-in-exile in the remote fortress city of Vilcabamba. Along with his extensive political, economic, and social reforms, Viceroy Francisco de Toledo also managed to destroy this last vestige of Inca resistance, capturing Vilcabamba and executing Tupac Amaru I in 1572. In the years that followed, numerous indigenous revolts and insurrections broke out, but most were relatively small-scale, spontaneous outbreaks of violence against specific abuses.

The second wave of indigenous resistance began with the revolt of Juan Santos Atahualpa, which spread from the Cerro de la Sal in 1742 and threatened Spanish control over populous highland provinces in central Peru. In the end, this conflict ultimately remained largely confined to a frontier zone. Neverthe-less, as the Crown began its eighteenth-century efforts to reform the empire, new outbreaks of unrest and violence escalated dramatically. Policies such as the infamous repartimiento de comercio and later efforts to heighten fiscal pressures, tighten administrative controls, and impose trade regulations all exacer-bated persistent political, social, and economic problems in the Andes. Ultimately, tensions arising from the reforms erupted into the bloody rebellions of Tomás Katari, Tupac Amaru II, and Tupac Katari, which inflamed much of Peru and Upper Peru for three long years (1780–83). These massive insurrections threatened the very foundations of Spanish rule in the Andes. In the years following their suppression, periodic smaller-scale rebellions still broke out, protesting continued Spanish abuses, particularly the disruptions occasioned by the Bourbon fiscal, administrative, and commercial innovations. As the colonial regime began its slow collapse after 1808, disgruntled Andeans participated actively on both sides of the independence struggles to advance their own agendas. Throughout this period of unrest, indigenous rebels developed distinctive forms of political consciousness, articulating their own vision of political and social justice. Still, the independent nation-states that emerged from these struggles were dominated by creoles, who seldom shared these Andean visions of freedom and liberty.

While the chronologies of political, socioeconomic, cultural, and religious developments all differed in the colonial Andean world, the seventeenth century stands out as a formative period. Although Francisco de Toledo attempted to circumscribe the political, social, and economic place of Andeans in the Viceroyalty of Peru, over time the indigenous peoples struggled to shape their own lives within the colonial order. As creoles slowly gained political clout, indigenous elites and commoners, denied any direct voice in government affairs, relied on access to the courts and extralegal resistance to defend their rights. Andeans also expanded their socioeconomic opportunities during the long seventeenth century by evading excessive taxes and the mita and by taking advantage of whatever limited opportunities existed in the colonial economy. While some indigenous elites managed to prosper in the more diversified colonial economy that emerged in the 1620s, most Andeans settled for fewer material rewards. Pervasive migration to the cities and Spanish rural enterprises by the 1680s created widespread social change as some communities endured, while others simply disappeared or forged new ethnic identities through the process of ethnogenesis. Likewise, in this era the principal trends in colonial culture and religion became firmly established. Alphabetic writing, forms of artistic expression, and conceptions of geographical space and property ownership all changed to accommodate European influences, while some indigenous modes of expression endured. The colonial cultural mix may have subordinated Andean influences, but it never extinguished them. Repeated attempts by some Roman Catholic clerics to extirpate Andean religious practices also proceeded apace, but by the eighteenth century Andean notions of religious compromise had largely prevailed, producing a hybrid set of religious beliefs that emerged so clearly in the rebellions of Tupac Amaru II and Tupac Katari in the 1780s. In short, during the seventeenth century Andeans survived the changes brought by the European invasion, and they worked to fashion new, but largely subordinate, roles for themselves in the mature colonial order. Like Toledo in the sixteenth century, the Bourbon reformers failed to impose a more centralized colonial regime, capable of reversing the evolutionary changes that emerged during the seventeenth century. Instead, Bourbon innovations contributed to the rebellions of the 1780s, and ultimately weakened royal authority enough to allow the independence movements to succeed by the 1820s.

Despite the overall failures of centralizers during the sixteenth and eighteenth centuries, the colonial regime still managed to hinder Andeans from reaping substantial benefits, in spite of their many contributions. Although Spaniards deprived Andeans of meaningful political power and forced them to integrate European social, economic, cultural, and religious practices, the indigenous peoples still served as the backbone of the colonial order. By working in the mines, on rural Spanish enterprises, or by tilling the soil in their own communities, the Andean peoples played a decisive role in the economic evolution of the Viceroyalty of Peru for three hundred years. Whatever benefits they enjoyed under colonialism, however, hardly matched their contributions. The people who had created so many advanced civilizations, culminating in Tawantinsuyu, too often became exploited and subordinated under colonial rule. At the same time, the indigenous peoples resisted oppression in obvious and subtle ways, and they tried to find compromises with those European political, social, economic, cultural, and religious changes pressing upon them. In so doing, the Andeans managed to preserve some elements of their traditional lifeways even to the twenty-first century. The events set in motion on 16 November 1532 at Cajamarca changed the Andes in incontrovertible ways, but visitors to the region can still see the many enduring legacies of the indigenous past that shape the present and undoubtedly will continue to influence the future.

GLOSSARY OF TERMS

This glossary includes Spanish, Quechua, and Aymara terms used and italicized at first mention in the text. Spanish terms are followed in parentheses by the code, **Sp**; Quechua terms, **Q**; and Aymara terms, **A**. Since there is no standard orthography for the indigenous language terms, when multiple spellings are commonly used in the scholarly literature, these variants are listed in parentheses after the code identifying the language of the word.

Aclla (Q, *aqlla*)—Chosen one; a group of chosen women who served the Sapa Inca and the state cults.

Aduana (Sp)—Customs house.

Alcabala (Sp)—Sales tax levied directly or indirectly on merchandise of Spanish origin; indigenous peoples and goods of native American origin were exempted in theory.

Alcalde del crimen (Sp)—Audiencia justice who heard criminal cases.

Alcalde de varayok (Sp)—Mayor in an indigenous town.

Amaru (Q)—Serpent, dragon; see katari.

Apu (Q)—Great lord or highest judge.

Audiencia (Sp)—Spanish colonial high court that heard criminal and civil cases and also issued laws.

Auto de fe (Sp)—A public ceremony of absolution and punishment, conducted by the Inquisition and during the idolatry inspections.

Ayllu (Q)—Local kinship group or a larger self-defined kindred, often defined by a common ancestry.

Azogue (Sp)—Mercury.

Azoguero (Sp)—Owner of a silver amalgamation mill and usually silver mines.

Cabildo (Sp)—City council.

Cacicazgo (Sp)—Jurisdiction of an indigenous ethnic leader or cacique; an indigenous leadership post.

Cacique (Sp)—Indigenous leader; hispanicized Arawak word, taken from Caribbean; see kuraka.

Caja real (Sp)—Most often referring to a royal treasury office, named for its strongbox.

Camayoc (Q)—Official or supervisor in charge of estates, fields, or craftsmen.

Capac (Q)—King, royal, one who has the support of many.

Capac apu (Q, capac apo, qhapaq apu)—Great and powerful lord.

Casta (Sp)—One of mixed racial ancestry.

Cédula (Sp)—A royal edict.

Ceque (Q, zeque)—A ceremonial line or path; one of forty-one imaginary "sight" lines radiating from the Temple of the Sun (Coricancha) in Cusco where all major holy shrines (huacas) were located and that integrated Inca kinship, cosmology, and calendrics; see ayllu; huaca.

Cercado (Sp)—Indigenous sector of Lima.

Champi (A)—Personal god of fertility; see conopa.

Chanca (Q)—Lineage god of particular significance to a specific social group, lineage, or family.

Chaski (Q, ch'aski)—Postal runner in Tawantinsuyu; a messenger.

Chicha (Q)—Fermented beverage, usually maize or corn beer used commonly on social and ritual occasions.

Cofradía (Sp)—Religious brotherhood or sodality organized to support a particular devotion.

Compadrazgo (Sp)—Godparentage.

Concierto (Sp)—A full-time, resident worker on a Spanish rural estate.

Conopa (Q)—Personal god of fertility.

Corregidor de indios (Sp)—Spanish rural magistrate in charge of an Amerindian province (corregimiento), usually larger than a parish and certainly smaller than an audiencia district; see audiencia.

Coya (Q, quya)—Queen consort of the Sapa Inca.

Cuenta (Sp)—An account, most commonly used to mean an official treasury office accounting of yearly income and expenditures.

Curaka (Q)—See kuraka.

Curandero (Sp)—Folk healer.

Doctrina (*Sp*)—A parish administered by members of the secular or the regular clergy, particularly in indigenous districts.

Encomendero (*Sp*)—Holder of an encomienda grant; see encomienda.

Encomienda (*Sp*)—A grant of indigenous towns to a creole or peninsular who had the right to receive a portion of the tribute collected in those communities in return for protecting the physical and spiritual welfare of the inhabitants.

Fanega (*Sp*)—A unit of dry measure, approximately 1.5 bushels.

Fianza (*Sp*)—A security bond, often posted by public officials to ensure their honesty in office.

Fiscal (*Sp*)—An attorney.

Forastero (*Sp*)—An Amerindian living as a resident alien in a settlement other than his/her place of birth; usually the resident alien paid a lower tribute rate than other permanent residents and did so at his/her home community, until the 1720s.

Gatera (*Sp*)—Urban peddler, usually indigenous and most frequently a woman.

Hanan (*Q*)—High or upper half or moiety of an indigenous community.

Huaca (*Q*, *waqa*)—A sacred or divine personage or a part of the landscape—such as a boulder, tree, river, or statue—associated with that divinity.

Hurin (*Q*)—The lower half or moiety of an indigenous community.

Indio de faltriquera (*Sp*)—Literally a "pocket" Indian; used to refer to those indigenous laborers who bought an exemption from corvée labor by paying in cash a sum equivalent to the salary of a wage laborer.

Indio ladino (*Sp*)—A hispanicized Amerindian, bilingual and usually literate in Castilian, and a Christian.

Jornalero (*Sp*)—Wage laborer, most often on a Spanish rural estate.

Juez visitador de idolatrías or visitador de idolatrías (*Sp*)—An inspector and judge of idolatry; an extirpator; a Catholic priest specifically commissioned to root out and punish forbidden Andean religious practices; see visita de idolatrías.

Junta (*Sp*)—Local committees that served as interim governments, most often dominated by creoles, after the abdication of King Charles IV in 1808.

Kajcha (*Q*)—Usually indigenous miners, who took advantage of a work holiday to mine silver ore for themselves.

Katari (*A*)—Serpent, dragon; see amaru.

Kero (Q, *qiru*)—A wooden drinking cup used in a variety of indigenous ritual and ceremonial occasions; frequently decorated with carving or painting.

Kuraka (Q, *curaca*)—Native lord or leader of an Andean community.

Lengua (Sp)—A translator, usually indigenous.

Llacta (Q)—An Andean territorial entity (town, village, or province) with its own local deities and with its own inhabitants, resources, and socioeconomic infrastructure.

Mallqui (Q, *malqui*)—The mummified remains of a venerated ancestor, often brought out to take part in religious ceremonies.

Mascapaycha (Q)—Red cloth tassel worn over the forehead as a crown by the Sapa Inca; later used by Andean nobles as a sign of their high rank and royal blood.

Mestizo (Sp)—A person of mixed Spanish and Amerindian blood.

Mindalá (Q, *plural mindalaes*)—Specialized, politically sponsored, and privileged long-distance trader in luxury goods in the North Andes.

Minga (Sp, *or* Q *variant mink'a*)—A grant of collective labor to an authority; a voluntary wage laborer at the silver mines (especially Potosí).

Mita (Sp)—Spanish reworking of Inca cyclical corvée; obligatory public service, especially at the silver mines.

Mit'a (Q)—Inca cyclical corvée, used most often for public works and the military.

Mitayo (Sp, Q, *mitayu, mit'ayuq*)—A person fulfilling state labor service.

Mitmaq (Q, *mitmaj, mitimae*)—Person sent from his/her place of origin to serve outside interests, usually those of the community or the Inca state.

Mullu (Q)—Spondylus; warm water mollusk, whose shells were used in offerings to Andean gods.

Obraje (Sp)—A Spanish woolen textile mill.

Obrajero (Sp)—Owner of an obraje.

Oidor (Sp)—Audiencia justice who heard civil cases.

Orejones (Sp)—Literally "big ears" or members of a high noble caste among the Inca who wore earplugs that stretched the ear lobe in a distinctive manner; frequently served as an imperial guard.

Originario (Sp)—Original resident of an Amerindian community with access to land who paid the full tribute rate assigned by the Spaniards; see tributario.

Pacarina (Q)—Place of origin of an Andean community; final resting place of the dead.

Padrón (Sp)—An official population census.

Panaca (Q)—A branch of the Inca nobility in Cusco assigned to venerate a deceased Sapa Inca and care for his lands and goods, probably encompassing all members of the dead Inca's lineage, except his successor; also from the land, lineage, or an acquaintance of someone; a cousin or sister of a man.

Páramo (Sp)—Humid, high altitude grasslands found in the North Andes.

Procurador (Sp)—A legal representative empowered to act on behalf of designated interest groups.

Puka kunka (Q)—Derisive term applied by Andean rebels to Spaniards, meaning literally "red necks."

Puna (Q)—Dry, high altitude grasslands, characteristic of the central and southern Andes.

Quillka (Q, *quillca*)—Writing, painting, or teaching using repetitive examples.

Quipu (Q, *khipu*)—Strings, knotted cords of different colors and shapes used to convey meaning, record numerical data, and record historical events.

Quipucamayoc (Q)—Learned person who could interpret or "read" a quipu.

Raymi (Q)—Religious feast, usually associated with a specific time on the Inca calendars, often involving solar celebrations.

Real provisión (Sp)—A legal document emanating from the Crown that usually concerned specific grants of land, offices, encomiendas, and so on to individuals or corporate groups.

Reducción (Sp)—Spanish-style town where the Andean peoples were forced to resettle (usually uniting many dispersed communities) mainly during the viceregency of Francisco de Toledo (1569–82).

Regatona (Sp)—Urban huckster, usually an Andean woman.

Relaciones geográficas (Sp)—Geographical survey of the Spanish Empire, conducted in the Andes between 1579 and 1583.

Repartimiento (Sp)—A Spanish regional administrative district.

Repartimiento de comercio (Sp, repartimiento de mercancías or shortened to reparto)—Forced distribution of European wares to Andean communities at prices fixed by the colonial regime; widely reputed to be a very abusive practice, which contributed to the unrest that eventually provoked the Great Age of Andean Rebellions.

Residencia (Sp)—A judicial review of all high-ranking Spanish officials.

Retasa (Sp)—A new tax evaluation, especially for Amerindian tribute.

Sapa Inca (Q)—"Unique" Inca or supreme ruler of Tawantinsuyu.

Saya (Q)—Inca administrative district, smaller than a province, and ruled by a trusted ethnic leader.

Sinchi (Q)—Andean war leader or tribal chief.

Sirvinacuy (Q)—Andean form of "trial" marriage.

Subdelegado (Sp)—Subdelegate; an official reporting directly to the intendant, who replaced the corregidor in supervising and collecting tribute in indigenous communities.

Supay (Q)—An Andean spirit who could be either benign or malevolent; frequently translated as "devil" by the Christian missionaries.

Suyu (Q, *suyo*)—An Inca administrative district; there were four suyu in the Inca realm.

Tampu (Q, *tampo, tambo*)—A roadside inn.

Tasa (Sp)—A tax rate assessed to Andean communities.

Taqui Onqoy (Q, *Taqui Unquy*)—Dancing sickness; an Andean resistance movement in the 1560s based on traditional religious deities who called for the expulsion of all Spaniards and an eradication of Christianity.

Taquiongo (Q, Sp, *takiunquero*)—Participant in the Taqui Onqoy movement.

Tiana (Q)—Low seat that signified high status among the Inca.

Torikoq (Q, *toricoq, tokriqoq*)—Inca governor of a suyu, who was usually a kinsman of the Sapa Inca.

Trajin (Q)—An Andean pack train, usually of llama or other indigenous beasts of burden, taking goods across the Andean cordillera.

Tribunal de cuentas (Sp)—Royal tribunal of accounts that sat in Lima and audited the annual tax records of each treasury office in the realm.

Tributario (Sp)—An indigenous male between the ages of eighteen and fifty, assessed a tax in specie, in kind, or both, payable twice annually.

Tucapu (Q, *tocapo, t'oquapu*)—Various squares or rectangle designs, mostly abstract, on Inca tunics or objects.

Uncu (Q)—A tunic that often signified high status.

Veedor—An overseer, an inspector in a treasury office.

Venta y composición de tierras (Sp)—An inspection and verification of land titles; anyone without legal title had to pay a tax assessed on the land's value or the property would be sold at public auction.

Visita (Sp)—An official government or clerical inspection tour.

Visita de idolatrías (Sp)—An investigation and trial of Andean religious practices, followed by religious instruction; see juez visitador de idolatrías.

Yana (Q, plural yanakuna; hispanicized Quechua, yanacona)—A social class of servants among the Inca and later the Spanish, treated as dependent and paid nominally; later a worker on a Spanish enterprise, especially a rural estate.

Yerba maté (Sp)—Paraguayan tea.

Yunga (Q)—Hot, subtropical lowlands.

NOTES

CHAPTER 1

1. A chronicle is a historical narrative of events, often written by a participant or contemporary of those events.

2. Hernando Pizarro to the *oidores* (civil justices) of the Audiencia (high court) of Santo Domingo, in Gonzalo Fernández de Oviedo, "Reports on the Discovery of Peru," trans. Clements R. Markham, *Hakluyt Society Papers* 47: 113–27 (Cambridge, England, 1872). Cited in John Hemming, *The Conquest of the Incas* (New York, 1970), 42.

3. Typically, this is called ethnographic work, and it involves living, observing, and working in an indigenous community to learn as much as possible about customs, culture, religion, and other facets of life. These data are often used to project backward (called upstreaming) in an effort to use present cultural practices as a means to understand the past.

4. The disruptions caused by warfare among the Spanish invaders and indigenous rebellions lasted until the 1570s, which impeded the collection of such information about the Andean peoples. During this nearly forty-year interval between the invasion and consolidation of the Spanish regime, Andean societies had been disrupted and much information was lost.

5. This probably stems from the time it took for indigenous intellectuals to gain a sufficient mastery over written Spanish to translate Andean ideas and cultural concepts into this European tongue.

6. This account was not discovered by scholars until 1908 in a library in Copenhagen, Denmark. How it got there is still unknown.

7. This manuscript apparently was compiled by Spanish priests attempting to stamp out indigenous religious practices. By that time, the Spanish had established an orthography for writing the most common Andean languages with the Latin alphabet.

8. Formulations of this type of synthesis have already been undertaken by some anthropologists, but they have not been applied systematically to Andean history. See, for example, George E. Marcus, "Contemporary Problems of Ethnography in the World System," in James Clifford and George E. Marcus, eds., *Writing Culture: The Poetics*

and Politics of Ethnography (Berkeley and Los Angeles, 1986), 166; Marcus and Michael M. J. Fischer, *Anthropology as Cultural Critique: An Experimental Moment in the Human Sciences* (Chicago, 1986), 77–110; and William Roseberry, "Beyond the Agrarian Question in Latin America," in Frederick Cooper, et al., eds., *Confronting Historical Paradigms: Peasants, Labor, and the Capitalist World System in Africa and Latin America* (Madison, Wis., 1993), 347–51.

9.   Marcus, "Contemporary Problems," 170.

CHAPTER 2

1.   Pedro de Cieza de León, *The Incas*, edited, with an introduction by Victor Wolfgang von Hagen, and translated by Harriet de Onis (Norman, Okla., 1959), 225, 227. Cited in Geoffrey W. Conrad and Arthur A. Demarest, *Religion and Empire: The Dynamics of Aztec and Inca Expansionism* (Cambridge, England, and New York, 1984), 111–12.

2.   Miguel Cabello de Valboa, *Miscelánea Antártica: Una historia del Perú Antiguo* (Lima, 1951), 301. Cited in Conrad and Demarest, *Religion and Empire*, 112.

3.   Rolena Adorno, *Guaman Poma: Writing and Resistance in Colonial Peru* (Austin, Tex., 1986), 5.

4.   One of the richest of these documents is an early census of the Huánuco region, which was discovered and analyzed by ethnohistorian John V. Murra. See Iñigo Ortiz de Zúñiga, "Visita de la Provincia de León de Huánuco en 1562," in John V. Murra, ed., *Documentos para la Historia y Etnología de Huánuco y la Selva Central* (Huánuco, 1967, 1972), 1: 8–266; 2:1–269.

5.   The chronicles indicate that several cross-cutting issues prompted this factionalism. The Inca had no formal rule of succession; the Sapa Inca was supposed to bequeath his crown to his most able son, but "competency" was frequently a matter of lively debate. One of Viracocha's brothers had already risen up in a bloody but unsuccessful revolt against the Inca, leaving division and bitterness at court. Likewise, Viracocha's apparent attempt to favor the god Tequi Viracocha (his namesake) and its priesthood over the traditional Sun god, Inti, stirred much popular resentment among the citizenry. See Conrad and Demarest, *Religion and Empire*, 113. For a discussion of the Chanca war, see María Rostworowski de Diez Canseco, *History of the Inca Realm*, trans. Harry Iceland (Cambridge, England, and New York, 1999 [1988]), 22–36.

6.   This explains the conflicting viewpoints in the passages at the outset of this chapter. To the supporters of Viracocha, Pachacuti was indeed a usurper, and Cieza de León's version apparently relied on an oral tradition sympathetic to the deposed Sapa Inca. The other version

obviously depended on informants who relayed a dynastic oral tradition more sympathetic to Pachacuti. See Conrad and Demarest, *Religion and Empire*, 111–12.

7. Rostworowski, *History of the Inca Realm*, 65–91.

8. The *ayllu* was apparently not always the basic social unit among ethnic groups in frontier zones, such as Ecuador or Chile.

9. Terence N. D'Altroy, *Provincial Power in the Inka Empire* (Washington, D.C., 1992), 132; Catherine J. Julien, "Inca Decimal Administration in the Lake Titicaca Region," in George A. Collier, Renato I. Rosaldo, and John D. Wirth, eds. *The Inca and Aztec States, 1400–1800: Anthropology and History* (New York, 1982), 129–32; Rostworowski, *History of the Inca Realm*, 144–45.

10. John Hyslop, *The Inka Road System* (Orlando, Fla., 1984), 222–24, and *Inca Settlement Planning* (Austin, Tex., 1990), 274–76.

11. The Andeans understood the concept of the wheel and even used versions of this device on toys, but they failed to employ it on large vehicles. In part, this apparently stemmed from the lack of a true beast of burden—the only effective animal carrier was the llama, but this fragile animal had a cargo limit of approximately one hundred pounds. The rugged terrain and the lack of a device such as the horse collar, which would have allowed the Andeans to utilize teams of llamas, also made wheeled vehicles impractical.

12. Hyslop, *The Inka Road System*, 215–24; Linda A. Newson, *Life and Death in Early Colonial Ecuador* (Norman, Okla., 1995), 126–28.

13. Rostworowski, *History of the Inca Realm*, 210–14; Susan E. Ramírez, "Exchange and Markets in the Sixteenth Century: A View from the North," in Brooke Larson and Olivia Harris, eds., with Enrique Tandeter, *Ethnicity, Markets, and Migration in the Andes: At the Crossroads of History and Anthropology* (Durham, N.C., 1995), 141–44.

14. Bernabé Cobo, *History of the Inca Empire*, trans. Roland Hamilton (Austin, Tex., 1996), 211.

15. Coca is a low tropical bush, whose leaves were commonly used in religious rituals. It was (and still is) commonly chewed by Andeans as a stimulant during work and travel in the highlands. Today, the coca leaf is refined by drug lords into various forms of the addictive narcotic, cocaine.

16. Quoted in Conrad and Demarest, *Religion and Empire*, 109.

17. According to Conrad and Demarest, this system of multifaceted gods utterly confused many Spanish clerics, who failed to understand that one god could have many characteristics that changed depending on the time and circumstance. Indeed, this lack of comprehension may even be visible in the previous quotation by Bernabé Cobo. Rather than lacking steadfastness in their worship, the Inca often emphasized different facets of the same gods. Nevertheless, this flexibility allowed

the Inca religious cults to subsume many of the traits associated with the deities worshipped by other Andean ethnic groups. See Conrad and Demarest, *Religion and Empire*, 100–109.

18. For a more detailed discussion of the *ceque* system, see chapter 5.
19. R. Tom Zuidema, "Guaman Poma and the Art of Empire: Towards an Iconography of Inca Royal Dress," in Kenneth J. Andrien and Rolena Adorno, eds., *Transatlantic Encounters: Europeans and Andeans in the Sixteenth Century* (Berkeley and Los Angeles, 1991), 151–202.
20. This concept is explored in Irene Silverblatt, *Moon, Sun, and Witches: Gender Ideologies and Class in Inca and Colonial Peru* (Princeton, N.J., 1987).
21. Felipe Huamán Poma de Ayala, *Letter to a King: A Picture-History of Inca Civilisation*, trans. Christopher Dilke (London, 1978), 85–86.
22. Newson, *Life and Death in Early Colonial Ecuador*, 119–23.
23. Conrad and Demarest, *Religion and Empire*, 126.
24. D'Altroy, *Provincial Power in the Inka Empire*, 75–77.
25. Ibid., 85–90.
26. Rostworowski, *History of the Inca Realm*, 106–10.
27. Huaman Poma, *Letter to a King*, 45.

CHAPTER 3

1. According to some chroniclers, Manco Inca's army began to disband after three or four months for want of food. The Spaniards apparently used their cavalry to disrupt attempts to resupply the huge force. Finally, the peasant soldiers returned home for the planting season and had to be reassembled later. See John Hemming, *The Conquest of the Incas* (New York, 1970), 204–5.
2. Despite Manco's retreat to Vilcabamba, he and his successors remained a military threat to the Spaniards, particularly during the ensuing years of civil war among the conquistadors. Ibid., 277–79.
3. For a short time, Almagro even tried to arrange a deal with Manco Inca: in exchange for allowing Almagro to take Cusco from the Pizarros, he would grant a pardon to the Inca and his Andean rebels. In the end, both sides mistrusted the other too much, and Almagro's attempt to betray the Pizarros and treat with Manco Inca failed. Ibid., 223–29.
4. Agustín de Zárate, *The Discovery and Conquest of Peru*, trans. J. M. Cohen (Harmondsworth, England, 1968), 236.
5. This institution had proven a useful temporary governing method during long wars of reconquest against the Muslims in the Iberian peninsula. It had served a similar purpose for the first Spanish settlers in the Caribbean and later in Mexico.
6. Among Núñez Vela's most controversial acts were the imprisonment of his predecessor, Cristóbal Vaca de Castro, and executing the royal

treasury official, Illán Suárez de Carvajal. Zárate, *Discovery and Conquest of Peru*, 236.

7. Lewis Hanke, *The Spanish Struggle for Justice in the Conquest of America* (Philadelphia, 1949), 96. According to William H. Prescott, Gonzalo Pizarro gave Núñez Vela an honorable burial. See Prescott, *History of the Conquest of Peru* (Philadelphia, 1871), 2: 312–14.

8. Hemming, *Conquest of the Incas*, 236.

9. Titu Cusi attained the crown in 1560 upon the death of Sayri Tupac, who had succeeded Manco Inca after his assassination in 1544. Hemming, *Conquest of the Incas*, 504.

10. The best recent edition of Toledo's ordinances is as follows: Guillermo Lohmann Villena, introduction, and transcription by Ma. Justina Sarabia Viejo, *Francisco de Toledo: Disposiciones gubernativas para el Virreinato del Perú*, 1569–1574, 2 vols. (Sevilla, 1986).

11. Information on the inspection tour, including several of the questions asked of local Andean community leaders may be found in Francisco de Toledo, "Libro de la visita general, 1570–1575," *Revista histórica* VII (1921): 125–77; and Roberto Levillier, ed., *Sus informaciones sobre los Incas* (1570–1572), vol. III, *Don Francisco de Toledo, supremo organizador del Perú: Su vida, su obra* (1515–1582) (Buenos Aires, 1942).

12. Hemming, *Conquest of the Incas*, 395.

13. Pedro de la Gasca, a prominent clergyman, was sent by the Crown to serve as president of the Audiencia of Lima in 1546. He arrived in Peru after the death of Viceroy Blasco Nuñez Vela, and he succeeded in raising an army and putting down the rebellion of Gonzalo Pizarro in 1548. Although he was never named viceroy, Pedro de la Gasca effectively ruled in the viceroyalty as president of its most prominent audiencia. After punishing the defeated rebels, he undertook a reallocation of encomienda grants and began the process of establishing orderly tribute assessments, before returning to Spain in 1550. See Teodoro Hampe Martínez, *Don Pedro de la Gasca* (1493–1567), *su obra política en España y América* (Lima, 1989).

14. Knowledge about the social position of *yanakuna* in Andean society is still quite sketchy, but they appear to have been people outside the traditional ayllu structure who worked as servants. During the colonial period the term was applied to many Andeans in private service to the Spaniards. *Forasteros* were migrants, living outside of their home communities; like the yanakuna they were subject to lower tribute rates and not subject to corvée labor. See Ann M. Wightman, *Indigenous Migration and Social Change: The Forasteros of Cuzco*, 1570–1720 (Durham, N.C., 1990), 31–33.

15. For a more detailed account of the fall of Vilcabamba and the execution of Tupac Amaru I, see chapter 7.

16. Creole refers to those of European ancestry born in the Americas.

Europeans born in the Iberian peninsula were usually referred to as *peninsulares*, *chapetones*, or even by the derogatory Quechua term *puka kunkas* (red necks).

17. Hemming, *Conquest of the Incas*, 395.

18. Ibid.

19. Francisco López de Caravantes, "Noticia general de las provincias del Perú, Tierrafirme, y Chile," vol. 3, 30 abril 1630, Manuscritos 1634, folio 182, Biblioteca del Palacio Real, Madrid; and Nicolás Polanco de Santillán to Crown, Lima, 31 julio 1663, Archivo General de Indias, Lima, 280.

20. Kenneth J. Andrien, "The Sale of Fiscal Offices and the Decline of Royal Authority in the Viceroyalty of Peru, 1633–1700," *Hispanic American Historical Review* 62 (February 1982): 49–71; Mark A. Burkholder and D. S. Chandler, *From Impotence to Authority: The Spanish Crown and the American Audiencias, 1687–1808* (Columbia, Mo., 1977).

21. Jorge Juan and Antonio de Ulloa, *Discourse and Political Reflections on the Kingdoms of Peru, their government, special regiment of their inhabitants, and abuses which have been introduced into one and another with special information on why they grew up and some means to avoid them*, edited and with introduction by John J. TePaske, and translated by John J. TePaske and Besse A. Clement (Norman, Okla., 1978 [1749]), 78.

22. According to traditional labor practices at Potosí and elsewhere, the workers had the privilege of mining ore for themselves every Sunday. Andean *mitayos* and even wage laborers frequently manipulated this custom to resist the miners' exploitation. During the week, they would secretly save some of the best pieces of ore for themselves and later retrieve it on Sunday for sale to silver traders in Potosí. By the eighteenth century gangs of indigenous laborers, called *kajchas*, would raid the mines and collect pieces of ore and tailings for sale.

23. See Jeffrey A. Cole, *The Potosí Mita, 1573–1700: Compulsory Indian Labor in the Andes* (Stanford, Calif., 1985), 23–33, 56–57.

24. See Cole, "An Abolition Born of Frustration: The Conde de Lemos and the Potosí Mita, 1667–1673," *Hispanic American Historical Review* 63 (May 1983): 307–33.

25. Manuel Atanasio Fuentes, ed., *Memorias de los vireyes que han governado el Perú, durante el tiempo del colonaje español*, 6 vols. (Lima, 1859), 1: 118–19.

26. See Cole, "Viceregal Persistence Versus Indian Mobility: The Impact of the Duque de la Palata's Reform Program in Alto Perú, 1681–1692," *Latin American Research Review* 19:1 (1984): 37–56.

27. Wightman, *Indigenous Migration and Social Change*, 43.

28. All of these figures are taken from the accounts of the Lima treasury office, which served as the clearinghouse for all public revenues from Peru and Upper Peru during this period. For an analysis of these figures, see Herbert S. Klein, *The American Finances of the Spanish Empire*:

Royal Income and Expenditures in Colonial Mexico, Peru, and Bolivia,
1680–1809 (Albuquerque, 1998).

29. Quoted in J. R. Fisher, *Government and Society in Colonial Peru: The*
    Intendant System, 1784–1814 (London, 1970), 12.

30. The intendancy system already existed in the Viceroyalty of the Río de
    la Plata from its foundation in 1776. The reform did not extend to the
    North Andean provinces that formed the Audiencia of Quito (modern
    Ecuador), which were then part of the Viceroyalty of New Granada.
    Instead, the *visitador* of that region, José García de León y Pizarro,
    appointed a series of special government agencies to collect taxes,
    including one for tribute. This removed the collection of this head tax
    from the *corregidores* and various private tax farmers. See Kenneth J.
    Andrien, *The Kingdom of Quito, 1690–1830: The State and Regional*
    Development (Cambridge, England, 1995), 190–215.

31. Klein, *American Finances of the Spanish Empire*, 31–54.

CHAPTER 4

1. Quoted in Peter J. Bakewell, *Miners of the Red Mountain: Indian Labor in*
   Potosí, 1545–1650 (Albuquerque, 1984), 4.

2. Quoted in Noble David Cook, *Demographic Collapse: Indian Peru,*
   1520–1620 (Cambridge, England, 1981), 199.

3. According to James Lockhart, the old Inca capital of Cusco was
   bypassed by the trunk line and remained more isolated on a main
   feeder line. See Lockhart, "Trunk Lines and Feeder Lines: The Spanish
   Reaction to American Resources," in Kenneth J. Andrien and Rolena
   Adorno, eds., *Transatlantic Encounters: Europeans and Andeans in the*
   Sixteenth Century (Berkeley, 1991), 109–10.

4. Modes of production refer to the social organization of production in
   a community. In this case, production encompasses not just an
   economic concept but also ecological, social, political, and social-
   psychological. See Eric R. Wolf, *Europe and the People without History*
   (Berkeley, 1982), 21.

5. Brooke Larson, *Colonialism and Agrarian Transformation in Bolivia:*
   Cochabamba, 1550–1900 (Princeton, N.J., 1988), 43.

6. John V. Murra, "Nos Hazen Mucha Ventaja: The Early European
   Perception of Andean Achievement," in Andrien and Adorno, eds.,
   Transatlantic Encounters, 85–86.

7. The bulk of what today constitutes modern Peru corresponds roughly
   to the Audiencia of Lima (see map 3).

8. See Cook, *Demographic Collapse*, 75–114; Linda Newson, *Life and Death in*
   Early Colonial Ecuador (Norman, Okla., 1995), 350; and Ann Zulawski,
   They Eat from Their Labor: Work and Social Change in Colonial Bolivia
   (Pittsburgh, Pa., 1995), 83.

9. Quoted in Louisa Schell Hoberman and Susan Migden Socolow, eds., *Cities and Society in Colonial Latin America* (Albuquerque, 1986), 55.

10. Susan Elizabeth Ramírez, "Exchange and Markets in the Sixteenth Century: A View From the North," in Brooke Larson and Olivia Harris, eds., with Enrique Tandeter, *Ethnicity, Markets, and Migration in the Andes: At the Crossroads of History and Anthropology* (Durham, N.C., 1995), 144–64.

11. Franklin Pease G. Y., "Curacas Coloniales: Riqueza y Actitudes," *Revista de Indias* XLVIII, 182–83 (1988): 93–95.

12. Quoted in Thierry Saignes, "Indian Migration and Social Change in Seventeenth-Century Charcas," in Larson and Harris, *Ethnicity, Markets, and Migration*, 168.

13. This discussion on indigenous *trajines* is taken from Luis Miguel Glave, *Trajinantes: Caminos indigenas en la sociedad colonial, siglos XVI/XVII* (Lima, 1989), 1–176.

14. Ann M. Wightman, *Indigenous Migration and Social Change: The Forasteros of Cuzco, 1570–1720* (Durham, N.C., 1990), 111–24.

15. Glave, *Trajinantes*, 305–62.

16. Martin Minchom, *The People of Quito, 1690–1810: Change and Unrest in the Underclass* (Boulder, Colo., 1994), 101–16.

17. Quoted in Newson, *Life and Death in Early Colonial Ecuador*, 157.

18. This information comes from Galo Ramón Valarezo, *La resistencia andina: Cayambe, 1500–1800* (Quito, 1987), 224–30.

19. Glave, *Trajinantes*, 201–14.

20. Bakewell, *Miners of the Red Mountain*, 28.

21. The Crown retained its system of monopoly ports in Spain and the Indies, but licensed individual ships to sail the Atlantic alone or in small groups at any time of the year, not in convoy.

22. Herbert S. Klein, *The American Finances of the Spanish Empire: Royal Income and Expenditures in Colonial Mexico, Peru, and Bolivia, 1680–1809* (Albuquerque, 1998), 40, 61.

23. Ibid., 44, 64.

24. Francisco A. Loayza, ed., *Fray Calixto Túpak Inka: documentos originales y, en su mayoría, totalmente desconocidos, auténticos, de este apóstol indio, valiente defensor de su raza, desde el año 1746 a 1760* (Lima, 1948 [1750]), 30.

25. See Olivia Harris, "Sources and Meanings of Money: Beyond the Market Paradigm in an Ayllu of Northern Potosí," in Larson and Harris, *Ethnicity, Markets, and Migration*, 297–328.

CHAPTER 5

1. This idea, from the work of Nicholas Thomas, has been applied to the case of Andean art in the following article: Tom Cummins, "Let Me See! Reading Is for Them: Colonial Andean Images and Objects 'como es costumbre tener los caciques Señores,'" in Elizabeth Hill Boone and

Tom Cummins, eds., *Native Traditions in the Postconquest World* (Washington, D.C., 1998), 96.

2.   This view has been articulated most clearly in Jack Goody, *The Domestication of the Savage Mind* (Cambridge, England, 1977) and in Walter J. Ong, *Orality and Literacy: The Technologizing of the Word* (London and New York, 1982).

3.   Frank Salomon and George L. Urioste, eds. and trans. *The Huarochirí Manuscript* (Austin, Tex., 1991), 41.

4.   This theoretical view is expressed in Brian V. Street, *Literacy in Theory and Practice* (Cambridge, England, 1984).

5.   Walter Mignolo, *The Darker Side of the Renaissance: Literacy, Territoriality, and Colonization* (Ann Arbor, Mich.), 15.

6.   Although dealing with medieval England, this more moderate view is expressed very clearly in M. T. Clanchy, *From Memory to Written Record: England, 1066–1307*, 2nd ed. (Oxford, England, and Cambridge, Mass., 1993), 9.

7.   Quoted in Rosaleen Howard-Malverde, *The Speaking of History: "Willapaakushayki" or Quechua Ways of Telling the Past* (London, 1990), 58.

8.   Quoted in Mignolo, *Darker Side of the Renaissance*, 84.

9.   See Gary Urton, in collaboration with Primitivo Nina Llanos, *The Social Life of Numbers: A Quechua Ontology of Numbers and Philosophy of Arithmetic* (Austin, Tex., 1997), passim.

10. Quoted in Mignolo, *Darker Side of the Renaissance*, 84–85.

11. Urton, "From Knots to Narratives: Reconstructing the Art of Historical Record Keeping in the Andes from Spanish Transcriptions of Inka Khipus," *Ethnohistory* 45:3 (summer 1998): 409–38.

12. For an additional discussion of Taqui Onqoy, see chapter 3 and especially chapter 6.

13. Quoted in Urton, "From Knots to Narratives," 430.

14. Quoted from a *cédula* issued repeatedly in 1535, 1540, 1579, 1619, and 1620 in Mignolo, *Darker Side of the Renaissance*, 53.

15. Quoted in Robert D. Wood, *Teach Them Good Customs: Colonial Indian Education and Acculturation in the Andes* (Culver City, Calif., 1986), 18.

16. Ibid., 20

17. Ibid., 46.

18. Ibid., 80–81.

19. Quoted in Bruce Manheim, "The Inka Language in the Colonial World," *Colonial Latin American Review* 1:1–2 (1992): 81–82.

20. Ibid., 75–91.

21. See Margarita Zamora, *Language, Authority, and Indigenous History in the Comentarios reales de los Incas* (Cambridge, England, 1988); José Antonio Mazzotti, *Coros mestizos del Inca Garcilaso: Resonancias andinas* (Lima and México, 1996); and D. A. Brading, *The First America: The Spanish Monarchy, Creole Patriots, and the Liberal State, 1492–1867* (Cambridge, England, 1991), 255–72.

22. Pierre Duviols and César Itier, eds., *Relación de antigüedades deste reyno del Pirú: Estudio Etnohistórico y Lingüístico* (Lima and Cusco, 1993), 28.

23. The definitive edition of this text is Felipe Guamán Poma de Ayala, *El primer nueva corónica y buen gobierno*, edited by John V. Murra and Rolena Adorno, translated and textual analysis of the Quechua by Jorge Urioste, 3 vols. (México, 1980). A partial English translation of an early edition of the text by Luis Bustíos Gálvez is Huamán Poma, *Letter to a King: A Picture-History of the Inca Civilization*, trans. Christopher Dilke (London, 1978).

24. Rolena Adorno, *Guaman Poma: Writing and Resistance in Colonial Peru* (Austin, Tex., 1986), 5.

25. This line of argumentation draws on Adorno's work, particularly *Guaman Poma: Writing and Resistance*, 3–56.

26. Ibid., 57–79.

27. This analysis is drawn from Mercedes López-Baralt, "From Looking to Seeing: The Image as Text and the Author as Artist," in Rolena Adorno, ed., *Guaman Poma de Ayala: The Colonial Art of an Andean Author* (New York, 1992), 28–31; and López-Baralt, *Icono y conquista: Guaman Poma de Ayala* (Madrid, 1988), 189–267.

28. Adorno, *Guaman Poma: Writing and Resistance*, 139–43.

29. S. Elizabeth Penry, "The Rey Común: Indigenous Political Discourse in Eighteenth-Century Alto Perú," in Louis Roniger and Tamar Herzog, eds., *Collective Identities, Public Spheres and Political Order: Latin American Dynamics* (Sussex, 2000), 230–33.

30. According to Guaman Poma, for example, the word *quillka* is associated with the *quipucamayoc*. See Tom Cummins, "The Uncomfortable Image: Pictures and Words in the *Nueva corónica y buen gobierno*," in Adorno, ed., *Guaman Poma de Ayala*, 58–59.

31. This analysis had been drawn from Joanne Rappaport and Tom Cummins, "Between Images and Writing: The Ritual of the King's *Quillka*," *Colonial Latin American Review* 7:1 (1998): 7–32.

32. Esther Pasztory, *Pre-Columbian Art* (Cambridge, England, 1998), 163.

33. Rebecca Stone-Miller, *To Weave for the Sun: Andean Textiles in the Museum of Fine Arts* (Boston, 1992).

34. Much of this discussion has been taken from R. Tom Zuidema, "Guaman Poma and the Art of Empire: Towards an Iconography of Inca Royal Dress," in Kenneth J. Andrien and Rolena Adorno, eds., *Transatlantic Encounters: Europeans and Andeans in the Sixteenth Century* (Berkeley and Los Angeles, 1991), 151–202.

35. Tom Cummins, "Representation in the Sixteenth Century and the Colonial Image of the Inca," in Elizabeth Hill Boone and Walter D. Mignolo, eds., *Writing without Words: Alternative Literacies in Mesoamerica and the Andes* (Durham, N.C., 1994), 205–7.

36. This analysis draws heavily upon Rolena Adorno, "The Nueva Coronica y Buen Gobierno: A New Look at the Royal Library's Peruvian Treasure," *Fund og Forskning* 24:7 (1979–80): 7–28; and Cummins, "The Uncomfortable Image," 50.

37. Adorno, *Guaman Poma*, 80–120, especially 94–95; and López Baralt, "From Looking to Seeing," 18–20.

38. This analysis is drawn from Cummins, "The Uncomfortable Image," 53–54. As Cummins indicates, since the toast is a gesture, rather than a speech act, the dialogue appears on the arm, instead of over the speaker's head, as is customary in Guaman Poma.

39. Teresa Gisbert, "The Artistic World of Felipe Guaman Poma de Ayala," in Adorno, ed., *Guaman Poma de Ayala*, 77–82; Maarten van de Guchte, "Invention and Assimilation: European Engravings as Models for the Drawings of Felipe Guaman Poma de Ayala," in Adorno, ed., *Guaman Poma de Ayala*, 93–94; Fernando Iwasaki Cauti, "Las panacas del Cuzco y la pintura Incaica," *Revista de Indias* XLVI:177 (1986): 59–74; Cummins, "Representation in the Sixteenth Century," 197–202; and Cummins, "Between Images and Writing," 16–20.

40. Thomas B. F. Cummins, "We Are the Other: Peruvian Portraits of Colonial *Kurakakuna*," in Andrien and Adorno, *Transatlantic Encounters*, 218. The analysis that follows is also drawn from this article, 204–12.

41. This analysis is drawn from Cummins, "We Are the Other," 204–12. For a detailed discussion of the Great Age of Andean Rebellions, see chapter 7.

42. The material in this paragraph has been drawn from the classic work of R. Tom Zuidema, *The Ceque System of Cuzco: The Social Organization of the Capital of the Inca* (Leiden, 1964); Zuidema, *Inca Civilization in Cuzco* (Austin, Tex., 1990), and Brian Bauer, *The Sacred Landscape of the Inca: The Cusco Ceque System* (Austin, Tex., 1998), 155–61.

43. Quoted in Catherine J. Julien, *Condesuyu: The Political Division of Territory Under Inca and Spanish Rule* (Bonn, 1991), 112.

44. Ibid., 122.

45. Susan E. Ramírez, *The World Upside Down: Cross-Cultural Contact and Conflict in Sixteenth-Century Peru* (Stanford, Calif., 1996), 42–87.

46. See Barbara E. Mundy, *The Mapping of New Spain: Indigenous Cartography and the Maps of the Relaciones Geográficas* (Chicago and London, 1996). Professor Mundy generously made this information on the *Relaciones Geográficas* for the Andean provinces available to me from her research notes at the Archivo General de Indias in Seville.

47. Joanne Rappaport, "Object and Alphabet: Andean Indians and Documents in the Colonial Period," in Boone and Mignolo, *Writing without Words*, 271–91.

48. Rolena Adorno, "Images of the Indio Ladino in Early Colonial Peru," in Andrien and Adorno, eds., *Transatlantic Encounters*, 232–70.

CHAPTER 6

1. Pablo José de Arriaga, *The Extirpation of Idolatry in Peru*, trans. L. Clark Keating (Lexington, Ky., 1968 [1621]), 72–73. Also quoted in Kenneth Mills and William B. Taylor, eds., *Colonial Spanish America: A Documentary History* (Wilmington, Del., 1998), 241.

2. Quoted in Kenneth Mills, *Idolatry and Its Enemies: Colonial Andean Religion and Extirpation, 1640–1750* (Princeton, N.J., 1997), 37.

3. According to Sabine MacCormack, even imperial Inca religion was "made up of clearly demarcated aristocratic and popular spheres." The Inca and their subject peoples saw the official state cults as dominant over lesser divinities, but not obliterating them or their influence over the everyday lives of people. See MacCormack, *Religion in the Andes: Vision and Imagination in Early Colonial Peru* (Princeton, N.J., 1991), 114.

4. Mills, *Idolatry and Its Enemies*, 39–74.

5. The Huarochirí Manuscript was a series of Andean religious traditions most likely compiled by the Spanish priest, Francisco de Avila, by the early seventeenth century. The most recent critical edition and translation is Frank Salomon and George L. Urioste, eds. and trans., *The Huarochirí Manuscript: A Testament of Ancient and Colonial Andean Religion* (Austin, Tex., 1991), 6–10, 54–92.

6. According to anthropologist Irene Marsha Silverblatt, the panoply of Andean gods and goddesses was arrayed in a hierarchy characterized by gender complementarity. She argues that male and female deities controlled parallel and complementary activities in the material world, with goddesses, such as Pacha Mama, overseeing largely female responsibilities and gods supervising male activities. As a result, the complementary roles of Paria Caca and Chaupi Ñamca were repeated in a host of other local deities. See Silverblatt, *Moon, Sun, and Witches: Gender Ideologies and Class in Inca and Colonial Peru* (Princeton, N.J., 1987), 3–20.

7. Mills, *Idolatry and Its Enemies*, 75–100; Arriaga, *Extirpation of Idolatry*, 28–30; and Nicholas Griffiths, *The Cross and the Serpent: Religious Repression and Resurgence in Colonial Peru* (Norman, Okla., 1996), 316–17.

8. Arriaga, *Extirpation of Idolatry*, 27–28; and MacCormack, *Religion in the Andes*, 390, 428–29.

9. This use of the Quechua notion of *mañay* has been taken from Luis Millones, *Historia y poder en los Andes centrales: desde los origenes al siglo XVII* (Madrid, 1987), 133–36.

10. Rubén Vargas Ugarte, *Historia de la iglesia en el Perú (1511–1568)* (Lima, 1953), I: 108–66, 199–228; and John Hemming, *The Conquest of the Incas* (New York, 1970), 308–9.

11. In the Acts of the Apostles, for example, Paul and Barnabas proclaimed that "[T]he Lord has commanded us, 'I have made you a light to the Gentiles, that you may be an instrument of salvation to

the ends of the earth,'" and later Paul proclaimed to the Athenians that already "you are very religious." *New American Bible* (New York, 1986), Acts 14:47, 17:23.

12. Sabine MacCormack, "The Heart Has Its Reasons: Predicaments of Missionary Christianity in Early Colonial Peru," *Hispanic American Historical Review* 65 (August 1985): 443–66; and MacCormack, *Religion in the Andes*, 205–48.

13. Pierre Duviols, *La destrucción de las religiones andinas (conquista y la colonia)*, trans. Albor Maruenda (México, 1977 [1971]), 98–100; 127–31. Rubén Vargas Ugarte, *Concilios Limenses (1551–1772)* (Lima, 1954), III: 1–24, 38–54, 54–113; Vargas Ugarte, *Historia de la iglesia*, I: 229–59; and Mills, *Idolatry and Its Enemies*, 20–24, 175.

14. Quoted in Vargas Ugarte, *Historia de la iglesia*, I: 126.

15. Ibid., 169.

16. Antonine Tibesar, *Franciscan Beginnings in Colonial Peru* (Washington, D.C., 1953), 36–41, 46–57, 73–90.

17. Norman Meiklejohn, *La iglesia y los Lupaqas de Chucuito durante la colonia* (Cusco, 1988), 43–73.

18. Regina Harrison, "'True Confessions': Quechua and Spanish Cultural Encounters in the Viceroyalty of Peru," *Occasional Papers of the Latin American Studies Center, University of Maryland* 5 (1992): 1–44.

19. A Spanish priest left an account of this last Inti Raymi, which is analyzed in MacCormack, *Religion in the Andes*, 75–79, 180, 367–70. According to the noted authority on Andean customs, Juan Polo de Ondegardo, these festivals preserved many customs present during Inti Raymi, and while he urged their extirpation, other Spanish officials and clergymen were more indulgent. See David Cahill, "Popular Religion and Appropriation: The Example of Corpus Christi in Eighteenth-Century Cuzco," *Latin American Research Review* 31:2 (1996): 67–110; Duviols, *La destrucción de la religiones andinas*, 115–21; Carolyn S. Dean, *Inka Bodies and the Body of Christ: Corpus Christi in Colonial Cuzco, Peru* (Durham, N.C., 1999), passim; Mills and Taylor, *Colonial Latin America*, 253–60; and Silvia Spitta, *Between Two Waters: Narratives of Transculturation in Latin America* (Houston, 1995), 106–12.

20. MacCormack, *Religion in the Andes*, 181.

21. According to Rafael Varón Gabai, Luis de Olvera harbored a strong animosity toward the Dominicans, who ministered along with the regular clergy in southern Huamanga and favored instead their newfound enemies, the Jesuits. Olvera actually wrote about Taqui Onqoy two decades later, when the Jesuits had already arrived in the Andes. His very public denunciation of Taqui Onqoy may have served two purposes: to call attention to the threat of the revivalist movement and to discredit the Dominicans. See Rafael Varón Gabai, "El Taki Onqoy: las raíces andinas de un fenómeno colonial," in Luis

Millones, ed., *El retorno de las huacas: Estudios y documentos sobre el Taki Onqoy (Siglo XVI)* (Lima, 1990), 388–89, 400–403; Steve J. Stern, *Peru's Indian Peoples and the Challenge of Spanish Conquest: Huamanga to 1640* (Madison, Wis., 1982), 55.

22. Stern, *Peru's Indian Peoples*, 68–71; and Hemming, *Conquest of the Incas*, 310–12.

23. Stern, *Peru's Indian Peoples*, 64.

24. Duviols, *La destrucción de las religiones andinas*, 139; and Mills, *Idolatry and Its Enemies*, 19.

25. Duviols, *La destrucción de las religiones andinas*, 185–89, 405–13; Mills, *Idolatry and Its Enemies*, 26–38; and Griffiths, *The Cross and the Serpent*, 28–32.

26. It is important to note that Avila wrote about these matters long afterward, as a dying canon in Cusco in the 1640s. See Mills, *Idolatry and Its Enemies*, 9; and Meiklejohn, *La iglesia y los Lupaqa*, 127–90.

27. Mills, *Idolatry and Its Enemies*, 26–38.

28. Before the publication of Arriaga's manual, Lobo Guerrero called a synod in 1613, which along with royal and viceregal legislation provided the legal and procedural foundations for the campaigns. See Duviols, *La destrucción de las religiones andinas*, 187–95; Griffiths, *The Cross and the Serpent*, 32–48; and Arriaga, *The Extirpation of Idolatry*, 107–38.

29. Kenneth Mills, "Bad Christians in Colonial Peru," *Colonial Latin American Review* 5:2 (1996): 184.

30. Griffiths, *The Cross and the Serpent*, 55–64; and Mills, *Idolatry and Its Enemies*, 33–38.

31. Despite the archbishop's theatrical send-off, the advanced age and poor health of the visitors kept most from accomplishing very much in their missions. See Mills, *Idolatry and Its Enemies*, 137–58.

32. Kenneth Mills, *An Evil Lost to View? An Investigation of Post-Evangelisation Andean Religion in Mid-Colonial Peru* (Liverpool, England, 1994), 61–83; and Griffiths, *The Cross and the Serpent*, 205–6.

33. Mills, *An Evil Lost to View?*, 87–91.

34. According to Griffiths, most idolatry inspectors were not so insistent on trying to link faith healing with a direct pact with the Devil. For the full details of this case, see Griffiths, *The Cross and the Serpent*, 112–46.

35. Mills, *Idolatry and Its Enemies*, 228–42.

36. Francisco Poma emerges as a complex figure in these events. On the one hand, he acknowledged participating in forbidden Andean religious rituals, yet he also gave damaging testimony against Hacas Poma and other local dogmatizers, probably both to discredit these enemies and to deflect any attention away from himself and those he wished to protect. See Mills, *Idolatry and Its Enemies*, 175–76; and Mills and Taylor, *Colonial Spanish America*, 236–49.

37. Mills, "Bad Christians," 183–207; Griffiths, *The Cross and the Serpent*,

191–93; and Duviols, *La destrucción de las religiones andinas*, 406–13.

38. Griffiths, *The Cross and the Serpent*, 132–35, 228–33; and Mills, *Idolatry and Its Enemies*, 167–69.

39. Griffiths, *The Cross and the Serpent*, 212–13, 222–30; and Mills, *Idolatry and Its Enemies*, 80–83, 88, 94–96, 168.

40. Verónica Salles-Reese, *From Viracocha to the Virgin of Copacabana: Representation of the Sacred at Lake Titicaca* (Austin, Tex., 1997), 131–71.

41. Manifiesto de los agravios, vexaciones, y molestias, que padecen los indios del reyno del Perú, Madrid, 2 septiembre 1732, Archivo General de Indias, Lima 442.

42. Jorge Juan and Antonio de Ulloa also complained that only the Jesuits among the regular clergy remained immune from such immorality, since they kept a tighter rein on their members, normally keeping them in monasteries or mission communities, instead of dispatching them for parish duty. See Juan and Ulloa, *Discourse and political reflections on the Kingdoms of Peru, their government, special regiment of their inhabitants, and abuses which have been introduced into one and another with special information on why they grew up and some means to avoid them*, edited by John J. TePaske, and translated by John J. TePaske and Besse A. Clement (Norman, Okla., 1978 [1749]), 106, 113–14.

43. Meiklejohn, *La iglesia y los Lupaqas*, 151, 162.

44. On the reform movement in Spain, see John Lynch, *Bourbon Spain, 1700–1808* (Oxford, England, 1989). For the impact of reform in the Andes, see Cahill, "Popular Religion and Appropriation," 67–104.

45. Frank Salomon, "Ancestor Cults and Resistance to the State in Arequipa, ca. 1748–1754," in Steve J. Stern, ed., *Resistance, Rebellion, and Consciousness in the Andean Peasant World, 18th to 20th Centuries* (Madison, Wis., 1987), 148–65.

46. Frank Salomon, "Nightmare Victory: The Meanings of Conversion among Peruvian Indians (Huarochirí, 1608?)," *Working Papers*, No. 7, Department of Spanish and Portuguese, University of Maryland, 1990.

CHAPTER 7

1. The Cañari had been defeated after a bitter struggle by the Inca armies of Huayna Capac (ca. 1500), and much of the population perished. Many survivors were resettled as mitimaes in the Cusco region, and they became early allies of the Spaniards. Tensions between the Cañari and the ethnic Inca plagued the city of Cusco for generations. See John Hemming, *The Conquest of the Incas* (New York, 1970), 155–56 ; and Carolyn Dean, "Ethnic Conflict and Corpus Christi in Colonial Cuzco," *Colonial Latin American Review* 2 (1993): 93–120.

2. The punishment of beheading was particularly odious to Andeans, who believed in mummifying prominent dead relatives to honor them

and to preserve their bodies. According to many indigenous religious beliefs, mutilating a body by beheading or burning would prevent the spirit of the deceased from entering pacarina, the final resting place of the dead. Hemming, *Conquest of the Incas*, 441–51.

3. Accounts of Tupac Amaru's death differ in the primary sources, and this version is largely drawn from Lillian Estelle Fisher, *The Last Inca Revolt, 1780–1783* (Norman, Okla., 1966), 236–38; Ward Stavig, *The World of Túpac Amaru* (Lincoln, Nebr., 1999), 246–48.

4. For a discussion of the siege of Cusco itself, see chapter 3.

5. Hemming, *Conquest of the Incas*, 189–256.

6. According to some accounts, Sayri Tupac was poisoned by a Cañari leader, Francisco Chilche, who wanted control over his estates in Yucay. Chilche was charged and imprisoned for the murder but never convicted. He later married the deceased Inca's wife, which allowed him to realize his goal of gaining control over these estates. See Carolyn S. Dean, *Inca Bodies and the Body of Christ: Corpus Christi in Colonial Cuzco, Peru* (Durham, N.C., 1999), 192–93.

7. Hemming, *Conquest of the Incas*, 333–38, 417.

8. Toledo had commissioned a lieutenant, Pedro Sarmiento de Gamboa, to compile a history of the Andes, which painted Tawantinsuyu as a corrupt, tyrannical empire. See Hemming, *Conquest of the Incas*, 414–15.

9. Ibid., 446–50.

10. The documentary evidence about the rebellion of Juan Santos Atahualpa is scanty. The principal secondary works used in constructing this account follow: Steve J. Stern, "The Age of Andean Insurrection: A Reappraisal," in Steve J. Stern, ed., *Resistance, Rebellion, and Consciousness in the Andean Peasant World, 18th to 20th Centuries* (Madison, Wis., 1987), 43–63; Stefano Varese, *La sal de los cerros: Una aproximación al mundo Campa* (Lima, 1973); Leon G. Campbell, *The Military and Society in Colonial Peru, 1750–1810* (Philadelphia, 1978), 11–12; and Alonso Zarzar, *Apo capac huayna, Jesus sacramentado: mito, utopia, y milenarismo en el pensamiento de Juan Santos Atahualpa* (Lima, 1989).

11. One of those implicated in the revolt was Fray Calixto de San José Tupak Inka, the mestizo Franciscan, who authored the 1750 protest against governmental abuse of the Andean peoples. See Francisco A. Loayza, ed., *Fray Calixto Túpak Inka: Documentos originales y, en su mayoría, totalmente desconocidos, auténticos, de este apóstol indio, valiente defensor de su raza, desde el año de 1746 a 1760* (Lima, 1948), 85–94.

12. Karen Spalding, *Huarochirí: An Andean Society Under Inca and Spanish Rule* (Stanford, Calif., 1984), 271–90.

13. Although legalized in 1751, the *repartimiento de comercio* did not actually operate within this legal framework until 1756. See Scarlett O'Phelan Godoy, *Rebellions and Revolts in Eighteenth-Century Peru and Upper Peru* (Köln, 1985), 99.

14. The *reparto* system never extended to the North Andes because the indigenous peoples had a long tradition of participating in colonial markets. Unrest and revolts in the north emerged from similar problems, but the repartimiento de comercio did not play the same role in exacerbating local tensions. See Segundo Moreno Yáñez, *Sublevaciones indígenas en la audiencia de Quito: Desde comienzos del siglo XVIII hasta finales de la colonia* (Quito, 1985 [1976]).

15. O'Phelan Godoy, *Rebellions and Revolts*, 99–118.

16. This analysis draws heavily on the path-breaking new work of Sergio Esteban Serulnikov, "Peasant Politics and Colonial Domination: Social Conflicts and Insurgency in Northern Potosí, 1730–1781," Ph.D. diss., State University of New York at Stony Brook, 1998, 167–241.

17. This discussion also relies heavily on another pioneering study by Sinclair Thomson, "Colonial Crisis, Community, and Andean Self-Rule: Aymara Politics in the Age of Insurgency (Eighteenth-Century La Paz)," Ph.D. diss., University of Wisconsin-Madison, 1996, 210.

18. Ibid., 209–14.

19. The best discussion of the problems caused by the reforms is found in O'Phelan, *Rebellions and Revolts*, 161–207.

20. Sergio Serulnikov, "Disputed Images of Colonialism: Spanish Rule and Indian Subversion in Northern Potosí, 1777–1780," *Hispanic American Historical Review* 2 (May 1996): 189–96, 198–218.

21. Ibid., 220.

22. Ibid., 218–26.

23. Fisher, *Last Inca Revolt*, 68.

24. Ibid., 38–52; O'Phelan, *Rebellions and Revolts*, 209–13; Stavig, *World of Túpac Amaru*, 207–9, 239–41; and Charles F. Walker, *Smoldering Ashes: Cuzco and the Creation of Republican Peru, 1780–1840* (Durham, N.C., 1999), 22–37.

25. Fisher, *The Last Inca Revolt*, 22–52, 95–117; O'Phelan, *Rebellions and Revolts*, 209–42; Stavig, *World of Túpac Amaru*, 207–56; and Walker, *Smoldering Ashes*, 37–42.

26. See Scarlett O'Phelan Godoy, *La gran rebelión en los Andes: De Túpac Amaru a Túpac Catari* (Cuzco, 1995), 23, 32–33; Mark Thurner, *From Two Republics to One Divided: Contradictions of Postcolonial Nationmaking in Andean Peru* (Durham, N.C., 1997), 8–11.

27. Numerous historians and anthropologists in the past twenty years have emphasized the importance of Inkarrí and other Andean resurrection myths as fundamental ideological components in the Tupac Amaru II rebellion. Some of the most influential are Jan Szeminski, *La utopia tupamarista* (Lima, 1983); Alberto Flores Galindo, *Buscando un Inca: identidad y utopia en los Andes* (Habana, 1986); and Leon G. Campbell, "Ideology and Factionalism during the Great Rebellion," in Stern, ed., *Resistance, Rebellion, and Consciousness*, 110–47. For a

discussion of the emergence of these resurrection myths, see Franklin Pease G. Y, *El dios creador andino* (Lima, 1973). In a recent study, Szeminski has also emphasized the Christian components of Tupac Amaru's ideology in "The Last Time the Inca Came Back: Messianism and Nationalism in the Great Rebellion, 1780–1783," in Gary H. Gossen and Miguel León-Portilla, eds., *Meso-American Native Spirituality: From the Cult of the Feathered Serpent to the Theology of Liberation* (New York, 1993), 279–98. More recently, the overwhelming importance of Andean resurrection myths in rebel ideology has been questioned, qualified, or balanced with other ideological components. Some scholars have even argued that different social classes or ethnic groups supporting the rebellion were attracted to different elements in the eclectic ideology of Tupac Amaru. Some of the most influential among these more recent works follow: O'Phelan Godoy, *La gran rebelión en los Andes*, 13–45; Stavig, *World of Túpac Amaru*, 236–34; Walker, *Smoldering Ashes*, 24–26, 39–40; and Thurner, *From Two Republics to One Divided*, 8–11.

28. O'Phelan Godoy, *Rebellions and Revolts*, 213–42; and Stavig, *World of Túpac Amaru*, 245–54.

29. O'Phelan Godoy, *Rebellions and Revolts*, 228–42, and "La rebelión de Tupac Amaru: organización interna, dirigencia, y alianzas," *Histórica* 3:2 (1979), 89–121; and Leon G. Campbell, "Social Structure of the Tupac Amaru Army in Cuzco," *Hispanic American Historical Review* 4 (November 1981): 688–89.

30. For opposing ideas on the meaning of these atrocities, see Szeminski, "Why Kill the Spaniard? New Perspectives on Andean Insurrectionary Ideology in the 18th Century," in Stern, ed., *Resistance, Rebellion, and Consciousness*, 166–92; and O'Phelan Godoy, *La gran rebelión en los Andes*, 105–37.

31. Walker, *Smoldering Ashes*, 41.

32. O'Phelan, *Rebellions and Revolts*, 245.

33. The name Amaru also means serpent in Quechua. Much of the analysis of the Tupac Katari revolt relies on the fine study of Sinclair Thomson. See Thomson, "Aymara Politics in the Age of Insurgency," 269–78.

34. Ibid., 279.

35. Ibid., 279–89.

36. Ibid., 279–300.

37. O'Phelan Godoy, *La gran rebelión en los Andes*, 121.

38. Thomson, "Aymara Politics in the Age of Insurgency," 301–31.

39. Leon G. Campbell, "Ideology and Factionalism," 130–32.

40. Walker, *Smoldering Ashes*, 59–83; and Núria Sala I Vila, *Y se armó el tole tole: tributo indígena y movimientos sociales en el virreinato del Perú* (Ayacucho, Peru, 1996), 23–64.

41. Walker, *Smoldering Ashes*, 59–83; and Sala I Vila, *Se armó el tole tole*, 65–99.

42. Sala I Vila, *Se armó el tole tole*, 118–28.

43. Walker, *Smoldering Ashes*, 84–105; Sala I Vila, *Se armó el tole tole*, 163–247; and David Cahill and Scarlett O'Phelan Godoy, "Forging their own History: Indian Insurgency in the Southern Peruvian Sierra, 1815," *Bulletin of Latin American Research* 11:2 (1992): 125–67.

44. This discussion of the *Tragedy of the Death of Atahualpa* and the notion of "hidden messages" is drawn from Raquel Chang-Rodríguez, *Hidden Messages: Representation and Resistance in Andean Colonial Drama* (Lewisburg, Pa., 1999), 36–58.

SUGGESTED READINGS

Adorno, Rolena. *Guaman Poma: Writing and Resistance in Colonial Peru.* Austin: University of Texas Press, 1986.

———, ed. *From Oral to Written Expression: Native Andean Chronicles of the Early Colonial Period.* Syracuse, N.Y.: Syracuse University, Maxwell School of Citizenship and Public Affairs, 1982.

———, ed. *Guaman Poma de Ayala: The Colonial Art of an Andean Author.* New York: The Americas Society, 1992.

Alchon, Suzanne Austin. *Native Society and Disease in Colonial Ecuador.* Cambridge, England, and New York: Cambridge University Press, 1991.

Andrien, Kenneth J. *Crisis and Decline: The Viceroyalty of Peru in the Seventeenth Century.* Albuquerque: University of New Mexico Press, 1985.

———. *The Kingdom of Quito, 1690–1830: The State and Regional Development.* Cambridge, England and New York: Cambridge University Press, 1995.

Andrien, Kenneth J., and Rolena Adorno, eds. *Transatlantic Encounters: Europeans and Andeans in the Sixteenth Century.* Berkeley and Los Angeles: University of California Press, 1991.

Arriaga, Pablo José de. *The Extirpation of Idolatry in Peru.* Translated and edited by L. Clark Keating. 1621. Reprint, Lexington: University of Kentucky Press, 1968.

Arzáns de Orsúa y Vela, Bartolomé, *Tales of Potosí.* Edited, with an introduction by R. C. Padden. Translated by Frances M. López-Morillas. 1735. Reprint, Providence: Brown University Press, 1975.

Bakewell, Peter J. *Miners of the Red Mountain: Indian Labor in Potosí, 1545–1650.* Albuquerque: University of New Mexico Press, 1984.

————. *Silver and Entrepreneurship in Seventeenth-Century Potosí: The Life and Times of Antonio López de Quiroga*. Albuquerque: University of New Mexico Press, 1988.

Bauer, Brian S. *The Sacred Landscape of the Inca: The Cusco Ceque System*. Austin: University of Texas Press, 1998.

Bolton, Ralph, and Enrique Mayer, eds. *Andean Kinship and Marriage*. Washington, D.C.: American Anthropological Association, 1977.

Boone, Elizabeth Hill, and Tom Cummins, eds. *Native Traditions in the Postconquest World: Symposium at Dumbarton Oaks, October 2–4, 1992*. Washington, D.C.: Dumbarton Oaks Research Library and Collection, 1998.

Boone, Elizabeth Hill, and Walter D. Mignolo, eds. *Writing Without Words: Alternative Literacies in Mesoamerica and the Andes*. Durham, N.C.: Duke University Press, 1994.

Brading, D. A. *The First America: The Spanish Monarchy, Creole Patriots, and the Liberal State, 1492–1867*. Cambridge, England, and New York: Cambridge University Press, 1991.

Bruhns, Karen Olsen. *Ancient South America*. Cambridge, England, and New York: Cambridge University Press, 1994.

Burkholder, Mark A., and D. S. Chandler. *From Impotence to Authority: The Spanish Crown and the American Audiencias, 1687–1808*. Columbia: University of Missouri Press, 1977.

————. *José de Baquíjano and the Audiencia of Lima: Politics of a Colonial Career*. Albuquerque: University of New Mexico Press, 1980.

Campbell, Leon G. *The Military and Society in Colonial Peru, 1750–1810*. Philadelphia: American Philosophical Society, 1978.

Chang-Rodríguez, Raquel. *Hidden Messages: Representation and Resistance in Andean Colonial Drama*. Lewisburg, Pa.: Bucknell University Press, 1999.

Clanchy, M. T. *From Memory to Written Record: England, 1066–1307*. 2nd ed. Oxford, England, and Cambridge, Mass.: Basil Blackwell, 1993.

Classen, Constance. *Inca Cosmology and the Human Body*. Salt Lake City: University of Utah Press, 1993.

Clifford, James, and George E. Marcus, eds. *Writing Culture: The Poetics and Politics of Ethnography*. Berkeley and Los Angeles: University of California Press, 1986.

Cobo, Bernabé. *History of the Inca Empire*. Translated and edited by Roland Hamilton. 5th reprint. Austin: University of Texas Press, 1996.

Cole, Jeffrey A. *The Potosí Mita, 1573–1700: Compulsory Indian Labor in the Andes*. Stanford, Calif.: Stanford University Press, 1985.

Collier, George A., Renato I. Rosaldo, and John D. Wirth, eds. *The Inca and Aztec States, 1400–1800: Anthropology and History*. New York: Academic Press, 1982.

Conrad, Geoffrey W., and Arthur A. Demarest. *Religion and Empire: The Dynamics of Aztec and Inca Expansionism*. Cambridge, England, and New York: Cambridge University Press, 1984.

Cook, Noble David. *Born to Die: Disease and New World Conquest, 1492–1650*. Cambridge, England, and New York: Cambridge University Press, 1998.

———. *Demographic Collapse: Indian Peru, 1520–1620*. Cambridge, England, and New York: Cambridge University Press, 1981.

Cooper, Frederick, et al., eds. *Confronting Historical Paradigms: Peasants, Labor, and the Capitalist World System in Africa and Latin America*. Madison: University of Wisconsin Press, 1993.

Cornblit, Oscar. *Power and Violence in the Colonial City: Oruro from the Mining Renaissance to the Rebellion of Tupac Amaru, 1740–1782*. Cambridge, England, and New York: Cambridge University Press, 1995.

Cossío del Pomar, Felipe. *The Art of Ancient Peru*. New York: Wittenborn & Co., 1971.

D'Altroy, Terence N. *Provincial Power in the Inka Empire*. Washington, D.C.: Smithsonian Institution Press, 1992.

Damian, Carol. *The Virgin of the Andes: Art and Ritual in Colonial Cuzco*. Miami Beach: Grassfield Press, 1995.

Dean, Carolyn S. *Inka Bodies and the Body of Christ: Corpus Christi in Colonial Cuzco, Peru*. Durham, N.C.: Duke University Press, 1999.

Dover, Robert V. H., Katharine E. Seibold, and John H. McDowell, eds. *Andean Cosmologies Through Time: Persistence and Emergence*. Bloomington: Indiana University Press, 1992.

Elliott, J. H. *Imperial Spain, 1469–1716*. New York: New American Library, 1977.

Fisher, J. R. *Government and Society in Colonial Peru: The Intendant System, 1784–1814*. London: University of London, Athlone Press, 1970.

————. *Silver Mines and Silver Miners in Colonial Peru, 1776–1824*. Liverpool, England: Centre for Latin American Studies, University of Liverpool, 1977.

————. *Commercial Relations Between Spain and Spanish America in the Era of Free Trade, 1778–1796*. Liverpool, England: Centre for Latin American Studies, University of Liverpool, 1985.

Fisher, Lillian Estelle. *The Last Inca Revolt, 1780–1783*. Norman: University of Oklahoma Press, 1966.

Goody, Jack. *The Domestication of the Savage Mind*. Cambridge, England, and New York: Cambridge University Press, 1977.

Gossen, Gary H., in collaboration with Miguel León-Portilla, eds. *South and Meso-American Native Spirituality: From the Cult of the Feathered Serpent to the Theology of Liberation*. New York: Crossroad, 1993.

Griffiths, Nicholas. *The Cross and the Serpent: Religious Repression and Resurgence in Colonial Peru*. Norman: University of Oklahoma Press, 1996.

Guaman Poma de Ayala, Felipe. *El primer nueva corónica y buen gobierno*. Edited by Juan V. Murra and Rolena Adorno. Translated by Jorge L. Urioste. México: Siglo Veintiuno, 1980.

Hanke, Lewis. *The Spanish Struggle for Justice in the Conquest of America*. Philadelphia: University of Pennsylvania Press, 1949.

Haring, C. H. *The Spanish Empire in America*. New York: Oxford University Press, 1947.

Harrison, Regina. *Signs, Songs, and Memory in the Andes: Translating Quechua Language and Culture*. Austin: University of Texas Press, 1989.

Hemming, John. *The Conquest of the Incas*. New York: Harcourt, Brace, and Jovanovich, 1970.

Hoberman, Louisa Schell, and Susan Migden Socolow, eds. *The Countryside in Colonial Latin America*. Albuquerque: University of New Mexico Press, 1996.

————. *Cities and Society in Colonial Latin America*. Albuquerque: University of New Mexico Press, 1986.

Howard-Malverde, Rosaleen. *The Speaking of History: "Willapaakushayki" or Quechua Ways of Telling the Past*. London: University of London, Institute of Latin American Studies, 1990.

Huaman Poma de Ayala, Felipe. *Letter to a King: A Picture-History of Inca Civilisation.* Translated by Christopher Dilke. London and Boston: George Allen & Unwin, 1978.

Hyslop, John. *The Inka Road System.* Orlando: Academic Press, 1984.

———. *Inka Settlement Planning.* Austin: University of Texas Press, 1990.

Juan, Jorge, and Antonio de Ulloa. *Discourse and Political Reflections on the Kingdoms of Peru, their government, special regiment of their inhabitants, and abuses which have been introduced into one and another with special information on why they grew up and some means to avoid them.* Edited and with introduction by John J. TePaske. Translated by John J. TePaske and Besse A. Clement. 1749. Reprint, Norman: University of Oklahoma Press, 1978.

Julien, Catherine J. *Condesuyo: The Political Division of Territory Under Inca and Spanish Rule.* Bonn: Seminar für Völkerkunde, Universität Bonn, 1991.

Keith, Robert G. *Conquest and Agrarian Change: The Emergence of the Hacienda System on the Peruvian Coast.* Cambridge, Mass.: Harvard University Press, 1976.

Klein, Herbert S. *The American Finances of the Spanish Empire: Royal Income and Expenditures in Colonial Mexico, Peru, and Bolivia, 1680–1809.* Albuquerque: University of New Mexico Press, 1998.

———. *Haciendas and Ayllus: Rural Society in the Bolivian Andes in the Eighteenth and Nineteenth Centuries.* Stanford, Calif.: Stanford University Press, 1993.

Korth, Eugene H. *Spanish Policy in Colonial Chile: The Struggle for Social Justice, 1535–1700.* Stanford, Calif.: Stanford University Press, 1968.

Larson, Brooke. *Colonialism and Agrarian Transformation in Bolivia: Cochabamba, 1550–1900.* Princeton, N.J.: Princeton University Press, 1988.

Larson, Brooke, and Olivia Harris, eds., with Enrique Tandeter. *Ethnicity, Markets, and Migration in the Andes: At the Crossroads of History and Anthropology.* Durham, N.C.: Duke University Press, 1995.

Lockhart, James. *Spanish Peru, 1532–1560: A Colonial Society.* Madison: University of Wisconsin Press, 1968.

Lynch, John. *Spain Under the Hapsburgs, 1517–1700.* 2 vols. Oxford, England: Basil Blackwell, 1981.

———. *Bourbon Spain, 1700–1808.* Oxford, England, and Cambridge, Mass.: Oxford University Press, 1989.

MacCormack, Sabine. *Religion in the Andes: Vision and Imagination in Early Colonial Peru*. Princeton, N.J.: Princeton University Press, 1991.

MacLachlan, Colin M. *Spain's Empire in the New World: The Role of Ideas in Institutional and Social Change*. Berkeley: University of California Press, 1988.

Malpass, Michael A. *Provincial Inca: Archaeological and Ethnohistorical Assessment of the Impact of the Inca State*. Iowa City: University of Iowa Press, 1993.

Mannheim, Bruce. *The Language of the Inka since the European Invasion*. Austin: University of Texas Press, 1991.

Marcus, George E., and Michael M. J. Fischer. *Anthropology as Cultural Critique: An Experimental Moment in the Human Sciences*. Chicago: University of Chicago Press, 1986.

Mignolo, Walter D. *The Darker Side of the Renaissance: Literacy, Territoriality, and Colonization*. Ann Arbor: University of Michigan Press, 1995.

Mills, Kenneth. *An Evil Lost to View? An Investigation of Post-Evangelisation Andean Religion in Mid-Colonial Peru*. Liverpool, England: University of Liverpool, Institute of Latin American Studies, 1994.

———. *Idolatry and Its Enemies: Colonial Andean Religion and Extirpation, 1640–1750*. Princeton, N.J.: Princeton University Press, 1997.

Mills, Kenneth, and William B. Taylor, eds. *Colonial Spanish America: A Documentary History*. Wilmington, Del.: Scholarly Resources, 1998.

Minchom, Martin. *The People of Quito, 1690–1810: Change and Unrest in the Underclass*. Boulder: Westview Press, 1994.

Morris, Craig, and Adriana von Hagen. *The Inka Empire and Its Andean Origins*. New York: Abbeville Press, 1993.

Mundy, Barbara E. *The Mapping of New Spain: Indigenous Cartography and the Maps of the Relaciones Geográficas*. Chicago: University of Chicago Press, 1996.

Newson, Linda A. *Life and Death in Early Colonial Ecuador*. Norman: University of Oklahoma Press, 1995.

O'Phelan Godoy, Scarlett. *Rebellions and Revolts in Eighteenth-Century Peru and Upper Peru*. Köln: Bohlau, 1985.

Ong, Walter J. *Orality and Literacy: The Technologizing of the Word*. London and New York: Methuen, 1982.

Pagden, Anthony. *Spanish Imperialism and the Political Imagination: Studies in European and Spanish-American Social and Political Theory, 1513–1830*. New Haven: Yale University Press, 1990.

Pasztory, Esther. *Pre-Columbian Art*. Cambridge, England, and New York: Cambridge University Press, 1998.

Phelan, John Leddy. *The Kingdom of Quito in the Seventeenth Century: Bureaucratic Politics in the Spanish Empire*. Madison: University of Wisconsin Press, 1967.

Powers, Karen Vieira. *Andean Journeys: Migration, Ethnogenesis, and the State in Colonial Quito*. Albuquerque: University of New Mexico Press, 1995.

Prescott, William H. *History of the Conquest of Peru*. 2 vols. Philadelphia: J. B. Lippincott & Co., 1871.

Ramírez, Susan Elizabeth. *The World Upside Down: Cross-Cultural Contact and Conflict in Sixteenth-Century Peru*. Stanford, Calif.: Stanford University Press, 1996.

Roniger, Louis, and Tamar Herzog, eds. *Collective Identities, Public Spheres and Political Order: Latin American Dynamics*. Sussex: Sussex Academic Press, 2000.

Rostworowski de Diez Canseco, María. *History of the Inca Realm*. Translated by Harry B. Iceland. 1988. Reprint, Cambridge, England, and New York: Cambridge University Press, 1999.

Salles-Reese, Verónica. *From Viracocha to the Virgen of Copacabana: Representation of the Sacred at Lake Titicaca*. Austin: University of Texas Press, 1997.

Salomon, Frank. *Native Lords of Quito in the Age of the Incas: The Political Economy of the North-Andean Chiefdoms*. Cambridge, England, and New York: Cambridge University Press, 1986.

Salomon, Frank, and George L. Urioste, eds. and trans. *The Huarochirí Manuscript: A Testament of Ancient and Colonial Andean Religion*. Austin: University of Texas Press, 1991.

Santa Cruz Pachacuti Yamqui Salcamayhua, Juan de. *Relación de antigüedades deste reyno del Pirú*. Edited by Pierre Duviols and César Itier. Lima: Institut français d'études andines; Cusco: Centro de Estudios Regionales Andinos Bartolomé de las Casas, 1993.

————. *Narratives of the Rights and Laws of the Yncas*. Edited and translated by Clements R. Markham. London: Hakluyut Society, 1923.

Silverblatt, Irene Marsha. *Moon, Sun, and Witches: Gender Ideologies and Class in Inca and Colonial Peru*. Princeton, N.J.: Princeton University Press, 1987.

Spalding, Karen. *Huarochirí: An Andean Society Under Inca and Spanish Rule*. Stanford, Calif.: Stanford University Press, 1984.

Spitta, Silvia. *Between Two Waters: Narratives of Transculturation in Latin America*. Houston: Rice University Press, 1995.

Stanish, Charles. *Ancient Andean Political Economy*. Austin: University of Texas Press, 1992.

Stavig, Ward. *The World of Túpac Amaru: Conflict, Community, and Identity in Colonial Peru*. Lincoln: University of Nebraska Press, 1999.

Stern, Steve J. *Peru's Indian Peoples and the Challenge of Spanish Conquest: Huamanga to 1640*. Madison: University of Wisconsin Press, 1982.

————, ed. *Resistance, Rebellion, and Consciousness in the Andean Peasant World, 18th to 20th Centuries*. Madison: University of Wisconsin Press, 1987

Stone-Miller, Rebecca. *To Weave for the Sun: Andean Textiles in the Museum of Fine Arts*. Boston: Boston Museum of Fine Arts, 1992.

Street, Brian V. *Literacy in Theory and Practice*. Cambridge, England, and New York: Cambridge University Press, 1984.

Tandeter, Enrique. *Coercion and Market: Silver Mining in Colonial Potosí, 1692–1826*. Albuquerque: University of New Mexico Press, 1993.

Thurner, Mark. *From Two Republics to One Divided: Contradictions of Postcolonial Nationmaking in Andean Peru*. Durham, N.C., and London: Duke University Press, 1997.

Tibesar, Antonine. *Franciscan Beginnings in Colonial Peru*. Washington, D.C.: Academy of American Franciscan History, 1953.

Urton, Gary. *At the Crossroads of the Earth and the Sky: An Andean Cosmology*. Austin: University of Texas Press, 1981.

Urton, Gary, in collaboration with Primitivo Nina Llanos. *The Social Life of Numbers: A Quechua Ontology of Numbers and Philosophy of Arithmetic*. Austin: University of Texas Press, 1997.

Varón Gabai, Rafael. *Francisco Pizarro and His Brothers: The Illusion of Power in Sixteenth-Century Peru.* Translated by Javier Flores Espinoza. Norman: University of Oklahoma Press, 1997.

Wachtel, Nathan. *Vision of the Vanquished: The Spanish Conquest of Peru Through Indian Eyes, 1530–1570.* Translated by Ben and Siân Reynolds. Hassocks, England: Harvester Press, 1977.

Walker, Charles F. *Smoldering Ashes: Cuzco and the Creation of Republican Peru, 1780–1840.* Durham, N.C.: Duke University Press, 1999.

Wightman, Ann M. *Indigenous Migration and Social Change: The Forasteros of Cuzco, 1570–1720.* Durham, N.C.: Duke University Press, 1990.

Wood, Robert D. *Teach Them Good Customs: Colonial Indian Education and Acculturation in the Andes.* Culver City, Calif.: Labyrinthos, 1986.

Zamora, Margarita. *Language, Authority, and Indigenous History in the Comentarios reales de los Incas.* Cambridge, England, and New York: Cambridge University Press, 1988.

Zárate, Agustín de. *The Discovery and Conquest of Peru.* Translated by J. M. Cohen. Harmondsworth, England: Penguin, 1968.

Zimmerman, Arthur Franklin. *Francisco de Toledo, Fifth Viceroy of Peru, 1569–1581.* Caldwell, Idaho: Caxton Printers, 1938.

Zuidema, R. T. *The Ceque System of Cuzco: The Social Organization of the Capital of the Inca.* Translated by Eva M. Hooykaas. Leiden: E. J. Brill, 1964.

Zuidema, R. Tom. *Inca Civilization in Cuzco.* Translated by Jean-Jacques Decoster. Austin: University of Texas Press, 1990.

Zulawski, Ann. *They Eat from Their Labor: Work and Social Change in Colonial Bolivia.* Pittsburgh, Pa.: University of Pittsburgh Press, 1995.

INDEX

Page numbers in *italic type* indicate a photo, map, or illustration.